Of
PRESBYTERS
and
KINGS

Of
PRESBYTERS
and
KINGS

Church and State
in the
Law of Scotland

Francis Lyall

Aberdeen University Press

First Published 1980
Aberdeen University Press
A Member of the Pergamon Group

© 1980 Francis Lyall

British Library Cataloguing in Publication Data
Lyall, Francis
    Of presbyters and kings
    1. Church and state in Scotland
    2. Scotland—Constitutional history
    I. Title
    342'.411'087   KD956

ISBN 0 08 025715 1

PRINTED IN GREAT BRITAIN
AT ABERDEEN UNIVERSITY PRESS

For
Fiona Elizabeth
Gillian Ann
and
Francis James

Contents

Preface

The following pages are the outcome of an interest of many years standing. In that Scotland is the primary home of Presbyterianism for most of the world I hope that it will be illuminating to see how the questions of Church and State have been and are organised within our legal system. The Law and the Church were the two elements preserved in the Treaty of Union with England in 1707. Curiously there is little formal treatment of the topic from the legal point of view, but due acknowledgement must be made to the pioneer work by A. Taylor Innes, *The Law of Creeds in Scotland*, 1867. The second edition of 1904 is less satisfactory, having to deal with much legal development, and is somewhat unfortunate in being published during the trial of the Free Church case of 1904.

This is a book about law, not theology. Though obviously the two disciplines inter-twine, I have not sought to explore the doctrinal thinking of participants in the tale more than is necessary. My approach has been influenced by, and to an extent follows, the lines of studies in Church and State in American legal writing, notably that of A. P. Stokes, *Church and State in the United States*, 1950, L. Pfeffer and S. R. J. Saunders, *Church, State and Freedom*, 1962, and Father J. J. McGrath, *Church and State in American Law: Cases and Materials*, 1962. What I have sought to do is to set the study in context, then deal with institutional relations, and finally and briefly show the interaction of Church and State in selected areas.

It will be seen that there is no extended discussion of the concept of an 'establishment of religion'. As noted in Chapter VIII, I take this concept as simply a state connection largely for ceremonial purposes, formally created by law. The concept is more properly discussed in works on political theory, such as J. N. Figgis, *Churches in the Modern State*, 1913, or H. J. Laski, *Studies in the Problem of Sovereignty*, 1917 (rep. 1968).

From the field of theological studies I have found helpful, T. G. Sanders, *Protestant Concepts of Church and State*, 1964, and J. Bannerman, *The Church of Christ*, 1869 (rep. 1960), though I have cited neither of these works. In Church History greater use has been made of J. H. S. Burleigh, *A Church History of Scotland*, 1960, than is apparent from the notes.

As I explain at several points, the standpoint of any writer affects his reading and evaluation of his subject. My theological standpoint is that of conservative evangelicalism. It should be made plain that although I served as a member of the Panel on Doctrine of the Church of Scotland (1971–9), the views I express are not to be taken as necessarily reflecting those of the Panel or committing it in any way. Again my view of the present state of the Church of Scotland is adumbrated at several points, but will require fuller balanced exposition in a separate work. Though critical, I am not without hope for the institution.

The effective date of the legal information in the following pages is 1 October 1979 though it has been possible to take later developments into account. Bibliographic references are in the notes and Table of Abbreviations. Those requiring a more extensive bibliography should consult the volumes of Bulloch cited in the Abbreviations.

I must record my thanks to those who, in a variety of ways, have helped this study to the light of day. In particular I would thank the supervisor of my original thesis, J. T. Craig, now Professor of Law in the University of Zambia, Lusaka, and my colleague Professor G. D. MacCormack, for much needed stimulus to complete that thesis. I would also single out Mrs. Alison L. Seager and Mr. D. J. Cusine of the Faculty of Law for their help and comments on both style and content. I accepted some of their advice. While they therefore bear some responsibility for some of the remaining errors and obscurities, the bulk of that responsibility is mine.

My thanks also go to the Panel on Doctrine, the General Administration Committee and W. R. Grieve, Esq., Q.C. (formerly Procurator of the Church of Scotland, now Lord Grieve, a Senator of the College of Justice in Scotland since June 1972) for permission to reproduce the Procurator's Opinion (App.III); to the National Church Association and D. Maxwell, Esq., Q.C., for permission to reproduce the Opinion secured by that Association (App.IV); and to the Controller of Her Majesty's Stationery Office for permission to reproduce the Church of Scotland Act, 1921. I would also thank the Scottish Council of Law Reporting, and the editor of Session Cases, The Incorporated Council of Law Reporting for England and Wales, Messrs W. Green and Sons, the publishers of The Scots Law Times, and Messrs Butterworths, the publishers of The All England Law Reports, for permission to use materials which appears in their reports and the editors of the Aberdeen University Review and the Juridical Review for permission to use material first published in their journals.

Finally my thanks go to Miss E. Carr, Mrs. F. Chaplain, Miss H. Somers, Miss M. Tough and Mrs. P. Simpson for making the manuscript legible, to my wife for encouraging me to persist, and to C. MacLean of The Aberdeen University Press for his interest and encouragement.

F. Lyall
Department of Public Law
University of Aberdeen
Scotland

Table of Abbreviations

Bettenson   H. Bettenson, *Documents of the Christian Church*, 2nd ed. 1967.

Bryce, Hist. Ret., **I and II**   James Bryce, *Ten : Years of the Church of Scotland from 1833 to 1843 with a Historical Retrospect from 1560*, 1850 2 vols. (The Historical Retrospect is separately paged in vol. I).

Buchanan, I and II   Robert Buchanan, *The Ten Years' Conflict : being a History of the Disruption of the Church of Scotland*, new ed. 1856 2 vols.

B.U.K.   *The Book of the Universal Kirk*, Bannatyne and Maitland Clubs, 3 vols. 1839–45.

Bulloch, I, II, and III   A. L. Drummond and J. Bulloch; *The Scottish Church, 1688–1843* (1973); *The Church in Victorian Scotland, 1843–1874* (1975); *The Church in Late Victorian Scotland, 1874–1900* (1978). (A fourth volume bringing the story down to date, is forthcoming).

Burleigh   J. H. S. Burleigh, *A Church History of Scotland*, 1960.

C.I.C.   *Codex Iuris Canonici*, 1911.

Cockburn, *Journals* I and II   H. Cockburn, *Journal of Henry Cockburn 1831–1854*, 2 vols. 1874.

Coleman-Norton   P. R. Coleman-Norton, *Roman State and Christian Church*, 1966.

Cox   J. T. Cox, *Practice and Procedure in the Church of Scotland*, 6th ed. D. F. M. MacDonald, 1976.

Dunlop   A. M. Dunlop, *Parochial Law*, 2nd ed. 1835.

Ehler   S. Z. Ehler and J. B. Morrall, *Church and State through the Centuries*, 1954.

Enchiridion Symbolorum   Denzinger, *Enchiridion Symbolorum Definitionum et Declarationum de Rebus Fidei et Morum*, 23rd ed. A. Schonmetzer 1965.

Erskine   John Erskine of Carnock, *An Institute of the Laws of Scotland*. 8th ed. J. Nicolson, 2 vols. 1871.

Fleming I   J. R. Fleming, *A History of the Church in Scotland, 1843–1874*, 1927.

Fleming II   J. R. Fleming, *A History of the Church in Scotland, 1875–1929*, 1933.

G. A.   Acts of the General Assembly of The Church of Scotland (cited by year).

G. A. Reps   Reports to the General Assembly of The Church of Scotland, (cited by year).

Innes I   A. Taylor Innes, *The Laws of Creeds in Scotland*, 1867.

Innes II   A. Taylor Innes, *The Law of Creeds in Scotland*, 1904. (Though stated as a 2nd ed. this book, taking account of developments from 1865–1904, is in many ways a new book).

J. R.   Juridical Review, 1889– .

Kidd   *Documents of the Continental Reformation*, B. J. Kidd ed., 1911 rep. 1967.

Knox, *History*   John Knox, *History of the Reformation in Scotland*, ed. W. C. Dickinson 1949, 2 vols.

P. L. Public Law 1956– .

R.S.C.H.S. Records of the Scottish Church History Society, 1921– .

Robertson, Auchterarder I and II C. O. Robertson, *Report of the Court of Session proceedings in the Auchterarder Case*, 2 vols. 1838.

S.B.S.H. *Source Book of Scottish History*, W. C. Dickinson, G. Donaldson and I. A. Milne eds., 3 vols. 2nd ed. 1968.

Sjölinder R. Sjölinder, *Presbyterian Reunion in Scotland, 1907–1921*, trans. E. J. Sharpe 1962 Acta Universitatis Upsalensis Studia Historico-Ecclesiastica Upsalensie No. 4.

S.S.C. *Statutes of the Scottish Church*, 1225–1559, D. Patrick ed., Scottish History Society vol. 54, 1907.

S.S.F.C.S. *The Subordinate Standards and other Authoritative Documents of the Free Church of Scotland*, 1955.

Stair Sir James Dalrymple, Viscount Stair, *Institutions of the Law of Scotland*, 5th ed. J. R. More, 2 vols. 1832.

Case Citation Abbreviations

The main Scottish series of Court of Session Reports are: Mor.—Morison's Dictionary of Decisions, 1540-1808, 1816; F.C.—Faculty of Advocates Collection of Decisions, 1787-1841; S.—Shaw, 1821-38; D.—Dunlop, 1832-62; M.—Macpherson, 1862-73; R.—Rettie, 1873-98; F.—Fraser, 1898-1906; S.C.—Session Cases, 1906 continuing; Sh.Ct.Rep.—Sheriff Court Reports; S.L.R.—Scottish Law Reporter, 1865-1924; S.L.T.—Scots Law Times, 1893 continuing. The additions (H.L.), (J.) and (Sh. Ct.) are references to the House of Lords, Justiciary and Sheriff Court Reports in the indicated volume. J.C. cases are Justiciary (criminal) cases bound in S.C. for the year. Other cited reports are: Bell, H.L. Cases, 1843-52; Bell's Cases, 1794; Paton, McL. & Rob. (McLean and Robertson) and McQ. (McQueen) are H.L. reports for 1757-1821, 1838-9 and 1851-65 respectively. Broun and Irv. are Broun's and Irvine's reports of Justiciary cases for 1842-5 and 1852-67 respectively.

The main English reports cited are: A.C. and App. Cas.—Appeal Cases (House of Lords); All E.R.—All England Reports; Ch.—Chancery; E.R.—a consolidation of early English Reports; I.R.L.R.—Industrial Relations Law Reports; J.P.—Justices of the Peace Reports; P.—Probate; Q.B. and Q.B.D.—Queen's Bench; W.L.R.—Weekly Law Reports. Other abbreviated single citations are: Rob. App.—Robertson's Appeals (H.L.) 1707-27; Rob. Ecc.—Robertson's Ecclesiastical Cases, 1844-53; Hag. Con.—Haggard's Consistorial Reports, 1789-1821; Leach—Leach's Criminal Cases, 1730-1814. Bligh, Cl. & Fin. (Clark and Finnelly), Dow and Mer. (Merivale) are references to early House of Lords Reports.

From other jurisdictions are: C.M.L.R.—Common Market Law Reports; P.D.—Israel Supreme Court Reports; Y.B. Eur. Conv. H.R.—Yearbook of the European Convention on Human Rights; U.S. and L.Ed—references to the official and Lawyers Edition of the U.S. Supreme Court Reports. Cranch is an early report of the U.S. Supreme Court.

CHAPTER I

Introduction, Theory and Context

I. *Introduction*

The relationship between the civil and the ecclesiastical authority has over the centuries produced theories, argument and literature, legislation, rebellion and war. Scotland has contributed her fair share to the various results. As Scotland is the primary home of the Presbyterian family of churches, her solutions to the problems of Church and State, the principles adopted and compromises struck, are of more than ordinary interest. But before exploring the Scottish solutions in their various aspects it would be well first to survey briefly the theory of Church and State and then to put the Scottish developments in their broad context. The evolution of the Scottish solutions was influenced by disputes elsewhere, notably in England and on the Continent. The general climate of opinion and the theories required by political factors all had an effect upon what happened in Scotland.

Discussion of the relations between Church and State has been current for many centuries. Some writers have directed their efforts towards actual situations and problems, while others have aimed at ideal solutions. Even today great diversity is to be found. Much difficulty derives from differing uses of the basic concepts involved, from the very ideas of 'church' and 'state' themselves, for there is no single agreed use of or meaning for these terms. The Public Law of Scotland and of the United Kingdom has not been consistent in its uses of the language: precise definition of the term 'church' or of the adjective 'religious', for example, is lacking. Further complications arise since there is no defined concept of 'the State' in Scotland.[1] However, it will be possible to proceed with the present enquiry using these several terms in their ordinary meaning. It is only at a later stage that the borderlands of definition will be approached. Broadly we may take 'the State' as the national legal order, and elaborate the position of 'the Church' within it. Difficulty will arise when discussing the mutual recognition and responsibilities of these *personae*. At that stage it may be better to consider rather the Church and the community, differentiating such discussion within legal parameters from the normal theological and social content of these ideas.

It is necessary also at the beginning of this enquiry to make clear that the core of a discussion of Church and State in Scotland must adopt a definition of 'church' which is within the broad traditions of Christianity. Problems of the recognition of and accommodation with other religions are growing, but it is unrealistic in discussing the present law to ignore its foundation of many centuries of Christian thought. Such influences go back even beyond Knox and Calvin, as may be shown by the latter's frequent citation of Early and Later Christian Fathers in his *Institutes* and *Commentaries*. Similarly it must be recognised that in the relationship between Church and State in Scotland the Established Church plays the largest formative part for reasons of both history and size. Other churches have important roles; for example that of the Roman Catholics is important in the development of church-state relations in the area of education, but the pre-eminent role is played by the Auld Kirk.[2] This fact conditions my approach to the topic.

The age-old question of the relationship between Church and State goes to the very heart of the nature of human political society involving as it does the divergent objectives of each institution. Religion is concerned with the relationship between a man and his God, and it may have important consequences in the relationship between man and man. The State is concerned with the relationship between man and man, with the due disposition and distribution of this world's goods in conformity with the basic ethos of the community, and with acting expediently for the good of the community. It was possible for Richard Hooker in the great Eighth Book of his work on *Ecclesiastical Polity* to consider that church and State were simply the same people under a different guise. Were that indeed so, and it may be doubted how true it was when Hooker wrote, the area of conflict between Church and State would be minimal. And yet even in that situation it is clear that questions will arise as to the supremacy between Church and State, for the political element will not be content to see itself simply as a department of the Church and the Church will not be content to see itself as an extension of the civil government; all quite apart from the cases, few though they may be, of those who feel that for reasons of conscience they may not follow the authorised state religion.

One way out of this is for there to be both a state religion and tolerance of other religions as well. Thus the ancient state of Rome had an official state religion of which the Pontifex Maximus (a title now used by the Pope) was the high priest. Not much is known of the Roman state religion, but it was considered that the gods of Rome presided over the safety of, and lived in, the essential city of Rome, the *Urbs Romana*. However, this Roman state religion was not intolerant of other religious manifestations, so long as these were not a threat to the civil government. Thus there occurred the spread of the great mystery cults, including, quite early, that of the Great Mother, and, later, the cult of Mithras around the time of the development of Christianity. Naturally such a solution depends upon the primary religion being one under which tolerance is possible. The function of the Roman state religion was the propitiation of the state gods, but these gods were not jealous gods, and, so long as they were duly sacrificed to on appropriate occasions, what the Romans did the rest of the time seems to have been a matter of indifference to them.

Christianity, in common with many other religions can not easily be used in such a way. Christianity is not only concerned with the relationship between a man and his God during life, but teaches that a living knowledge and love of Christ is essential for salvation. In other words, what a man believes and does in this life has permanent consequences for him. It follows that institutional

Christianity will lay down certain patterns of conduct and belief which are difficult for the individual to recede from when invited by the State to do something which conflicts with these patterns. It also follows that bigoted Christians (if such be Christian) may attempt by various means to make alternative patterns of behaviour and belief difficult, even impossible, and at the least uninviting. This may even operate as between different varieties of Christian belief. There may therefore be the two possibilities, that the State will find that some 'Christians' are unwilling to follow its dictates, and secondly that some 'Christians' will attempt to use the institutional framework of the State for what they conceive to be the best interests of the citizens; in terms of the parable 'to compel them to come in' (Luke 14:23). In fairness it should be said that this attitude of mind is not confined to 'Christians' but is found in men of very divergent convictions. Although for obvious reasons this inquiry is largely confined to questions arising between versions of Christianity and the State, yet the basic principles have application wherever individuals or a group of individuals with strong beliefs or a missionary zeal, conceive of divergence between the State and their beliefs.

The distinction between Church and State has a long history. It is to be found as early as Romans 13, and is inherent in certain of the early Christian Fathers. However, it seems that St. Augustine's *City of God*[3] was the major work giving it popular expression. The Gelasian theory of the Two Powers, current throughout the Middle Ages was put forward by Pope Gelasius I in A.D. 494 in a letter to the Byzantine Emperor to justify his argument that Imperial interference in Church affairs was illegal.[4] This expression gives basic form to the separation of Church and State which all parts of the Church have contended for at various times. Questions as to the supremacy of one or other of the powers arose, and the two sides took different stances. Thus Charlemagne argued the State's duty not only to support the Church but also to 'strengthen within it the knowledge of the Catholic Faith'.[5] On the other hand Gregory VII strongly asserted the Papal supremacy[6] and Innocent III explained this supremacy by the famous analogy of the Sun and the Moon.[7] The highest exposition of the doctrine of the Two Powers, expressed this time as the Two Swords, and of the papal supremacy, was reached in the Bull *Unam Sanctam* issued by Boniface VIII in 1302.[8]

The Reformers saw no reason to depart from the doctrine of the Two Powers. For them it was adequately grounded in the teaching of the New Testament. That there is a division of function between the civil magistrate and the Church is inherent in Calvin's discussion of the topic in his *Institutes of the Christian Religion*[9], and naturally forms a pre-supposition of the various reformed Confessions including the Scots and Westminster Confessions. The fundamental division between the powers is a continuing feature, though the precise balance of authority between them differs. Thus there is a spectrum from the erastian concepts of Lutheranism, through the disciples of Zwingli, to the Calvinist position of the Genevan reformers. It is this last which appears in

Scotland in Andrew Melville's *Second Book of Discipline*, the leading source of the presbyterian government of the present Church of Scotland.

II. Theoretical Solutions

Logically there may be four different solutions to the problems of the relationship between Church and State. The State may be supreme; the Church, or one Church, may be supreme; there may be strict separation between Church and State; and there may be a balance between the two, each supreme within its own area of competence. In history there have been manifestations of each of these crude classifications. Some of these manifestations have been sophisticated, some rudimentary, and it is necessary to outline these principal possible solutions in order to understand the conceptual background of the Scottish position.[10]

Erastianism

It is usual to call any view which gives supremacy to the State over the Church 'erastian'. In so doing we classify together many different shades of opinion, and may misrepresent the original thesis, but today the label has come to be used in this general way. J. N. Figgis gives the basic meaning of erastianism as being the theory that 'religion is the creature of the state'.[11] He illustrates the theory by the statement of Selden, 'Whether is the Church or the Scripture the judge of religion? Of truth neither, but the State'.[12] Where erastianism is applied the State is the supreme authority in religious affairs, with consequent dangers for freedom of belief; the possibility that expediency will override reason; and the possibility that belief will be subjected to political convenience. It seems that these dangers were not apparent to Thomas Erastus, whose name the theory bears.

Erastus was a Doctor of Medicine, most of his writing being in that field, though later in his career he became well-known for this theological writing. He was a friend of Beza, Calvin's biographer and successor at Geneva, and of Bullinger, the successor of Zwingli at Zurich. Erastus's theories owe much to the ideas of Zwingli, and less to those of theocratic Geneva.

The occasion of Erastus's thinking was the presentation and defence of a thesis on Excommunication by George Wither at the theological faculty in Heidelberg in 1568, where Erastus was professor of therapeutics. Erastus had argued the relationship of Church and State in excommunication, fearing the establishment of a rigid clericalism when the introduction of excommunication had been proposed by some incomers from Geneva, but the Wither thesis precipitated a fuller study. This extended treatment was not, however, published until after Erastus's death, though it was in private circulation before then. The *Theses of Erastus touching Excommunication* when published in 1589 caused great controversy among theologians and politicians, and it is the use made of principles found in, or developed from, the propositions of the

Theses, that fixed the word 'erastian' in our language. The actual *Theses* did not appear in English translation until 1659, being re-translated in 1682, and again by Dr. R. W. Lee in 1844 in an attempt to refute allegations of erastianism made against Moderates during the Disruption controversy in Scotland.

Erastus argued that the discipline of excommunication was not for the Church to exercise because it was not sanctioned by the Bible, and because in a Christian State it is for the civil magistrate, not the Church, to punish all offences. But Erastus did not give the civil magistrate power over doctrine, and did not envisage the civil authority having, or being able, to choose between religious systems and beliefs. In this lies the difficulty of his doctrines. For he assumed that in the State all citizens are members of the same Church, believing the same truths. Therefore the magistrate had no need to pick and choose between doctrines, nor might he set himself above religious questions. As a theoretical position there is much to be said for this, but life is not that simple, and adapting Erastus's theory to life has occasioned much abuse of it. His ingenious arguments are attractive in a variety of ways. To the politician they give opportunity to escape from clerical domination; to ecclesiastics, opportunity to consolidate their civil power, depending upon how one stresses the arguments.

But it is all very well to argue that in a Christian State ecclesiastical and secular jurisdiction belongs exclusively to the magistrate, where beliefs are fully agreed. It is too easy a step from that to suggest that the magistrate can impose whatever religious opinions seem good to him, and that under these circumstances there is still the same duty to obey. Nonetheless, drawing on the example of Constantine and his successors, as well as on Moses, writers such as John Jewel found it possible to defend the Elizabethan supremacy[13], though he had to differentiate between ecclesiastical jurisdiction and doctrine, excluding the latter on the grounds of its being beyond human interference. Ecclesiastical jurisdiction was, however, within the magistrate's power, since he, owing his position to God, was under a duty to see that ministers performed their office properly. In addition, since all citizens were members of the Church it was obvious that the magistrate had responsibilities and authority in ecclesiastical matters.

Richard Hooker, in the Eighth Book of *The Laws of Ecclesiastical Polity* (written by 1593, but not published until 1648) took the same line as Jewel. However, Hooker went somewhat further by suggesting that Church and State are in essence the same people under different guise, and extending the duty of the magistrate to support orthodox religion against deviance much as the magistrate supports orthodox behaviour through the criminal law. This of course could involve persecution. The magistrate's highest duty was in securing the salvation of his subjects, and so untrue religion had to be suppressed. Yet Hooker does not seem to have considered that this could mean that the subject had to believe as the monarch said. He rather thought that to refuse to the monarch the power to govern in religious matters meant either that truth was not capable of being distinguished, or that the magistrate could not so distinguish. In either event the institution of a national church would have been struck at, and that institution was Hooker's great aim.

The basis of Hooker's views was the correspondence in membership between the Church and State. Since Church and State are co-extensive it was for him a short step to argue as he does in Book Eight, that the Crown in Parliament is the essence of government of the Church. His basis for this argument was that all authority in the kingdom was grounded on the consent of the people—a strange argument having regard to the political facts of his time, and perhaps the reason why he did not publish Book Eight during his life. If, then, the Church is to be governed through Parliament, and the people are bound to obey Parliament, it is curious to find that Hooker himself did not see that this form of argument leads to the conclusion, drawn three years after the publication of Book Eight in 1648, that the State can dictate religious belief.

The most thorough-going erastianism (sometimes known as Caesaro-papalism) is to be found in Chapter Forty-two of Hobbes' *Leviathan* published in 1651. It amounts to holding that the State may establish whatever religion it pleases and exact obedience for the sake of conscience, creating and altering the forms of church government as it desires. Erastus himself did not assert more than that the State possesses all coercive authority, but he considered that the true religion is supposed to be established in the State, none other being allowed and that the magistrate has no power to transgress the teaching of the Bible. This is of course detached from political reality in a way which Hobbes is not. Yet it may well seem that Hobbes has performed a *reductio ad absurdum* of the erastian position by holding that religion is under the absolute control of the State's dictates. In fairness it must be noted that Hobbes does allow one reservation in the case where the State denies the Incarnation but, as Figgis says, he leaves little doubt that the duty to obey the State is paramount.[14]

Charges of erastianism were levelled against the Moderates in Scotland particularly at the time of the conflict between Church and State which occasioned the Disruption of 1843. To a degree these were justified as it was made clear by the House of Lords and the Court of Session, and by the refusal of Parliament to overset their decisions, that the Church of Scotland had only such power as the State afforded it. But thorough-going erastianism has never been present in Scotland. We have had periods in which the civil power has attempted to state and to enforce particular forms of church government and doctrine, but these have been temporary. Such instances as the Laud Prayer Book, James VI's attempt to impose Bishops, and the operation of the Test Acts were all erastian operations, the magistrate taking the initiative. But they were all attempts for political ends, the content of doctrine being secondary to these. At the Disruption the conflict was occasioned by objections by a party in the Church to an establishment in which the State had the last word, but, whatever the theory of the matter, it is clear that the State was not at that time going to impose doctrine, though it would enforce the patronage laws. This came close to interference in spiritual matters, and was presented as such by the evangelicals, but this was not the erastianism to be found even in the Church of England.[15]

Clericalism

The inverse of erastianism is the system in which the Church is supreme. But a distinction must be drawn between true examples of such a system and cases where it happens that the civil authority is also and primarily the ecclesiastical authority. Thus one can not classify the Papal States of the Fourteenth to Nineteenth centuries as an example of Clericalism. There the Church was the civil authority, but clearly was acting in a civil capacity and according to the normal political forms without religious purpose and intent. One might however arguably classify the present Communist states as examples of such a mode, for Communism is a form of religious belief.

The city of Geneva during the ascendancy of Farel and during the period that Calvin was the guiding spirit would seem to be a good example.[16] There, and to a lesser extent in Basle, Berne and Zurich, the position of the Church was such that it dominated the city, but for religious ends. Again there may be argument as to the degree of theocracy in Scotland after the Reformation. It is, however, clear that in Scotland there was never the degree of Clericalism that there was in Geneva. Although the Scottish Parliament passed the various statutes abolishing the jurisdiction of Rome and the Roman religion, it was not willing to enact *The First Book of Discipline*, and by the time of the death of Knox the political elements of the State were once more in the ascendant. The Church was a strong element thereafter.[17] It resisted episcopacy, and insisted upon the establishment of Presbyterianism in 1592 and 1690. The Scottish Presbyterians attempted unsuccessfully to make the whole of Britain Presbyterian, in exchange for their help against Charles I. The doctrine, worship, government and discipline of the Church of Scotland were secured in the negotiations with England for the Union of 1707. But the Church did not achieve the position of dominance inherent in true Clericalism, probably due to the conciliar nature of Presbyterianism, which militates against the creation of a clerical institution of sufficient political weight and continuity to act as a political force. The fact is. that the Church in Scotland has not controlled the State, though it has greatly influenced it at times.

Total Separation

The absolute separation of Church and State is an attractive idea in theory, but it has practical difficulties. The First Amendment to the Constitution of the United States provides *inter alia*:

'Congress shall make no law respecting an establishment of religion or prohibiting the free exercise thereof; . . .'

According to Jefferson it was the intention of the whole American people thus to build 'a wall of separation between Church and State.'[18] This statement was first quoted judicially by Chief Justice Waite in *Reynolds* v. *United States* (1879) 98 U.S. 145 at 164, but merely as the context of an observation by Jefferson on the ability of courts to reach actions, and not thoughts. However, it was resurrected in *Everson* v. *Board of Education* (1947) 330 U.S. 1, and has been a much used slogan since.[19]

The United States experience in separation is not happy, and has shown that while it may be easy for Church and State to inter-mingle in erastian or clerical modes, strict separation is not possible. Thus in the United States there has been developed a series of categories of state aid to religion, which are held not to contravene the First Amendment.[20] In so doing the United States has arguably placed itself in the fourth possible category, that of balance between Church and State. But in constitutional terms the separation remains. Not only do the two powers have separate jurisdictions, but under the constitution these two powers do not overlap. There remain, however, areas of common interest and interaction in education, broadcasting, and similar areas in which both powers have interests.

The concept of separation has strong doctrinal basis, and is a relatively simple development from the idea of the two powers. It is to be found in the writings of John Locke and of Roger Williams[21] among many others, and from these men became the principle of the First Amendment. But the basis of this view was not the seeking of the health of either power, but rather the avoidance of persecuting and intolerant attitudes gaining positions of authority from which they might take action. We have not required strict separation for these reasons in Scotland though in the last century dis-establishment of the state church was sought, since its position of privilege was felt by some to be unjustified, and by others unscriptural.

Cooperation

That the Church and the State may cooperate seems the sensible solution in a situation where there is a single church to which the majority of the citizens adhere. Pre-eminently this is the case where the proportion of Church members of one denomination is very high. In that instance cooperation is a good solution. Clearly there are areas within which the Church and State do not conflict and therefore 'acting within their respective spheres may signally promote each other's welfare'.[22] The difficulty comes with the determination of the limits of the proper sphere of each power. It is attractive to talk of co-ordinate jurisdiction, and alluring to use the imagery of the Sun and the Moon, but the difficulties of definition may be acute.

There are further difficulties for the law in such a situation. Normally the State will cooperate with one Church, establishing that Church as being the expression of the national religious consciousness. But the Church established will usually expect some form of State endowment, in Scotland represented by the teinds and similar feudal burdens.[23] This expression of the duty of the civil magistrate to promote the established religion has given rise to problems in

Scotland. Beyond that there is inherent in the establishment idea the possibility that the Church will seek the aid of the State in the suppression of error, with consequent difficulties for minority groups. It is this type of activity which occasioned the writings of Roger Williams and John Locke, referred to above, seeking to escape from persecution by the strict separation of Church and State. Scotland has not been without such difficulties, though Presbyterianism may claim to have been less blood-thirsty than some other faiths.

Such then are the four principal theoretical solutions to the relationship between Church and State. A variety of intermediate positions are also possible, and, as indicated, none of the principal positions are or have been found purely in history. Argument and struggle over the precise accommodation of the principles involved are to be seen in every century.

The Scottish position at present is that an amalgam has been created between cooperation and separation, varying in different topics and in respect of different denominations. There has been preserved a national recognition of religion connected with the special, though not necessarily favoured, position afforded to one denomination—which hardly amounts to establishment in the sense that word was used in in prior centuries—and yet the law also enshrines principles of toleration which have been worked out over the years by statute and case law, by practice and tacit agreement. Whether this amalgam is satisfactory depends to a degree at least on one's own convictions and persuasions. It is the purpose of the succeeding pages to set out the facets of the arrangement so that the reader can assess the position for himself. At the same time it would be less than honest for me totally to conceal my own opinions and reactions.

III. Contexts

Finally before we turn to the law and its development it is convenient very briefly to indicate political, economic and social contexts within which the Scottish developments occurred. These affected the changing intellectual climates and attitudes of the centuries, and also had political effects, which in turn affected the Scottish law on Church and State. It would be unwise for a mere lawyer to attempt fully to assess the extent of the impact of these factors—for different disciplines will present different analyses—but their existence ought to be noted as in part conditioning our law.[24] At the same time I would urge strongly that, while these factors are to be kept in mind, to undervalue or underplay the elements of religious belief and conviction in the Scottish developments is hopelessly to distort and misrepresent the situation.

Most obviously political and economic factors play a part in the Scottish Reformation, and this will be indicated at the appropriate point. Suffice it here to say that the Roman Catholic Church was to a degree emblematic of the French Alliance, and that the intervention of Elizabeth in 1560, which sealed the success of the Reformers, giving them opportunity to take political power, was actuated by the self-interest of eliminating a possible route for an invasion.

The Scottish development did not occur in isolation. At the time of the Scottish Reformation there was much traffic with the Continent, and the struggles there between Protestant and Catholic theorists, to say nothing of politics, was not without effect. It is interesting therefore to find that the Scottish Reformation was a reformation of religion, and only secondarily a departure from Catholicism. It soon also became a cause round which nationalism might thrive, and the pride in government by Presbytery is not entirely grounded in religion. There were political forces at work, at first to avoid a restoration of Catholicism, for that would have meant the resumption of the French link and perhaps an unwanted war with England. Then within the kingdom itself there was the struggle to restrict the power of the Crown. The efforts of James VI to impose episcopacy, and the theory of the later Stuarts of the Divine Right of Kings, were attempts in part to produce a political system closer to the Austinian model (see note 27) than was then available to monarchy. This had obvious effects on the Union of 1707.

At the time of the Disruption controversy a variety of factors may be noticed. In religious organisation of the time there was a seeking of independence on the part of churches. Thus in France the Gallican Declaration of 1682 had marked the beginning of the French Church's attempt to secure a degree of independence from the Papacy, which eventually produced the Liberal Catholic movement associated with the names of Lamennais, Montalembert and Dupanloup, and later Gallicanism. Opposed to this De Maistre's writings gave rise to Ultramontanism, the supreme expression of which was the pontificate of Pius IX, under whom the famous *Syllabus of Errors* of 1864 was issued and the dogma of Papal Infallibility was proclaimed at the Vatican Council of 1870. But fundamentally both these movements, though opposed in doctrine, were united in their concepts of the Church as being at any rate free of state control, and, in the thinking of some, as being the absolute authority. Of course the State also had an interest. It objected to control of part of the life of the people being vested in Rome. Bismarck's Kulturkampf is the expression of the same dilemma, from the State's side.[25]

Nearer home the British government during the Disruption seems to have had its eyes more upon developments in the Church of England,[26] and may have confused the establishment of that Church with the quite different establishment in Scotland. At any rate within the English Church there was also a movement, dating perhaps from 1829, and certainly from John Keble's sermon on 'National Apostasy' preached at St. Mary's, Oxford on 14 July 1833 before His Majesty's Justices of Assize. To this sermon may be dated the beginning of the Oxford or Tractarian Movement, which shook the Church of England during the following years. John Henry Newman had already been publishing the series of *Tracts for the Times,* but following the Assize Sermon the movement increased in vitality. In contrast to the Scottish position, however, the initial point of dispute was not an objection to interference under the establishment, but the fact that the State seemed to be about to give away the patrimony of the Church and to dismantle the establishment. The Tractarians sought a return to pure principles, and their studies in search of authority and Apostolic Succession led many, including Newman, into the Roman Catholic Church. The importance of this movement for the present enquiry is this. The Tractarians in order to protect the patrimony of the Church became anti-erastian. But they were not of great political weight, and the erastian structure of the Church of England allowed the government to remain inactive. The government seems to have carried this attitude over into its dealings with the Scottish Church.

Other factors may also be noted. In legal and political theory in the Nineteenth Century there was much emphasis on the concept of "the sovereign" as the single source of authority.[27] This almost necessarily led to the views expressed by the Courts in the various Disruption cases. The Church had only the power which "the sovereign" gave it. The only remedy was parliamentary intervention, but this was not forthcoming and the Disruption of the Church of Scotland occurred.

Such ideas also affected the development of the law relating to the churches outside establishment, but ideas of tolerance helped give these associations legal personality and status. Pluralism gave a theoretical basis for many developments, helping to spread the idea, abhorrent to earlier generations, that there might be separate societies of spontaneous growth within the State, which it was the duty of the State to recognise and protect, even though strictly they did not owe their origin or 'jurisdiction' to the State.[28]

Within the field of theology itself, the rise of Higher Criticism had an effect upon the relations of Church and State. The doubts which that movement threw on former Church concepts of truth and doctrine were not without effect on views of the Church itself. Accordingly a wider view of the Church, with greater freedom to rule itself, and to alter and modify its standards and beliefs became current. Changing views of the desirable church constitution and of the political theory of the State made it possible to achieve the solution of the Church of Scotland Act 1921. The ideal of a free Church in a free State was therefore approached.

CHAPTER II

From the Reformation of Religion to the Union of the Parliaments

The Reformation of religion in Scotland, usually dated to the adoption of the Scots Confession and the anti-Catholic statutes of 1560, is the most appropriate point for a study of Church and State in Scotland to commence. The statutes of that Reformation imply in places that there was a Church of God in Scotland under Roman Catholicism, but the statutory repudiation of the external manifestations of Catholicism and its beliefs is such that there is little value in our delving into prior history. What was done after 1560 elaborates and builds upon the events of that time, making them form, from the vantage of the present day, a major watershed.[29]

The outbreak of the Scottish Reformation was due to a variety of factors, political and economic as well as religious, and the exact balance between these at any given time, and in the motives of any given participant, may be a matter of dispute. The principal facts were that the Roman Catholic Church in Scotland was corrupt and wealthy. It was also a major landholder. By a variety of devices the Crown in the late Fifteenth and early Sixteenth centuries had obtained what amounted to the right to present to major church appointments. Most of the abbeys and priories were in the hands of relatives of nobility who were without interest in the spiritual functions of their offices, and the personal lives of such were common scandal.[30] By the time of the Reformation the Church was beginning to seek to reform itself[31], but the matter had passed out of its hands. Protestant doctrines had been preached in the kingdom soon after Luther had begun his work on the Continent[32], and the martyrdom of George Wishart in 1546 added to the zeal of friends and followers throughout the country. Three months after the burning of Wishart, Cardinal Beaton, who had condemned him, was assassinated in his own castle in St. Andrews, and the castle was seized by the Protestants. After a siege by the French troops of Mary of Guise, who was the Queen Mother and Regent during Mary Stuart's minority, the Protestants, including John Knox who had joined them and been called to be their minister, were transported to French prisons and galleys.[33]

These events were religious in origin, but they also introduced a political factor by involving the French alliance, and there was a tendency in the following years for those opposed to that alliance to side with the Reformers. Some also gave their support being keen to seize the lands held by the Roman Catholic Church. But it would be unfair to imply that the basis of the Scottish Reformation was not primarily religious. However, at this time, although Protestant doctrines were being more and more widely preached by Catholic priests as well as by men from the Continent, there was no defined body which could be considered to be the Church of Scotland.

Historically the roots of the institutional Church of Scotland might be traced back to the First Covenant of December 1557, in which various persons bound themselves to maintain, nourish and defend the whole congregation of Christ against the attacks of the 'congregation of Satan' which they expressly renounced.[34] Notwithstanding this language, it did appear at first that the desired reformation of religion might be obtained within a system of tolerance, but this hope vanished following a riot in Perth in 1559. The Lords of the Congregation took up arms to defend themselves, and, naturally, the Crown sought to suppress the insurrection. Elizabeth of England intervened to give support to the rebels, and, Mary of Guise having died, the Crown forces, which were mainly French, sought peace. A mutual withdrawal of French and English forces was agreed by the Treaty of Edinburgh.[35] Under Concessions attached to this Treaty Queen Mary was to take no reprisals against her rebellious subjects, and the Convention of Estates was appointed to meet in August 1560. That meeting was to name commissioners to go to France and discuss the religious questions which were at the root of the rebellion.

Parliament duly met in August 1560, but without having been summoned by the Crown, and without its normal balance of composition.[36] Although the Concessions required only the appointment of commissioners to discuss the religious question with the Crown, Parliament was petitioned to abolish popery. This it was willing to do, and by the Papal Jurisdiction Act 1560 c.2, it abolished the jurisdiction of the Pope in Scotland. Further the Act 1560 c.3 abolished idolatry, and c.4 proscribed the Mass.

Being unwilling simply to leave a vacuum, the Estates asked a small Committee of ministers to prepare a statement of the new belief. In four days this Committee under John Knox produced a draft of what came to be known as the Scots Confession.[37] After discussion this was adopted by Parliament in the Confession of Faith Ratification Act 1560 c.1. The Confession was agreed as being;

'The Confession of Faith professed and believed by the Protestants within the realm of Scotland, published by them in Scotland, and by the Estates thereof ratified and approved as wholesome and sound doctrine, grounded upon the infallible truth of God's Word.'

Certain things are notable about this formula. The Confession does not bear to be enacted by the civil authority for the Church. It is the Confession published by the Protestants in Scotland, and *ratified and approved* by Parliament. The civil authority does not act, it approves a statement formulated outside of itself. Again, the Confession is not the Confession of the Church of Scotland at this stage. Nor is it adopted or put forward by authority of that Church. It is the Confession of the Protestants in Scotland, and no institutional church is referred to. Finally the Confession is not a Confession: it is truth.[38]

It is noticeable that this, the first enactment dealing with the Church, does not contain any detail on the relations of the Church and the State. Indeed, reflecting its theological origin, the Confession does not contain a concept of the Church or of the State in their modern aspects. The Church is seen in its theological aspect as the company of believers, though it is recognised that there may be 'filthy synagogues', and the 'false Kirk' is dealt with.[39] The civil magistrate is stated to have his proper sphere, including the duty of maintaining true religion and suppressing all idolatry and superstition.[40] But all this is without truly defining the institutional Church with which the State has relations. The Church is simply the congregation of believers. It may therefore be questioned whether the Church of Scotland existed at this stage, or was thought of as The Church in Scotland. The further question therefore emerges, whether the Church of Scotland is the origin of its creed and doctrines, or whether the creed and doctrines are the origin of that Church.

Unfortunately the 1560 Parliament was unwilling to go beyond these steps, and there was no settlement of ecclesiastical polity, nor was there any attempt to deal with the colossal question of the endowments of the Roman Catholic Church. The Privy Council had appointed six men, John Douglas, John Winram, John Row, John Spottiswoode, John Willock and John Knox to form a committee charged with the drawing up of a constitution for the Church. The Committee speedily reported to the Council, laying a variation of the *First Book of Discipline* before it on 20 May 1560, and a revision was submitted to Parliament in 1560 and 1561. *The First Book of Discipline*[41], prepared by Knox and his colleagues did formulate a system of church government, based on a modified episcopal concept. It envisaged a Christian commonwealth in which the Church and the State would cooperate, the Church being responsible for the welfare of the people, while the civil authority would govern. The Church would deal with all such matters as education[42], and poor relief[43] in addition to its more obvious functions of preaching and discipline. But in order to carry out these schemes Knox and his friends considered that it would be necessary for the new Protestant church to be given the endowment of the Roman Catholic Church as a patrimony.[44] This was not acceptable to the Lords, some of whom had seized estates, some of whom had relatives in positions of authority over estates, and some of whom (including the Crown itself) received large payments from ecclesiastical estates. In retrospect the *Book's* failure to receive the approval of Parliament was inevitable. The financial and economic upheaval consequent upon such a redistribution of the economic assets of the country would have been tremendous, though the ends were eminently desirable. But the endowments were left virtually intact, and the polity of the old church was left undisturbed, though the ministers were effectively prohibited from preaching by the Reformation statutes. The provision for the ministers of the new faith was limited to giving them the right to receive the 'thirds of benefices' as a temporary measure.[45]

The failure of the State to deal with the endowments of the Catholic Church, and of the Reformed Church to organise itself properly without state approval, produced a curious situation. The old Church continued in existence, with its estates and revenues, but forbidden to preach and celebrate its sacraments, while the new Church struggled to establish its polity with insufficient resources. Thus two churches were in existence and continued so for some years. The Reformers seem at this time to have considered that there was little point in pressing the take-over of the institutional church, and there was force in this view, especially since the Catholic Church was closely allied to the Crown through the presence of Queen Mary. Her abdication in 1567[46] changed matters as the regent on behalf of the infant James VI, the Earl of Moray, was a Protestant. The Acts of the 1567 Parliament repealed the Acts in support of the Papacy (c.4), and ratified the abolition of the Pope's jurisdiction (c.3) and the Mass (c.5). The Confession of Faith was once more engrossed in the register of Parliament. But now steps were taken to establish the reformed Church.

The Church Act 1567 c.6 'Anent the trew and haly Kirk and of thame declarit not to be of the same' gave legal establishment to the Church of Scotland. Defectively printed in 1567, but re-enacted with due explanation in 1579 as c.6 of that year, it provides:

'. . . . Oure souerane lord with auise [advice] of his thrie estaitis . . . . hes declarit and declaris the ministeris of the blissed euangel of Jesus chryst quhome god of his mercie hes now raisit vp amangis ws [raised up amongst us] Or heirefter sall [shall] raise aggreing with thame that now levis [live] in doctrine and administratioun of the sacramentis And the people of this realme that professis Jesus christ as he is now offerit in his evangell and do communicat with the haly sacramentis as in the reformit kirkis of this realme ar publictlie administrat according to the confessioun of the fayth To be the only trew and haly kirk of Jesus christ within this realme.'

In this way the Church of Scotland was first legally defined and given place as an institution of the realm. The statute defines the standards, and hence the doctrinal identity of the Church, in terms of its known teaching and the Scots Confession. But though the Church is defined in terms of its existing standards, and is declared to be the true Church, the Act goes beyond a mere acknowledgement of the Church. The terms of the Act, striking at other beliefs, establish the Church as the only Church recognised by law in the kingdom.

The next step was the settlement of the jurisdiction of the Church. The Church Jurisdiction Act 1567 c.12, narrated that the Crown:

'declarit and grantit iurisdictioun to the said Kirk quhilk [which] consistis and standis in preicheing of the trew word of Jesus Christ correctioun of maneris and administratioun of haly Sacramentis . . . .'

and went on to declare that:

'. . . . thair is na uther face of Kirk nor uther face of Religion than is presentlie be the fauour of God establischeit within this Realme And that thair be na uther iurisdictioun ecclesiasticall acknawlegeit within this Realme uther than quhilk [which] is and salbe [shall be] within the same Kirk or that quhilk [which] flowis thairfra concerning the premissis . . . .'

This was not entirely satisfactory to the Church, but no remedy was forthcoming. The terms of the Act do not make it clear whether the State was recognising that jurisdiction which the Church had undoubtedly been exercising from 1560, or whether the 'grant' additional to the declaration involved a conferral of power by the State. It was interpreted in the latter form during the Disruption cases, conforming to the then prevalent legal theory, but this may have been wrong. However it is interpreted, the Act nonetheless is fundamental to the position of the Church as having legal jurisdiction within Scotland.

The third Act connected with the establishing of the Church was the Coronation Oath Act 1567 c.8, requiring all future monarchs to swear to protect the true Church as established, and to root out all those opposed to its teaching. This was of more political than legal interest, though as we shall see it provided the first complaint of the Claim of Right against James VII.

These Acts then represent the establishment of the Protestant Church in Scotland. They may be viewed as recognising the existing Church, or they may be interpreted as constituting the conditions of the establishment of the Church, and conferring, and therefore limiting, its powers. That ambiguity was to be productive of much strife in the future. It is, however, noticeable, that the statutes do not attempt in any way to deal with the form of government of the Church. In fact for the next twenty-five years the Church was without a defined polity, and moved from quasi-episcopacy to quasi-presbyterianism and back, depending upon a variety of factors.

The endowment of the Church was another topic not dealt with in 1567. The Act 1567 c.7 provided benefices for the maintenance of ministers:

'. . . . ay and quhill [until] the Kirk come to the full possessioun of their proper patrimonie, quhilk [which] is the teindes . . . .'

thus enforcing the previous provisions made by the Privy Council. But curiously in view of the ascendancy of the Church in 1567 and in later years, the State was unwilling to give the provisions of The First Book of Discipline statutory effect. Steps were taken not so much to disendow the Roman Catholic Church as slowly to take over its benefices. Thus the Act 1567 c.10 provided for the patronage of benefices to remain in the hands of the existing patrons, but for the reformed Church, through its superintendents, to be the judge of the qualifications of a presentee. This was intended to result in a gradual placement of reformed ministers as the Catholic benefices fell vacant, and this remedy was further extended by the Concordat of Leith of 1572, under which episcopal sees falling vacant were to be filled by Crown appointment, subject to examination of the qualifications of the presentee by the Church. But the system was open to abuse, and was used by the Crown to establish its control of the Church, the bishop's oath of office recognising the Royal supremacy in matters religious.[47]

Further in 1572 the Act 1572 c.3 enacted testing legislation, requiring subscription of the Confession by ministers so 'that the adversaries of Christ's Evangell sall [shall] not injoy the Patrimonie of the Kirk'. This Act made possible the deposition of ministers who refused to conform to the Confession, and was partially effective. It was also used by the Crown once more to exact a recognition of the Royal supremacy. The total effect of the Acts of 1567 and 1572 was slowly to convert the benefices to the use of the Church. However, the legislation only dealt with benefices occupied by ministers. Nothing was done to recover benefices which had been put under secular control, or to deal with institutions such as monasteries and abbeys which had not been taken over by the Kirk.

When Andrew Melville returned to Scotland from Geneva in 1574 he found that the episcopal system then in force was being used by the Crown to control the Church, and by the nobility to continue to divert Church funds into their coffers. Further, despite the legislation, the ordinary ministers were subject to grave financial limitations as the laws were not being properly administered. To meet this situation he formulated *The Second Book of Discipline*[48] which was approved by the General Assembly in 1578. This work was crucial in the development of the Church of Scotland as we know it today, containing as it does the basic elements of Presbyterianism.[49]

The *Second Book* condemned episcopacy due to its possible abuse, and set out clearly and cogently the presbyterian doctrine of the parity of ministers, and the normal presbyterian form of conciliar church government. The *Second Book* stated, rather than argued, the independence of the Church from civil authority, Church powers and authority being derived from God. It also argued that the Church had the right and duty to instruct the civil authority in matters of conscience and religion, and indeed the right to tell the civil arm how to exercise its own peculiar civil authority in accordance with the Word of God.[50] This argument threatened the introduction of a theocracy, and, not surprisingly, was avoided and indeed attacked by the Crown as being subversive of the Crown's own authority and powers.

It is unnecessary here to go into the history of the struggles between the Church and the State, and between episcopacy and presbyterianism over the next few years. James sought to control the Church, the major alternative power within the kingdom, and yet, for political reasons, he was forced to accept many of the Church's demands. Thus in 1579, as we have seen, the Church Act c.6, re-enacted the establishment of the Protestant Church, affirming that the 'only trew and haly Kirk of Jesus Christ within this realme' was composed of those who professed the Scots Confession. The Church Jurisdiction Act 1579 c.7 re-stated the jurisdiction of the Church. In 1581 the King and his household subscribed the Negative Confession[51], denying all doctrines contrary to those of the Scots Confession. Despite all this, the Black Acts of 1584 sought to re-impose episcopacy, and placed all authority, including ecclesiastical authority, under the Crown. But by 1590 the presbyterian party was once more in the ascendant, resulting in the Act 1592 c.8, establishing the presbyterian government of the Church of Scotland.

The General Assembly Act 1592 c.8, sometimes referred to as the Great Charter of the Church, is the statutory foundation of the presbyterian character of the Church of Scotland. In it the former Acts regarding the Protestant religion were ratified and approved (though not the Black Acts of 1584) and the civil authority went on to ratify and approve the form of Church government by way of General Assembly, Synods, Presbyteries and Kirk Session. These have power and jurisdiction in matters ecclesiastical. In so providing the Act repeated statements from Ch.VII of *The Second Book of Discipline*, and gave foundation to the present established Church in law. But though this Act was and is of great importance in settling the polity of the Church, for it was grafted in to the constitution of the country at the Union, nonetheless James himself was able by a variety of astute moves to diminish the importance of the enactment. Thus the Act expressly preserved patronage, a device which could be used by the civil authority. Again the calling of General Assemblies was left as a matter for the Crown, and James used this power to call Assemblies at a variety of venues less under Presbyterian control than Edinburgh. In short, in the space of a few years James was able to secure the re-creation of bishops, and through their agency was able to control the Church[52], but only after his accession to the English throne in 1603.

The next century saw a struggle between Church and State, and between rival theories of church government[53]. For a time episcopacy was enforced, and there were the famous struggles of the Covenanters. The Divine Right of Kings, propagated by the later Stuarts at least in part on a basis of erastian theories[54], was met by Rutherford's *Lex Rex*, arguing that the law is king, not an autocrat, and that there is a sovereignty in the people to which the monarch is subject. This view was based upon Covenanting principles, and called for the end of any form of episcopacy as part of a general revision of the constitutional stru.   , a revision which the people had the right to require in the face of abuses.

One of the most important developments occurred in the middle of this period. During the struggles between Charles I and the English Parliament, the English Parliament resolved on the reformation of the liturgy, discipline and government of the English Church. Accordingly it convened the Westminster Assembly, to which the Church of Scotland sent Commissioners to participate in an advisory capacity. The Assembly hoped to produce a settlement of religion which would secure the presbyterian government of the Church throughout the United Kingdom, but this enterprise failed. Nonetheless the Assembly drew up the Form of Church Government, the Directory of Public Worship, and the Longer and Shorter Catechisms. The central result of the Assembly was, however, the Westminster Confession of Faith, the main part of the hoped for uniformity of religion in Britain. The Confession is a much more careful and precise document than the Scots Confession. It purports to contain the sum and substance of reformed doctrine, rather than being the belief of a group of Protestants in one country, and it fairly reflects the general theological position of its day in most points. In 1647 the General Assembly of the Church of Scotland adopted—with minor modification, explanations and reservations —the Westminster Confession of Faith as the Confession of the Church[55], and two years later required all ministers and elders to further its teaching. On 7 February 1649 the Scots Parliament approved and ratified the Confession and Catechisms, but the legislation of this Parliament was struck down by the Recissory Act 1661 c. 46.

Under Charles II episcopacy was restored, and persecution began again to crush the Presbyterianism of the Covenants. In 1669 the Act c.2, the Act of Supremacy, once more asserted the Royal supremacy over all persons and in ecclesiastical matters. The famous Test Act of 1681 c.6, was introduced to require the renunciation of the National Covenant and the Solemn League and Covenant by all persons in positions of public trust and to assert the Royal supremacy.[56] In all this the Westminster Confession was not mentioned.[57] However, after the Revolution and the flight of James VII in 1688 the re-settlement of church affairs gave the Westminster Confession the position which it held for many years thereafter. The Revolution itself was a mainly English affair, but in Scotland its consequent legislation was used once more to guard the Scottish Church against episcopacy (the instrument through which the Crown had sought to subject the Church to itself) and to re-enact legislation establishing presbyterian Protestantism as the form of church government within the realm. More particularly the legislators sought to secure that never again would the civil authority have power lawfully to repeat the severities of the attempts to suppress the Covenanters.

The first section of the Claim of Right of 1689 c.28[58] narrates that James VII had forfeited the throne, on the conveniently hitherto forgotten ground that he:

> 'Being a profest papist did assume the Regall power and acted as King without ever takeing the oath required by law wherby the King at his access [accession] to the government is obliged to swear To maintain the protestant religion and to rule the people according to the laudble lawes . . . .'[59]

More importantly he did:

> 'By the advyce of wicked and evill Counsellers Invade the fundamentall Constitution of this Kingdome And altered it from a legall limited monarchy to ane Arbitary Despotick power and in a public proclamation asserted ane absolute power to cass annull and dissable all the lawes particularly arrainging the lawes Establishing the protestant Religion and to the violation of the lawes and liberties of the Kingdome.'

For these and other specified reasons the Estates of the kingdom of Scotland found and declared that:

> '. . . . he hath forfaulted [forfeited] the right to the Croune and the throne is become vacant.'

2

The throne was therefore offered to William and Mary in confidence that they would more properly carry out the duties of monarchy.

The first parliament of the new reign abolished prelacy by the Act 1689 c.4, but it was not until the next year that major questions of the government of the church were dealt with. The Act 1690 c.1 repealed the Act of Supremacy, 1669 c.2. The Act 1690 c.2 re-instated in their parishes all the ministers who had been dispossessed of their parishes during the previous troubles due to their adherence to Covenanting principles, and the Act 1690 c.53 provided for the abolition of patronages, by their being bought out. But the key of the Revolution Settlement in relation to Church and State is the Confession of Faith Ratification Act 1690 c.7 'Ratifying the Confession of Faith and settling Presbyterian Church Government'.

As in the case of the Act 1560 c.1 and the Scots Confession, the Act 1690 c.7 deals with a settlement of religion which it describes as true, as Protestant and as according to the truth of God's Word, but it adds to these statements that this religion is secured 'as it hath of a long time been professed within this land', which, in view of history, was rather sweeping. The Presbyterian government of the Church was once more ratified, and all the laws against Popery and papists were revived and perpetually confirmed, as were the laws for the maintenance of the true Reformed Protestant religion and of the Church of Christ. Further the Westminster Confession of Faith subjoined to the Act was voted and approved as the public and avowed Confession of the Church of Scotland.[60] The Presbyterian form of church government was once more given statutory approval as it had obtained in 1592 and the Church was enjoined to 'try and purge out all Insufficient, negligent, scandalous and erroneous Ministers'.

There were some problems in the Act as passed; for example it enacted the Confession, but without the reservations and explanatory notes of the 1647 General Assembly, which had the effect *inter alia*, of allowing the Crown alone in law to call Assemblies—a defect which was not put right until 1927.[61] But the Act stands as the second foundation of the Church of Scotland. Nonetheless, other questions arose and had to be settled. Of these an important one was whether the Confession of Faith had to be subscribed by ministers as their Confession, since a Confession need not be a standard. In the debate William intervened to aid the former episcopalian ministers who wished to join the Church, and then, the Church delaying, Parliament passed the Ministers Act 1693 c.38 'An Act for Setling the Quiet and Peace of the Church'. This required subscription of the Confession by ministers, and their submission to the Presbyterian form of government.[62] It also required them to observe uniformity of worship 'as the samen are at present performed and allowed' in the Church or would in the future be declared by authority of the Church. This was a useful intervention in the short term, but it did raise justified fears that it implied that the church establishment under law might be more subject to the will and legislation of the civil power than would have been welcomed by Andrew Melville.

The projected Union between the Parliaments of England and Scotland was the next major step in the development of the relations of Church and State in this country. In the last years of his reign, notwithstanding the abolition of prelacy and its condemnation in The Confesson of Faith Ratification Act 1690, William had attempted to secure control over the Church by swinging the Church back to episcopacy.[63] Accordingly in view of this and of previous history, it was the Scots intention in the Union negotiations that the presbyterian polity of the Church should not be affected in any way. This was done in two main ways. Firstly the Act 1705 c.50 appointing the Scottish Commissioners for the negotiations concluded with the provision:

'That the said commissioners shall not treat of, or concerning, any alteration of the worship, discipline, and government of the Church of this kingdom as now by law established.'

Religion was thus removed from the negotiating table and did not form part of the discussion.

The second step was the passing of the Protestant Religion and Presbyterian Church Act 1706 c.6, (the Act of Security)[64] which was appointed to be inserted into any legislation to enact a Treaty of Union with England:

'And that the [Act] shall be therein expressly Declared to be a fundamental and essential condition of the said Treaty or Union in all time comeing.'

The Act 1706 c.6 narrated its predecessors, and, considering that it was necessary that 'the true Protestant religion as presently professed' should be 'effectually and unalterably' secured, it stated that the Queen:

'with the advice and consent of the said Estates of Parliament, Doth hereby Establish and confirm the said true Protestant Religion and Worship Discipline and Government of the Church to continue without any alteration to the people in this land in all succeeding generations . . . .'[65]

To that end the Confession of Faith Ratification Act 1690 c.7, and the relative Acts, were all ratified and confirmed. The Presbyterian form of Church government and discipline were secured, and, after lesser provisions relating to subscription of the Confession by professors, the continuance of the universities and colleges of the realm, and forbidding the imposition of oaths contrary to the established religion, the Act provides for future sovereigns on their accession to take an oath to preserve inviolable this settlement of the Protestant religion and presbyterian church government.

As required the Act of Security was inserted in the Union with England Act 1706 c.7, and also appears in s.2 of the Union with Scotland Act 1706, its English counterpart. The Union duly became effective on 1 May 1707, and the new Parliament began its life. But it soon appeared that the provisions for the security of the Church of Scotland were not as effective as had been thought, and that the position of the Church was weaker in respect of state interference and action than had been intended. In particular in the case of *Greenshields* v.

Magistrates of Edinburgh (1710) Rob. App. 12, a successful appeal was made to the House of Lords (itself a possible breach of the Union agreements) against the refusal of the Court of Session to disturb a decision of the Edinburgh Magistrates to imprison Greenshields unless he undertook to close the place of worship he had opened in 1710. Greenshields was an episcopalian, and had been ordained after the abolition of Episcopacy in 1690. The Presbytery of Edinburgh had therefore found him not qualified to minister within their bounds, and the magistrates had attempted to sanction their finding.

Further steps were taken in 1711, with the passing of the Scottish Episcopalians Act 1711 affording toleration to that denomination in Scotland as a matter of law, which caused much offence to the Presbyterian Church. But the passing of the Church Patronage (Scotland) Act 1711 re-establishing patronage was productive of more strife and difficulty. It will be discussed more fully in the next chapter in connection with the Disruption controversy, but suffice to say here, that these two Acts showed that the Union Parliament was not unwilling to legislate in matters which at the time the Scottish Church considered to lie more within its province.[66] The basis of such legislation was there already, for the Acts of the Revolution Settlement, and even those of a hundred years previously, had shown that in law the civil authority might legislate for the Church. Whatever the original position, even if it were true that the Church had been recognised and not created by the State, there were sufficient instances of legislation to make it arguable that the State had the right so to legislate.

A modern argument might be that the General Assembly Act 1592, the Confession of Faith Ratification Act 1690, the Protestant Church and Presbyterian Church Act 1706 and all the others had merely recognised an already existing, self-existent and self-regulating community separate from the State and not requiring State sanction for the validity of its institutions and decisions. But in the then prevalent political requirements of monolithic authority, such an argument would not have been put. The theory of the single sovereign from whom all power is drawn, expressed in Hobbe's *Leviathan*, and later in the legal theory of John Austin[67], was in the ascendant. The church history of the next years shows it developing through the Scottish Church, under the influence of Moderatism, spread through the institution of patronage. The Church was seen increasingly as subject to the laws of the State, without any more freedom than that which might be directly spelled out of the legislation. The Disruption of the Church in 1843 was the direct result of the collision of such a theory of the monolithic State with the idea of the independent Church which had earlier been expressed to a degree in Andrew Melville's *Second Book of Discipline*.

CHAPTER III
The Disruption

The period 1834–1843 which ends with the Disruption of the Church of Scotland is generally referred to as the 'Ten Years' Conflict'.[68] During it the State and the Church collided over the whole question of their relationship and inter-connection within the concept of establishment. The opinions then uttered by both civil and ecclesiastical courts, and the actions and statements of the governments of the time, have helped form the present law. The civil courts held the church limited in its powers by the statute law of the realm. Government refused any remedy or redress. One section of the Church therefore, unable or unwilling to accept what it considered to be that erastian position, seceded to form the Free Church of Scotland. When in the early decades of this century there were moves to re-unite, satisfactory provision had to be made within the constitution of the 'new' Church of Scotland on the matter of the church-state relationship, a topic we will come to in Chapter V. Here we are concerned with the injury, not the subsequent repair work.

The core of the dispute was the old question of supremacy and control, with also an added element from the movement towards popular government which in civil matters had produced electoral reform in the Reform Act 1832 and the Representation (Scotland) Act of the same year.

The occasion of the conflict was the legislative action of the General Assembly of 1834 in passing, first, the Veto Act, which affected the operation of civil statute law relating to the appointment of ministers—the question of patronage—and second, the Chapel Act, which affected the law laid down by the state on the question of the membership of the courts of the Church, and their operation.

The parties to the dispute were the Evangelicals and the Moderates within the Church of Scotland and, brought in by the latter, the civil courts of Scotland, and then the government and Parliament of the time. These should not, however, be considered as separate contenders, many active disputants being present in a variety of characters. Some in the Courts, government and Parliament were of course not Church of Scotland members, and indeed arguably their lack of knowledge or familiarity with the Kirk, and in some cases their adherence to other forms of church government, contributed to the problem rather than its solution. But many were members of the Kirk, and these can roughly be classified as Evangelicals and Moderates. Though many of their ministerial leaders (e.g. Chalmers) were Tories, the Evangelicals tended to be liberal in politics. They were active in the Church, doctrinally laying stress on individual conversion, being individually 'enthusiastic' and, as a consequence wishing to free the Kirk from the deadening fetters of 'worldly institutions'. It is difficult to define 'Moderatism' save as being 'moderate', and in being generally opposed to what was seen as the wildness and ungentlemanly enthusiasm of Evangelicalism. In professed doctrine most Moderates were in form as orthodox as Evangelicals. However, some doubt may be cast on the reality or depth of their doctrinal positions. They were rationalist, devoting only part of their time, talents and energies to their work. Satisfactory performance of their tasks comprised in 'administering the ordinances of religion' —an almost ceremonial approach with little apparent depth of care for their parishioners as fellow human beings.[69] In politics they were aligned with the Tories. These two attitudes, opposed in their fundamental views of the ministerial function, and in the extent of their desire to see doctrine mould personality and behaviour, collided over the Veto and Chapel Acts.

I The Veto and Chapel Acts, 1834

The Veto Act

The Veto Act tackled the question of patronage in the Church. For our purposes Patronage may be shortly defined as the right to present a man to be the minister of a particular charge or congregation. It went beyond a matter of nomination, and effectively meant that, unless the individual was so incompetent that Presbytery could not with any vestige of good faith proceed to induct him to that parish, the nominee of the patron would be settled as minister of the parish.

The idea of patronage was present in the civil law before the Reformation, and a body of law on the matter was built up over the years.[70] Usually the right to present to a benefice was vested in someone owning property in the parish, but this was not necessarily the case. A person who had built or endowed a church, or his successors, often held the patronage to that church, and the right to present to a charge was considered as a right of property which could be sold or purchased like any other property right. More rarely where a congregation itself came together to build a church, the right to choose a minister might be vested in the members of that congregation, and exercised by free election among them.

The institution of Patronage was attacked over the years for its many obvious defects. It could mean that the selection of a minister was in the hands of someone out of touch with parochial opinion, and who might have no real interest in the welfare of the congregation. The patron might not be capable of assessing the merits of possible appointees and the qualities required for ministry in that particular charge. Though in general the system seems to have worked through informal consultation, yet it could produce unfortunate results,[71] and, in law there was no formal place or standing given to the opinion of church members. Although there was the safeguard that Presbytery could refuse to induct a presentee on grounds of qualifications,[72] this was very unlikely, and ineffective in practice.

In that presentation to a charge had important financial and other benefits for the presentee, giving him legal right to the glebe produce, the stipend and whatever other emoluments went with the post,[73] and in that patronage was considered as a property right it was some time after the Reformation before steps were taken to deal with it. Although it was frowned on by both the *First* and *Second Book of Discipline* it was not swept away intil the Act 1649 c. 39.[74] That Act was, however, struck down by the Recissory Act 1661 c. 46, which cancelled all the Acts of the 1649 Parliament.

When the opportunity arose in 1690 again to consider the question of patronage as part of the settlement of Church and State affairs, the clauses regarding patronage were expressly exempted from the Confession of Faith Ratification Act 1690 c. 7, and 19 July of that year the Patronage Act 1690 c. 53 was passed, abolishing patronages, subject to the payment of compensation to the former patrons.[75]

Such was the position regarding patronage which was integral to the arrangements for the protection of the constitution, worship and discipline of the Church which were built in to the negotiations for the Union, the Treaty, and the Union legislation described at the end of the last chapter. However, as noted also there, the protection of the Treaty and enacting legislation proved ineffective. The Church Patronage (Scotland) Act 1711 re-establishing patronage was a major infringement of the terms of the Union and it, along with the Scottish Episcopalians Act, also of 1711, was protested by Principal Carstares and other commissioners of the Church in a memorial presented to Parliament which was afterwards appointed by the General Assembly of 1715 to be held as the deed and mind of the Assembly. The protest was further repeated by the General Assembly annually throughout the eighteenth century, but to no effect. The ground of protest was not the toleration of episcopalian worship, but the clear implication that the protective devices of the Union were not as fundamental and inviolable as had been intended or hoped.

Part of the memorial of protest specifically stated that: 'by the Act restoring the power of presentation to patrons the legally established constitution of this church was altered in a very important point.'[76] That point of principle was underlined by the emergence of various difficulties with patronage in succeeding years, most notably where the patron was unable or unwilling to present a man to a charge. The attempts of the Church to solve these problems were not particularly successful, and partially gave rise to the secessions of 1733 and 1752.[77] Patronage therefore came to form a focus of discontent. It is not too much to say as Lord Macaulay did in his speech on the Test in the Scottish Universities:

'The British Legislature violated the Articles of Union and made a change in the Constitution of the Church of Scotland. From that change has flowed almost all the dissent now existing in Scotland. . . . Year after year the General Assembly protested against the violation, but in vain; and from the act of 1712 undoubtedly flowed every secession and schism that has taken place in the Church of Scotland.'[78]

Further contributions to dissatisfaction with patronage within the Church came from outside it. The rise of the evangelical movement throughout Britain in the latter half of the eighteenth century and the first half of the nineteenth is associated with the Wesleys, Whitefield, Robert Raikes and Sunday Schools, with the Church Missionary Society, the Society for the Promoting of Christian Knowledge and the Clapham Sect, including Wilberforce and the other social reformers. The movement spread into Scotland through the Haldanes, and, having first been productive of independent congregations slowly infiltrated the established Church. As part of normal evangelical attitudes the concept of patronage was doubted as being incompatible with freedom and responsibility. Indeed most evangelicals vehemently opposed patronage, though curiously perhaps, Thomas Chalmers, the eventual leader of the Evangelicals during the attack on patronage, was openminded on the matter.[79]

The seam of opposition to patronage within the Church was further strengthened by the so-called Voluntary controversy. As stated the initial effect of the evangelical revival had been the creation of independent congregations. It was a principle of such that the Church of Christ should not be financed or beholden in any way to the State. Strict separation of Church and State was their watchword, and they therefore attacked the established church. Naturally, as in so many theological disputes, the most acrimonious dispute was between the Voluntaries and the evangelicals within the Kirk, that is between those who were otherwise closest doctrinally. While the evangelicals were willing to contend for a principle of establishment, they were not willing to defend the concept of state-created patronage. There were two lines of attack. First, the clear theological concept of the church as stated by the Voluntaries required separation. Patronage was an element in the argument, being evidence of the fettering of the Kirk to worldly institutions for financial gain. Secondly, and more practically, the Voluntaries did not see why they, as non-members of the Kirk and opposed to the state connection, should be required by law, if property owners, to defray the costs of construction and maintenance of established church buildings.

It was the view of Chalmers, stated in 1826, and re-stated in 1838 in a series of public lectures which attracted much attention, that the establishment of the Church of Scotland was not attended by the demerits with which it was usually credited. His view was that Assemblies and Presbyteries were legally capable of doing anything they wished.[80] Following him, evangelicals asserted the power of the Church to govern its own affairs: and the curbing of lay patronage by Act of Assembly without the intervention of Parliament would have been a demonstration of such omnicompetence.

Means were found in the concept of and procedure for the 'call' of a minister to a parish. The 'call' had been introduced prior to the re-establishment of patronage in 1711, and had been retained as a formal part of the procedures despite its inconsistency with the right of patronage.[81] In 1833 an attempt to make use of such a device narrowly failed,[82] and the Moderate majority of Assembly carried a Declaratory Act which permitted 'objections of whatever nature against the presentee or against the settlement taking place' to be made by heads of families 'in full and regular communion with the Church' to Presbytery. The Presbytery was bound to investigate these complaints: if it found them valid, the presentation was to be rejected as the presentee was not found qualified.[83]

This was a major innovation, which probably went to the limit of church settlement under the law as it was to be construed in the succeeding years.[84] But it did not satisfy the Evangelical party, and they, forming a majority at the next General Assembly, carried their own view into the law of the Church. The Act XII, 1834, declaring it to be a fundamental law of the Church of Scotland that no minister should be intruded upon a congregation contrary to the will of the people, has gone down into history as the Veto Act.[85] Presbyteries were instructed when considering a call to a vacant pastoral charge to reject the presentation of a person in whose favour the call was proposed to be moderated if it were proved that a majority of the male heads of families, being members of the congregation, should disapprove of him. No reason had to be given for such disapproval, nor was Presbytery required to consider the merits of the case. So long as each disapprover was willing if called on to declare that he was actuated by no malicious or factious motives, and to swear that he was motivated solely by a conscious regard to the spiritual interests of himself and of the congregation, the settlement should not proceed.

The Veto Act can be (and was) criticised. It is rather vaguely framed, perhaps regrettably vaguely. People may 'disapprove' of the call, though inconsistently the call is the free gift of the people. Disapproval implies some test of qualification though the test of qualification was a matter for Presbytery. And so on: there were many arguments and much sophistry, all now dead. It may be that better drafting would have avoided some of the later difficulties, but this is criticism from hindsight.

At any rate the important point was and is this: under the Veto Act machinery was established by which the will of at least the heads of families in a congregation was accorded primary status in the selection and settlement of a minister. That their dissent should be taken as conclusive that a man has not the gifts appropriate to teach, instruct and edify that particular congregation seems elementary,[86] though I accept that it is a proposition unwelcome to much clerical opinion.

Prior to the Assembly some dubiety was expressed as to the competency of the Assembly in enacting the Veto Act. The motion, however, was supported by the counsel, advice and indeed active participation of men conversant with the Law. Most notably the Lord Advocate (Jeffrey) and the Solicitor General (Cockburn) considered the Act entirely competent, and the report which immediately gave rise to the Act was moved by Lord Moncrieff, one of the judges of the Court of Session.[87]

After the decision was taken by a margin of 184 to 139, 106 members of the

Assembly dissented from the step. The grounds of dissent were argued by Dr.
D. Mearns, Professor of Divinity in King's College, Aberdeen, and his statement was referred to repeatedly in the civil courts during the ensuing debates.
However, his arguments did not challenge the competency of the Church to
legislate as it had done. That challenge is only to be found in the fourteen
reasons for dissent given in separately in writing by a single individual who is
pilloried by Buchanan as being the author of the Disruption, since he later
came to a position of eminence from which he could and did make his opinion
felt. This was the Dean of the Faculty of Advocates, Mr. John Hope. He
entered his dissent on the grounds that, since the Assembly had purported to
restrict the right of patronage, it had acted beyond its powers. However, at this
stage Mr. Hope did not suggest that the civil courts could do anything other
than alienate the benefice, that is award the financial and civil rights stemming
from the particular appointment to the rejected presentee.[88] It was not until he
was advising in the First Auchterarder case that he sought to have the Church
compelled by the civil authority to act in accordance with the civil law.

The Chapel Act

The purpose of the Chapel Act, Act IX 1834, was the giving of Chapels of
Ease and their ministers a more effective place within the structure of the
Church general.[89] The Chapel of Ease had been one response to population
growth and mobility since the foundation of the original parish churches. It was
not the only response, as there existed procedures for the establishing of 'full
churches', parishes *quoad omnia*, by the division of existing parishes, but that
procedure was subject to the consent of the heritors, a consent not often forthcoming as it involved the heritors in the expense of construction and maintenance of more buildings.[90] Accordingly the Church found it convenient to
erect Chapels of Ease, which were preaching stations within the confines of the
parish *quoad omnia*. That 'full parish' continued its responsibility for civil
matters (eg. education and poor relief) in the 'territory' of the new charge, and
had jurisdiction in matters of discipline.

However, the chapels of ease were not popular with the church authorities,
especially as they were normally filled with an evangelical ministry. Equally
importantly these chapels of ease were created free of the yoke of patronage,[91]
and government resisted attempts to impose such a yoke. It followed that the
ministers of the chapels, and the chapel congregations were in a way freer in
their activities than the normal full charge. Although Buchanan states the
point extremely, it does appear that the Moderates did impede the
development of the chapel system, and did attempt to lower the ecclesiastical
status and influence of their ministers. In the 100 years from 1730 the population of Scotland doubled, but that need was met by an increase of 40 churches
under special Act of Parliament and by 62 Chapels of Ease in the established
Church. In the same time about 100 churches had been erected by the much
smaller and poorer non-established denominations.[92]

To meet the problem in part the Chapel Act enacted that all ministers of Chapels of Ease then existing, or as might be created, should be received and regarded as members of presbyteries and synods, should be eligible to sit in the General Assembly, and should enjoy the full powers of a parish minister. This was therefore a return to the presbyterian doctrine of the parity of ministers which had gone by default in previous years. Notwithstanding the Act was dissented from by the Moderate side specifically on the question of the competence of the Assembly so to enact. Dr. George Cook of St. Andrews pointed out that presbyteries and parishes functioned not only as ecclesiastical courts but also as organs of civil government. The ecclesiastical court which was the Assembly could not empower ministers of churches which were not recognised by the civil legislation to act in temporal matters.[93] This is a powerful argument, but it is scarcely one which could have swayed those who were impatient with any suggestion that their jurisdiction was derived from civil enactment.

Finally, before turning to the cases themselves, one general point may be made. Although the Veto Act produced the greater volume of litigation, affected more individuals in more congregations, stirred the emotions, provided an easily grasped point of principle, and was in crude terms a better political platform, it is arguable that in law the Chapel Act was the greater and more interesting innovation. Had the Chapel Act been acceptable to the civil courts the Church of Scotland would have been decided to have that freedom of self-government which later had to be sought by legislative enactment. But the conflict was acute, and was largely conducted on the field of the Veto Act. When the Chapel Act did come up for scrutiny many 'veto' cases had been decided already, and the monolithic concepts of sovereignty of John Hope and, let it be said, of a number of episcopalian or sacramentalist judges, had been well aired. Reading the judgements one cannot escape the feeling that it had become more important to win the argument than to do the best,[94] and this at a time when judges were less concerned with precedent than often nowadays.

In any event in the next nine years many court cases were brought and argued, and the questions of the relationship between the Church and the State in Scotland in these matters were to be submerged in the more general and more vital one: whether the Church had any spiritual jurisdiction independent of the control of the civil authority.

II The Conflict

The intelligible presentation of the Disruption cases is not the least of the difficulties of this book. The various decisions occur over what is in legal practice a very short period of time and many were proceeding simultaneously, though at different stages. Their impact on both the general public and the more active disputants in the Conflict were therefore cumulative, but not linear. However for ease of apprehension it is better to take each case or cases respecting a particular parish as a single unit, and only later to arrange them in a chronological order, at which stage the emerging pattern of jurisdictional conflict will be better understood. At that point the trend of decision and the reasons for the demand for relief become clear, as the opinions of the majority in the cases, which in the legal literature are usually called after the name of the parish involved, provide an increasingly strong statement of a strict theory of state control.

The Veto Act Cases
The Auchterarder Cases
1. *Earl of Kinnoull and Rev. R. Young* v. *Presbytery of Auchterarder* (1838) 16 S. 661:aff'd (1839) McL. & Rob. 220. C. G. Robertson, *Report of Court of Session proceedings in the Auchterarder Case,* 1838
2. *Earl of Kinnoull and Rev. R. Young* v. *Rev. John Ferguson and others (a majority of the Presbytery of Auchterarder)* (1841) 3 D. 778:aff'd (1842) 1 Bell 662.
3. Same, (1843) 5 D. 1010.

The essential facts of the First Auchterarder case were that on the occurrence of a vacancy in the parish Mr. Young was presented to the charge. In accordance with the Veto Act and relative regulations, after Mr. Young conducted a service there a 'call' in the normal form inviting him to take the charge was presented for signature to the people. Of 300 residents in the parish only 2 signed the call, and a third added his signature invalidly. Then when opportunity was duly given to the male heads of families on the communion roll, of 330 entitled to exercise the privilege 287 recorded their names as dissentients against the 'call'. After other procedure, and a reference to the General Assembly of 1835,[95] the Presbytery of Auchterarder rejected Mr. Young. An appeal to synod was intimated, but at this stage the matter was removed from the courts of the Church. The case was ideal to test the validity of the Veto Act. Clearly the bulk of the congregation did not want Mr. Young as their minister, and if the voting and dissents did not bring into play the principle of the Veto Act, that 'no pastor is to be intruded in a congregation contrary to their will', it could only be because the Veto Act itself was invalid.

The bringing of the matter into the civil courts was not of itself unusual. They were accustomed to dealing with patronage questions in so far as they affected private right.[96] As first drafted the case would not have been remarkable. What was initially sought was simply a declaration that Young had been validly presented, and therefore had right to the civil pertinents of the charge, the manse, stipend and glebe. But the Dean of the Faculty, John Hope, who had separately dissented from the passing of the Veto Act at the 1834 Assembly, was counsel for the pursuers, and he had the summons amended directly to raise the validity of the Veto Act, and the powers and functions of the Church in what many considered spiritual matters. The Court was asked, first, to hold that the Presbytery was bound to make trial of the qualifications of Mr. Young, (which under the Veto Act they could not do in the face of the proportion of dissentient heads of families); second, to hold that its acting in accordance with the Veto Act was illegal by reason of statute law. That might have been enough for one day, but the summons also asked the Court to declare that if the Presbytery after examination of his qualifications found Mr. Young qualified, then it was bound to admit him as minister of the charge.[97] The Presbytery was therefore not only to be told what it had done wrong, but also what it must do to do right. It was to be instructed in the performance of its duties. And, of course, underlying all the minutiae and legal language was the basic premise that the civil courts had jurisdiction in the matter as thus presented, and also power to hold as was asked.

Due to the importance of the case, the First Division of the Court of Session required that it be argued before the whole court: and eventually each of the thirteen judges then on the Bench delivered a separate opinion. Pleading began on 21 November 1837 and concluded on 12 December. The Bench began to deliver their opinions on 27 February and concluded on 8 March. The importance and complexity of the case and decision are therefore clear, and are underlined by several facts. In the sixteenth volume of Shaw's reports of Session cases the report of the initial decision begins at p. 661 with the summary of the argument. The opinions of the judges commence at p. 735 and run to p. 811, but at p. 735 the reporters regret that due to the unprecedented length of the opinions, they could only provide an abridgment of the opinions. The full report is available only in the two volume case report edited by C. G. Robertson, cited above, which was published by authority of the court in 1838.

By a majority of 8 judges to 5 the decision of the Court of Session was substantially that the Presbytery had acted illegally and contrary to the statute law of the realm, in particular the Patronage Act 1711, in refusing to take Mr. Young on trials.[98] The Church by law established had only such powers as were granted it under statute, and no other. Since statute did not sanction the passing of the Veto Act, it and acts done in conformity with it were unlawful.

The view of the minority on the other hand was that the Veto Act was legal and, even if it were not, the Court of Session did not have jurisdiction to interfere with the purely spiritual proceedings of the ecclesiastical courts. The most that might be done would have been to adjudge the temporalities to Mr. Young (as the first form of the summons had intended), but the civil court could not compel the Presbytery to take Mr. Young on trials. Even the Lord President, Charles Hope, father of John Hope, inclined to that view of the civil court's powers in the matter.[99]

The decision at first instance was therefore unsatisfactory. The Court of Session was by no means unanimous, split 8 to 5, and that head count was based only on the statement of the judges as to whether they found in favour of pursuers or defenders. The reasons each judge gave for his opinion varied, and it is difficult to harmonise some which led to the same conclusion. Further it was not left clear by the decision what could or would be done, though some in the majority did give warning that the court might have to take steps to render its judgement effective.

In the resulting confusion there were many overtures to the 1838 General Assembly asking it to clarify the situation. Mr. Young had demanded to be taken on trials, and, when the Presbytery of Auchterarder had demurred and asked synod for advice, he had indicated he might seek money damages. Over the protest of the Moderates the 1838 Assembly adopted a resolution affirming the spiritual independence of the Church and its competence to enforce obedience upon all its office-bearers and members in the exercise of their ecclesiastical authority. The next day the Synod of Perth and Stirling proposed that the Auchterarder decision be appealed to the House of Lords, and this was agreed to.

The House of Lords had no difficulty in affirming the judgement of the Court of Session. Reported at (1830) McL. & Rob. 220, the judgement of the Lords involved two propositions expressed most cogently by Lord Brougham (pp. 247–315) and Lord Cottenham, the Lord Chancellor (pp. 315–50). They considered that the Church was the judge of the qualifications of a presentee to the office of minister of a charge *by statute*, and by the consequential case law. 'Qualification' so construed was a technical term having reference to doctrine, literature and life of the presentee. In the absence of proven allegations of ignorance, immorality or heresy Presbytery could not reject a presentee. It followed that such an Act as the Veto Act, giving place to dissent, was illegal, and *ultra vires* of the Church.

Beyond this (and revealingly) the House considered that in matters of induction the Presbytery was simply in the same executive position as a bishop of the Church of England. In all matters where civil right was involved or affected the proceedings of church courts were subject to review in the civil courts. At p. 307 Lord Brougham was quite explicit. Only where a matter was proved to be of exclusively ecclesiastical competence would the civil court lack jurisdiction—a far-reaching position. Finally at pp. 314–5 Lord Brougham also dealt with the question of enforcement of the civil courts' decree. For him the proposition that the Court of Session and House of Lords might hold the Assembly and Presbytery had acted in error but that the Assembly and Presbytery could or would persist in that error had only to be stated to be seen to be erroneous.

Such reasoning was unacceptable to the Evangelicals. As Chalmers said to the 1839 Assembly meeting two weeks after the decision, not only had the legislative power of the Church been stated to be subject to the confines of civil statute, but the judicial power of the Church had also been brought under the jurisdiction of the civil courts. For example, the decision of Presbytery as to the qualifications of a presentee had a clear effect on his civil rights. On the reasoning of the House of Lords the matter might therefore be taken from the church courts into the civil courts.[100] Despite an attempt to revise church law in terms of the Auchterarder opinion, because the appeal had been the initiative of the Church—and integrity required obedience, whatever the result—the

Assembly accepted Chalmers' view and affirmed its intention to abide by the principle that a minister should not be intruded on a congregation against its will.[101] A committee was also set up to seek to negotiate a satisfactory solution to the conflict between civil and ecclesiastical law. As far as Auchterarder was concerned, the Presbytery was instructed to offer no further resistance to the claims to the temporalities, and not to appoint a minister to the parish for the period. But the Assembly was not in control of events. Mr. Young had a court decree in his favour.

The Presbytery of Auchterarder was faced with the instruction of the Assembly which barred it from proceeding with a settlement, though allowing Mr. Young the civil consequences thereof, and also with a court decree ordering it to try Mr. Young's qualifications, and if it found him qualified under the pre-Veto Act procedures and law, to admit him to the parish. It asked the next Commission of Assembly, which was to meet in August 1839, for advice. A claim for damages was intimated, and a minority of Presbytery then expressed their willingness to give effect to the decrees of the civil court. The majority was then sued as individuals for £15,000, being £5,000 damages for the patron, the Earl of Kinnoull, for the interference with his rights, and for £10,000 for Mr. Young, made up of £8,000 for the wrongful refusal of Presbytery to do its duty by taking him on trials, and £2,000 in reparation for the injury done to his character and usefulness and to his status in the Church of Scotland, and as recompense for the injury done to his feelings (solatium) by the illegal acts of the Presbytery. (case no. 2, the Second Auchterarder case)

The defenders pleaded that the action was irrelevant, a technical defence which may be expressed as a plea that, even if all the facts alleged were proved, the law would not afford the remedy sought. First, the summons was improperly directed against them as individuals. Second in referring the matter to the Commission of Assembly the Presbytery had acted as a legal court within its jurisdiction, and not as an inferior court refusing to obey the order of a superior court. Lastly, the claim for damages was incompetent because damages were being asked for the non-performance of an obligation which the Court of Session could not enforce. Admission to a pastoral charge implied ordination, which was an exclusively ecclesiastical act, and the Court of Session had no jurisdiction to compel the grant of ordination.

On grounds of its difficulty the Lord Ordinary referred the case to the Inner House of the Court of Session, and discussed in a lengthy Note whether the matter should be restricted simply to the temporalities, or whether the judgement in the First case went beyond that. This point was taken up, particularly in the opinion of Lord Hope, the Lord President, who elaborated his statements in the prior case. At p. 797 of (1841) 3 D. he stated that while it was true that the Court could not order the Presbytery to ordain, it could in terms of the 1711 Patronage Act order them to receive and admit a minister to a parish. Where a person is not only empowered but also may be ordered to do something 'it is necessarily implied that they are to take the means necessary for accomplishing the end.' If ordination were a necessary part of reception and admittance to a parish, this amounted to the Court of Session having jurisdiction to order ordination. Further, the Inner House held that the question at issue was simply one of failure to comply with a decree of the civil court. It was unnecessary to aver malice, and damages could be sought. Given the decision in the First Auchterarder case it was not possible for the Presbytery lawfully to refuse to give effect to the judgement. The decision of the majority to disobey the judgement therefore exposed them to an action for damages.

This decision also was appealed to the House of Lords, which on 9 August 1842 had no difficulty in affirming the lower court's decision, (1843) 1 Bell 662. The decisions of the civil court have to be obeyed. Thus, in contrast to his easy dismissal of the possibility of disobedience in the First case, the opinion of Lord Brougham concludes at pp. 716-7:

'it is fit that these men (sc. the majority) learn at length the lesson of obedience to the tribunals which have been appointed over them; a lesson which all others have long acquired, and which they, as learning it, should also practise. It is just that they should make reparation to those whom their breach of a plain duty has injured. The duty is not doubtful. The Courts have laid it down. Their failure is not a mistaken opinion; their fault is not an error of judgement. They knew what they ought to have done, and they refused to do it. The penalty of their transgression is to make compensation to those whom they have injured by their pertinacious refusal to perform their duty, and yield obedience to the law.'

Lord Campbell was similarly stringent. At pp. 733-4 he dealt with the argument that the majority had followed their conscience, acting according to their deep-rooted beliefs as to the true relations between church and state. His view was that as members of the establishment these men had to obey its rules, modification of those rules being possible only through parliamentary action.

'I do not think, my Lords, that, where the law is clear, the hardship of being obliged to obey it is a topic that can be listened to in a court of justice. There can be nothing more dangerous than to allow the obligation to obey a law to depend upon the opinion entertained by individuals of its propriety, that opinion being so liable to be influenced by interest, prejudice, and passion,—the love of power, still more deceitful than the love of profit,—and that most seductive of all delusions, that a man may recommend himself to the Almighty by exercising a stern control over the religious opinions of his fellow men.' ((1843) 1 Bell 662 at 735).

For Lord Campbell the matter was clear, the defiance of Courts of Justice and of the Legislature led inevitably to confusion and mischief, and 'a perseverance in such ill-advised counsels must either end in the total subversion of the establishment, or in a schism which would for ages impair its respectability and usefulness.'

The last stage in the Auchterarder cases, the Third case (1843) 5 D. 1010, arose from the continued failure of the Presbytery to obey the injunctions of the civil courts. The pursuers sought a court order that the minority, willing to obey the courts, might constitute the Presbytery for the purpose of taking Mr. Young on trials, and ordaining and admitting him if he were found qualified. The majority was to be interdicted from interfering with such proceedings. The jurisdiction of the Court of Session and the competency of this action were sustained by a majority of 6 to 3, and after argument the matter was remitted to the Lord Ordinary to proceed as asked. By a majority of 8 to 5 the Court of Session considered that in law there was nothing to hinder the action, and that the remedies sought by Mr. Young and the Earl of Kinnoull were appropriate to prevent and repair the wrongs which had been done to them.

This was the effective end of the Auchterarder dispute, for the whole matter was swallowed up in the Disruption of the Church of Scotland, which occurred within two months of the decision being given.

The Lethendy Case

Clark v. *Stirling* (1839) 1 D. 955. C. G. Robertson, *Report of the Proceedings in the Court of Session in the Lethendy Case*, 1839.[102]

In the Lethendy case the facts were rather different. The pursuer the Rev. Thomas Clark had been presented by the Crown as patron as colleague and successor to the incumbent, the Rev. Laurence Butter. His settlement was vetoed, and when both the Presbytery of Dunkeld and the 1836 Assembly refused him induction, Clark raised a civil action. Before that action was decided the incumbent died, and the Crown presented a Mr. Kessen to the vacancy, considering that, as Clark had not been settled during the life-time of the previous incumbency, that presentation had lapsed. Kessen was acceptable to the congregation, but Clark sought to interdict his settlement in the charge. Interdict was granted, but the 1838 Assembly ordered the Presbytery to proceed. A further interdict was granted, the Presbytery refusing to appear or plead in the matter. However, it felt it advisable to refer for advice to the August Commission of Assembly, which instructed it to proceed, and also indicated that unless Clark withdrew his interdicts the Presbytery would be in order in proceeding against him for the ecclesiastical offence of seeking to bring the government and discipline of the Church under the control of the civil courts.

When the Presbytery duly met to proceed with the induction of Mr. Kessen, a letter was read to it containing the opinion of the Dean of Faculty, John Hope, as to the competence of its intended action. Amongst other things this opinion stated that it was idle to expect the supreme civil court to let its interdict be defied, and that if Presbytery did proceed in defiance of the interdict its members would infallibly be committed to prison, and that 'most justly for an offence of the most grave nature, in the more aggravated in proportion of the status by whom it is committed.'[103]

The fulminations of the Dean seem, if anything, to have strengthened the resolve of Presbytery, which proceeded to induct Mr. Kessen to the charge of Lethendy. Clark complained of the breach of interdict to the courts which ordered the appearance of the members of the Presbytery at the Bar of the court. The whole question of Clark's title to apply for the interdicts, the jurisdiction of the court, and whether the respondents had been guilty of breach of interdict, was fully rehearsed. It was decided that Clark had title to sue, that the Court had jurisdiction to issue the interdicts, and that the breach amounted to contempt of court. Enforcement was clearly called for. However, apparently by a majority, the Court decided simply to censure the Presbytery, but made it plain that a similar offence in the future by any Presbytery would be treated more harshly.[104]

Clark subsequently was awarded damages of several thousand pounds against the Presbytery, but the Lethendy case was never fully settled. After the Disruption the Presbytery (or such of it as had not left the Church) found proved a libel that Clark was a drunkard, and deprived him of his licence to preach.[105]

The Daviot Case

MacIntosh v. *Rose* (1839) 2 D. 253.

Shortly after the Presbytery of Dunkeld was censured in the Lethendy case, the Second Division dealt with a dispute from the parish of Daviot and Dunlichity in the Presbytery of Inverness. In 1838, in an attempt partially to meet popular opinion on the question of congregational views, the Crown had indicated that it would informally seek the opinion of parishioners before exercising its patronage rights. Accordingly a list of two names was circulated, but local feeling was in favour of a third, the Rev. Archibald Cooke. Of the two men listed, Mr. MacIntosh was acceptable to the heritors, and to three of the ten heads of families entitled to act under the Veto Act.

MacIntosh was duly presented to the charge, and lest he be 'vetoed', he presented a note of suspension to the Court of Session, asking that the other seven heads of families be interdicted from objecting to his settlement without alleging and proving special objections to his life or doctrine. In support of this request he stated that the Auchterarder case had held it illegal and contrary to statute for Presbytery to reject a presentee without cause shown.

The three judges of the Second Division were not as sweeping in their statements as MacIntosh's application, but did grant interim interdict in the case. I have not, however, discovered its eventual outcome as it is overshadowed in the literature and controversy by the Strathbogie (Marnoch) case, an important stage of which was reached three days after Daviot, and which is the case next reported in 2 Dunlop.

The Strathbogie Cases (Marnoch)[106]

1. *Presbytery of Strathbogie and Rev. J. Cruickshank and Others,* Suspenders (1839) 2 D. 258.
2. Same (1839) 2 D. 585.
3. Same (1840) 2 D. 1047; id. 1380.
4. *Rev. J. Edwards* v. *Rev. J. Cruickshank and others (a majority of the Presbytery of Strathbogie) and Rev. J. Robertson and others (a minority of the said Presbytery)* (1840) 3 D. 282.
5. *Presbytery of Strathbogie* (1842) 4 D. 1298.
6. *Rev. J. Cruickshank* v. *Gordon* (1843) 5 D. 909.
7. *Rev. J. Edwards* v. *Rev. H. Leith* (1843) 15 Jurist 375.

The patronage of the parish of Marnoch in Strathbogie was vested in the Earl of Fife and Huntly, whose trustees presented a Mr. John Edwards to the charge when it fell vacant in 1837. Only one parishioner, the local inn-keeper, could be found to sign the call, and 261 heads of families dissented from the settlement in terms of the Veto Act. As Edwards had acted as an assistant in the parish previously, and had been withdrawn from the post at the request of the parishioners, their reaction to his proposed settlement should not have been unanticipated.[107] Both the Synod of Moray and then the Assembly being appealed to by both sides, the instruction of both bodies was to reject Edwards.

This the Presbytery did, and Edwards raised an action in the Court of Session against the Presbytery on the grounds that in refusing to take him on trials it had acted illegally and in violation of the statute law of Scotland. The writ was served just after the Court of Session decided the First Auchterarder case, and the Presbytery, realising the import of that decision for their own problem, applied again to synod for advice. At this stage an interesting development became fully apparent. Only a minority of the Presbytery wished to comply with the synod and Assembly instructions. However, on the appeal of the minority, the synod again instructed Edwards' rejection as did the Assembly of 1839 on the appeal of the majority. In the meantime the patron, assuming that there was a legal vacancy, presented a Mr. Hendry to the living. Mr. Edwards was granted an interim interdict against his settlement.

On 17 July 1838 the Presbytery decided again by a majority that its duty was to delay the settlement at Marnoch until the Auchterarder question had been finally dealt with. The Court of Session had jurisdiction in settlement cases as enunciated by the First Auchterarder case, and that Court had interdicted the Presbytery of Strathbogie from proceeding further. The Synod affirmed that admission to a pastoral charge was an entirely ecclesiastical act, but referred the matter on to the 1839 Assembly, which itself passed the matter to its Commission of Assembly, which met for the purpose as soon as the Assembly adjourned.

The Commission found the conduct of the Presbytery in entertaining the thought that the Court of Session might have jurisdiction in the matter was censurable, and it specially forbad the taking of any further steps towards the induction of Mr. Edwards. In the meantime Edwards obtained a further court order requiring the Presbytery to take him on trials. It appears that the majority of the Presbytery might well have obeyed the court order before the instructions of the Commission were formally received, but the then moderator of the Presbytery forestalled this by delaying to call a Presbytery meeting when such was requisitioned by the majority. His action caused further dispute, aggravating the politics of the situation, but without further legal importance. That came with the next ordinary meeting of the Presbytery on 4 December 1839, when the Presbytery by a majority of 7 to 3, in the knowledge of the proceedings and instructions of the Assembly and the Commission of Assembly, and in view of the decrees of the Court of Session, resolved to take Mr. Edwards on trial as presentee to the church and parish of Marnoch.

On 11 December 1839 the Commission of Assembly thoroughly reviewed the Marnoch case and reversed the whole proceedings of the Presbytery of Strathbogie. By approving and disapproving of various of the actions of the parties the majority of the Commission made clear that it was hostile to any suggestion that the civil courts had any jurisdiction in spiritual cases. Most importantly, however, the Commission suspended from pastoral and judicial functions the seven ministers of Strathbogie who had formed the majority of the Presbytery in its actings, and the Commission granted the remaining four ministers of the Presbytery full powers to act in the name of the Presbytery. (This may have been beyond the competence of the Commission).

The seven suspended ministers protested by the hand of their agent, and their protest was referred to the next Assembly by the Commission. Notwithstanding, they proceeded to meet as a Presbytery within four days of their suspension, disowned the Commission's authority to have acted, and sought the aid of the civil courts (case no. 1 above). They asked the courts to order first, that no-one should invade their exercise of their usual functions; second, that despite the decision of the Commission of Assembly the minority should not discharge the full powers of a Presbytery; and third, that no-one should intrude into their parishes either to intimate the suspension or to perform any of the normal duties of a ministry.

At first the Court of Session did not fully grant the orders it was asked for, and restricted its decrees to interdicting service of the sentence of the Commission, and prohibiting the minority and others from using the church, churchyard and school house of the affected ministers. These were civil matters, and in obedience to a sentence of the civil court which they considered within its competence the ministers appointed by the Commission to intimate the suspension did so in the open country of the area. In addition they held services in the open air.

This last was too much for the suspended ministers, and they asked the court for a further interdict to exclude other ministers of the established church from access to 'their' people. Interdict was refused by the Lord Ordinary,

(Murray), but was granted by the First Division on appeal, Lord Fullerton dissenting (i.e. by a 2 to 1 majority) (case no. 2 above). However, in fact this interdict was broken freely without the civil court seeking its enforcement.[108]

The matter came up again at the March 1840 meeting of the Commission of Assembly at which Dr. Chalmers gave fair notice to the state authorities that, if the interdicts in the Strathbogie case were continued, the Church would accept whatever consequences stemmed from disobedience. The Assembly meeting in May cited the seven ministers to appear before the August Commission of Assembly, and instructed it to libel them if it found them remaining contumacious. The seven therefore immediately went back to the Court of Session complaining of the illegality of the Assembly's proceedings as its actions were based on ecclesiastical legislation which had been declared unlawful. On 11 June 1840 they obtained an interim decree of suspension and interdict against the whole proceedings of the Assembly concerning themselves, and therefore also reponing them in the eyes of the civil authority, that is cancelling their suspension as ministers and restoring them to full status. When the Assembly failed to lodge answers in respect of the interim decrees or to defend the action the decrees were made perpetual on 11 July 1840 (case no. 3 above).

Consequent upon these decrees, when the Commission met in August, the seven ministers stated that they could not 'without acting inconsistently, recognise or sanction any part of the proceedings which had been suspended as illegal.' Such comment was considered by the Commission to be in itself contumacious, and it proceeded to libel the seven, by a majority of 180 to 66.[109] Mr. Edwards was similarly libelled.

At the November 1840 meeting of the Commission the relevancy of the libels was attacked by counsel for the ministers and Mr. Edwards. Written defences argued that the Commission was without jurisdiction, not being a court established by the statute law of the land, and that, since the sentence of the Assembly under which the libels proceeded had been suspended as illegal and therefore itself was void, the libels were similarly a violation of the law of the land. These arguments were not accepted, and proof in the cases was set for the March meeting of the Commission.

Between the November and March meetings further developments occurred. Mr. Edwards had been examined and found qualified by the suspended ministers in February 1840. Now, with the consent of the seven, he raised an action against the Presbytery of Strathbogie, both suspended and un-suspended members, asking the court to order it to admit him as the minister of Marnoch. On 18 December 1840 the First Division of the Court of Session, Lord Fullerton again dissenting, granted decree as craved on the ground that this was the logical corollary of the previous proceedings. As the Court had jurisdiction to determine the duty of Presbytery on such facts, it had the power to order that duty be performed (case no. 4 above, cf. opinion of Lord President Hope at p. 308).

The 'Reel of Bogie', which gave rise to a famous cartoon, is still so remembered in the annals of the area. The settlement of Mr. Edwards by the suspended ministers was to take place in January 1841, the depths of winter. Despite the weather many turned up at the church. The floor of the church was reserved for the parishioners of Marnoch, the gallery for spectators. Mr. Thomson of Keith, one of the suspendees, acted as Moderator of the 'Court of Session' Presbytery and constituted the meeting by prayer. One of the elders of the congregation then challenged the authority of the 'Presbytery' to act, and eventually an agent for the parishioners protested the whole proceedings, and the parishioners retired. Others present then made it impossible for the settlement to proceed, until a magistrate was called. Mr. Edwards was then admitted and received to the charge.[110]

The case against the seven ministers was prepared by the Commission, and presented to the 1841 Assembly. The first act of that Assembly was indicative of its reception. This was the deletion from its Roll of Commissioners of those commissioned by the suspended seven, acting as the Strathbogie Presbytery. When the case came up there was a wide ranging discussion of the whole question of the power of the civil magistrate, and the responsibilities of ministers to obey (cf. Romans 13). But the majority accepted the arguments of Chalmers, Cunningham and A. M. Dunlop, a lawyer, that in this instance the ministers in obeying the civil power had violated their ordination vows in recognising a head of the Church other than Christ. Sentence of deposition was passed. The Moderate party formally protested this on the ground that the established Church was bound to 'be subject to the civil power in all matters declared' by the supreme Civil Authorities of the country to affect temporal rights'.[111]

The next act was almost ludicrous in its ineptness. The Court of Session granted a further interdict to the seven, this time against the 1841 Assembly proceedings, and a court messenger sought to serve it on the Assembly. He was refused admission to the Assembly Hall, and a deputation was sent to inform the Lord High Commissioner as representative of the sovereign. It was, of course, improper for the messenger to seek to serve the writ in the presence of the Commissioner, but after some debate it was agreed to permit the interdict papers to be placed on the table of the Assembly, where they were ignored except for a protest at the intrusion of the secular arm of the state into the ecclesiastical province.[112]

When the 1842 Assembly came round the now deposed seven, constituting themselves as the Presbytery of Strathbogie on the authority of the earlier decrees in their favour, sought again to send Commissioners to it. Again the Assembly refused to receive individuals so commissioned, and accepted commissions from the minority, also constituted as Strathbogie Presbytery. Although the seven then obtained an interdict from the Court of Session against the minority's commissioners sitting, the Church again refused to regard the civil authority, and once more protested its interference (case no. 5 above).[113]

The end of the Strathbogie cases came in 1843, when first, on 10 March, six judges of the Court of Session (Lords Medwyn and Cuninghame at great length, and Lord Fullerton dissenting) held that that court had jurisdiction to declare that the prior interdicts were still operative, and that the court could also reduce (i.e. quash) the sentence of deposition passed on the seven ministers by the 1841 Assembly. The majority of the judges had no time for any argument that the depositions involved matters of ecclesiastical discipline, and therefore were for the sole jurisdiction of the Church courts. The supreme power of the State required them to intervene where the Church was acting in contravention of the very statutes upon which its powers rested (case no. 6 above). In harmony with that decision on the very next day, 11 March 1843, the court held that the induction by the 'minority' Presbytery of Mr. Hendry to the parish of Marnoch on 29 July 1842 was a breach of the prior court decrees (case no. 7 above).[114] However, all was soon swallowed up in the Disruption itself, though it may be noted that Mr. Hendry had a very successful ministry thereafter as the Free Church minister in Marnoch.

Be that as it may, the Strathbogie cases had underlined the conflict between church and state. The civil courts had proved willing to intervene in all matters where a civil element was present, and, going beyond the First Auchterarder case, had shown that it was prepared to instruct the Church how to act, and to review the internal proceedings of the Assembly. The cancelling of the suspension of the seven ministers (case no. 3) and of their deposition (case no 6) took matters very far indeed. In addition the effect of the long saga was the crystallisation of the attitudes of both parties, and indeed arguably resulted in more extreme positions being taken up than were necessary, and from which neither side could extricate itself without at least the appearance of surrender.

The Culsalmond Case[115]

Middleton v. Anderson (1842) 4 D. 957.

When in 1841 the incumbent of the parish of Culsalmond in the Presbytery of Garioch became too infirm to act, the patron presented Mr. William Middleton who had been acting as assistant in the charge. Out of a parish of around 1000, 45 persons were willing to sign the call, and of the 139 heads of families 89 dissented from the settlement in terms of the Veto Act. By this time Assembly regulations required that any such dispute be referred to the Assembly, but the Presbytery considered that a sufficient proportion of the congregation and heads of families were in favour of the settlement, and that the settlement should proceed. Aggrieved parishioners and members of the Presbytery duly appealed, and matters were further complicated, for the dissentient parishioners not only sought simply to dissent, but put forward special reasons which would have fallen within the categories laid down as proper by the House of Lords in the First Auchterarder case. They referred to the life and conduct of Mr. Middleton.

The Presbytery dismissed these special objections, and at a rather confused meeting on 11 November 1841, inducted Mr. Middleton to the charge.[116] Six days later the Commission of Assembly took the matter up, and as an interim measure prohibited Mr. Middleton from acting as minister. Middleton, the majority of the Presbytery, and the patron applied to the Court of Session to have the Commission proceedings suspended, and the dissentients interdicted from molesting the Presbytery, or complaining to the courts of the Church. The Lord Ordinary (Ivory) refused, considering that no question of civil right had been raised. On appeal, however, the petition was granted on an interim basis by Lord President Boyle and Lords Gillies and Mackenzie (Lord Fullerton dissenting). The grounds of the majority were that the basis of the whole proceedings was the Veto Act, which had already been declared unlawful as being *ultra vires* of the Church in previous cases. Any attempt therefore to operate that Act was *ipso facto* null, vitiating the whole proceedings. Further, Mr. Middleton's civil rights had been affected by his suspension, as suspension had unwarrantably stigmatised him in his status as a minister of the gospel.

The latter ground of decision is very wide. No question of stipend, glebe or emoluments, or of the patron's right to present, were involved. Only the personal character of the minister was called in question. That would happen in any disciplinary proceeding held by the Church, and therefore the reasoning opened up new vast areas of the Church's jurisdiction to the reviewing powers of the civil court. An appeal to the House of Lords was therefore marked, and in law the case ended by a failure to prosecute that appeal, the decision of the First Division becoming final.[117] But the reason for the failure to continue the case was not acquiescence in the decision. By adopting the Claim of Right, the Assembly of 1842 took a stand on the spiritual independence of the Church, requiring the State to make answer, as will be seen, and Culsalmond was overtaken by other cases which more directly led to the Disruption.

The Chapel Act Cases

So far the cases dealt with have concerned the legality of the Veto Act and proceedings thereunder. The question of the lawfulness of the Chapel Act did not come up for proper decision until quite late in the Ten Years' Conflict, though there were indications of trouble to come given *obiter* in some cases concerning the Widow's Fund and in Poor Law matters.[118] The case of *Livingstone* (1841) 3 D. 1278, brought out the possibilities of trouble more clearly.[119]

In 1840 the Rev. Archibald Livingstone, minister of Cambusnethan, was libelled by the Presbytery of Hamilton for various acts of theft, and was found guilty of five of the charges. For technical reasons the matter was then referred to the General Assembly, but, before that body met, Livingstone asked the Court of Session to suspend the past proceedings, and to interdict future action against him. His argument was that the Presbytery meetings which had dealt with his case had been attended by ministers of chapels of ease. Their entitlement to participate was based on the Chapel Act. But, argued Livingstone, that Act was illegal, being *ultra vires* of the Church, and contrary to statute law. It followed that the actions taken against him were not taken by a lawfully constituted court, but by some anomalous body composed partly of members of Presbytery, and partly of others. The actions of such a body were therefore incompetent, illegal, null and void.

Lord Ivory referred the question to the Inner House, observing that while the Chapel Act had been incidentally before the courts, its legality had not been pronounced upon, and the prior cases indicated some division of opinion with the courts. The Inner House decided to call the parties, and Lords Gillies and MacKenzie gave some indication that they felt the Church did not have the power to change its constitution at its own hand, by introducing new ministerial members, not being ministers of 'full' charges, into its Presbyteries. However, neither the Presbytery nor the Assembly responded, and the interim decree became final in their absence. The case therefore only raised, and did not settle, the question of the Chapel Act.[120]

Livingstone's argument was next taken up by the pursuer in *Wilson* v. *Presbytery of Stranraer* (1842) 4 D. 1294, who sought to prevent his case being heard at all by the Presbytery on the ground that the decision to proceed had not been taken by a properly constituted Presbytery. Again the legality of the Chapel Act was not settled as again the Church courts failed to respond, and decree was given in their absence. But it may be noted as indicative of the temper of the time that Wilson was summarily deposed from the ministry for contumacy in seeking the aid of the civil court in what the Assembly considered an ecclesiastical matter.[121] The legality of the Chapel Act was, however, by this time before the Court of Session as the Stewarton case had begun.

The Stewarton Case

Cuninghame v. *Presbytery of Irvine* (1843) 5 D. 427.[122] W. Cuninghame, *Mutual Cases, record and appendix in causa W. Cuninghame and others, heritors of Stewarton v. Presbytery of Irvine*, 3 parts, 1842. *The Stewarton Case*, J. M. Bell ed. 1843 (the Stewarton Report).

Under the Chapel Act all ministers of *quoad sacra* charges, that is of churches created within the boundaries of the older parishes for preaching purposes only, were admitted to full membership of the courts of the Church. From 1834 there was an increase in the number of these churches because the Evangelical party, following Chalmers' own earlier example, was diligent in their founding. In addition during the period a number of smaller associations of non-established churches sought to unite with the established church, in part because they were in sympathy with the standpoint and efforts of the Evangelicals. Among these was the denomination known as the Associate Synod which had seceded from the established church in 1733 as part of the movement led by Ebenezer Erskine.[123] To facilitate this union the established

Church provided in 1839 for the admission of ministers and congregations of the Associate Synod, and rules were laid down under which the Associate Synod churches were to be incorporated in to the existing parochial system as *quoad sacra* charges, and their minister made members of the appropriate presbyteries using the Chapel Act provisions.

In August 1839 the Associate Synod church in Stewarton in the Presbytery of Irvine sought to be received into the Church of Scotland using the new procedure. This was done. But when the Presbytery set up a committee to consider the creation of a parish *quoad sacra* for the new charge within the boundary of the existing parish *quoad omnia*, the patron of the older charge, Mr. Cuninghame of Lainshaw, and others, heritors of that parish, decided to take action. They opposed both the subdivision of the existing parish, doubtless as that would reduce income at the older church, and the admission of the minister of the newly incorporated church, Mr. James Clelland, to a seat and vote in the Presbytery of Irvine.

After procedures within the church courts, Mr. Cuninghame and his supporters asked the Court of Session to interdict Mr. Clelland from sitting and acting as a member of the Presbytery of Irvine, and to interdict the Presbytery both from erecting the proposed new parish, and from giving Mr. Clelland any standing thereanent. They argued that by the Act 1706 c. 10, the power to create new parishes was given to the Court of Teinds (by this time the Court of Session with another hat), and that the Church therefore did not have the power to create new parishes of its own motion. Decrees were granted on an interim basis until the question could be fully argued. However despite this the internal procedures of the church courts continued, and in due course the Presbytery was ordered to proceed with the erection of the new parish *quoad sacra*.

After an offer further to confer with the opposers was turned down, the Presbytery set up the new parish on 10 December 1840, despite the interdicts being served on them anew. They also passed a resolution expressing puzzlement, being unable to understand the interdict as being intended to prevent them carrying out a spiritual act, which was within the province of the church alone, and which in no way affected civil rights.

Cuninghame complained to the courts, but it was decided that there was no urgency, and matters could be deferred until his action was more fully tried. Accordingly the case proceeded, with a variation. By the time the action came up on the court lists the Church had decided that normally actions in respect of the disputed Acts should not be defended, lest it appear that by so doing the Church was acknowledging that the civil courts had some authority in these matters. However, it was decided to defend in the Stewarton case so as to prevent the Presbytery being caught between the mills of the civil and ecclesiastical courts. (I have the impression, though I cannot prove, that another reason was that, unlike the Strathbogie case, the Church had no ecclesiastical jurisdiction over the pursuers allowing it to deal with them as contumacious).

In the action Cuninghame and the other pursuers sought to have the proceedings of the Presbytery suspended as illegal. Statute gave the power regarding the creation of charges to the Court of Teinds, and the Church was therefore barred from taking powers in the matter. The argument was concise, as for the previous interim interdicts. The defences of the Presbytery were the right of the Church to regulate the membership of its own courts, and a want of jurisdiction in the Court of Session in the matter, since the matters at issue were spiritual and therefore of exclusively ecclesiastical competence.

As in the Auchterarder case, the matter was referred to a Bench of the Whole Court, which decided by 8 to 5 in favour of Mr. Cuninghame and the heritors. The ground of the majority's decision was far-reaching, and is best summarised by a short passage in the opinion of the former Dean of Faculty, John Hope, who had by now been raised to the Bench as Lord Justice-Clerk:

'I cannot admit that an establishment instituted by statute, can claim or legally possess any authority from a source, which the State, constituting the establishment, may not have thought fit to acknowledge as belonging to it; and, of course, I cannot admit that an establishment can ever possess an independent jurisdiction, which can give rise to a conflict as between two separate and independent jurisdictions. The establishment being instituted by the State, the competency of *all* its acts must be subject to the determination of the supreme court of law. If it were admitted to possess any power as an establishment not sanctioned by the provisions of the State, and so to possess from a separate source jurisdiction, producing a proper conflict of authority, then it would follow that the church must be entitled to determine for itself the extent of that authority, and hence no one act which the Church chose to ascribe to that authority could be inquired into in a court of law.'[124]

From such a base the majority held the proceedings of the Presbytery in acting upon the Chapel Act were void, because that Act was itself *ultra vires* of the General Assembly of the Church, being passed without the authority of the state. The interdicts in the case were therefore made perpetual.

The decision in the Stewarton case was given in January 1843. It served as additional fuel to the opinions of those who felt that the authority claimed over the Church for the State by the court decisions since 1838 was beyond reasonable bounds. The earlier cases holding the Veto Act unlawful were concerned with the judicial activities of the Church, and with its performance of its obligations. *Stewarton* now decided that in matters of legislating for its own internal constitution and composition, the Church had only such powers as were laid down by the statutes constituting the establishment. This development, taken along with the other cases which were reaching conclusions around the same time, and with the newly formed Government's reply to the Church's request for relief, indicated that radical steps would have to be taken.

A single flicker in the gloom came from the Court of Session on 21 February

1843 when the First Division unanimously, though only with the grudging assent of Lord President Boyle, decided not to intervene in the case of *Campbell* v. *Presbytery of Kintyre* (1843) 5 D. 657. An appeal to the General Assembly against the Presbytery's decision on a matter of drunkenness had not been proceeded with and the matter had been remitted back to Presbytery. It was held that as the matter did lie within the competence of Presbytery, and that as the Presbytery had no *quoad sacra* members it was properly constituted in terms of the Stewarton decision of the previous month, the mixed membership of the Assembly was irrelevant. The Court therefore seems to be striving to be dispassionate, but the main trend of its decisions was by then clear. On 10 March the Third Auchterarder and Third Strathbogie cases were decided, and the die finally cast.

III   The Disruption

We can now summarise the more important of the Disruption cases, chronologically, both to illustrate the development of the civil courts' attitude, and to show that the cases, previously outlined as separate units, were concurrent, and formed an emerging pattern.[125] Indeed as time went on the pattern was made quite apparent within them by the frequent citation and explanation of previous opinions within the series.

The First Auchterarder case, the *Earl of Kinnoul* v. *Presbytery of Auchterarder* 27 Feb. 1838, (1839) 16 S. 661; aff'd (H.L.) 3 May 1839, (1839) Mc. & Rob. 220), decided that it was unlawful for a presbytery to reject a presentee under Veto Act procedure, where the presentation by the patron was duly made. By so doing the Presbytery violated its duty and acted contrary to statute law. In the Lethendy case, *Clark* v. *Stirling* (14 June 1839, (1839) 1 D. 955), it was held that a preacher, rejected following the unlawful Veto Act procedure, could obtain a civil interdict against the Presbytery taking a second presentee on trials, and could obtain a declarator concluding that he himself should be so taken, and, if found qualified, be admitted to the charge, all of which showed the civil courts willing to intervene in what was previously considered an exclusively ecclesiastical area. Further, the court could punish infringements of the decrees. In the Daviot case, *MacIntosh* v. *Rose* (17 Dec. 1839, (1839) 2 D. 253) in an undefended action interdicts were granted against heads of families dissenting from a settlement in terms of the Veto Act without their proving special objection to the life and doctrine of the presentee.

In the First Strathbogie case, *Presbytery of Strathbogie* (20 Dec. 1839, 14 Feb., 11 June and 11 July 1840, (1839–40) 2 D. 258, 585, 1047, 1380), the suspension by the General Assembly of ministers who had proposed to disobey the Veto Act because it had been declared unlawful in the Auchterarder and Lethendy cases, was itself suspended by the civil courts and the Church interdicted from acting on it, ((1840) 2 D. 585). Interdict was also granted against the service and intimation of the Church sentence, and other ministers were barred from preaching or otherwise intruding into Church properties within the area. In the Second Strathbogie case, *Edwards* v. *Cruickshank* (18 Dec. 1840 (1840) 3 D. 282) decree in absence had been given in favour of Edwards the vetoed presentee, declaring that the Presbytery was bound to take him on trials, and admit him to the charge if he were found qualified. The suspended ministers, whose suspension had been suspended in the First case, so found, and Edwards asked the court to order the Presbytery to receive and admit him. The majority of the Presbytery (i.e. the suspended ministers) consented to decree, and it was granted in the face of argument by the minority of the Presbytery that the Court of Session had no jurisdiction so to order.

The Second Auchterarder case, *The Earl of Kinnoull* v. *Ferguson* was decided on 5 March 1841, ((1841) 3 D. 778; aff'd (H.L.) (1842) 1 Bell 662). There it was decided that damages could be awarded, without proof of malice, for the refusal of the Presbytery to take Mr. Young, the presentee, on trials, and admit him were he found qualified. The refusal of the majority of the Presbytery to act in accordance with the decision in the First Auchterarder case rendered them liable as individuals. All that was involved was a simple disobedience of the authority of the civil court. The next year, on 10 March 1842 in *Middleton* v. *Anderson* (1842) 4 D. 957, the Culsalmond case, the Court of Session suspended an order of the Commission of the General Assembly suspending a presentee, who had been settled by his Presbytery contrary to the Veto Act, and prohibiting him from officiating in the parish until the matter had been to the General Assembly. Interim interdict was also granted against other ministers intruding into the parish. The basis of the decision was the invalidity of the Veto Act, which vitiated the proceedings against Middleton, and the civil effect of his suspension by the Church.

In January 1843 came the first proper decision on the Chapel Act. As had been foreshadowed, most clearly in *Livingstone* (20 July, 1841, (1841) 3 D. 1278) and in *Wilson* v. *Presbytery of Stranraer* (27 May 1842, (1842) 4 D. 1294), the decision was adverse. In the Stewarton case, *Cuninghame* v. *Presbytery of Irvine* (20 Jan. 1843 5 D. 427), the Chapel Act was decided to have been beyond the legislative competence of the General Assembly as that competence was laid down by statute law. Interdicts were therefore granted against the creation of a new parish *quoad sacra* within the boundary of a 'full' parish, against the constitution of the new Kirk Session having jurisdiction over the proposed new parish, and against the minister of the 'new' charge sitting and voting as a member of the Presbytery. The previous procedures of the Presbytery directed to these ends were invalid by reason of the unlawfulness of the Chapel Act, and by the Presbytery being improperly constituted at the time, containing 'members' whose presence was justified only by that Act.

The final important decisions both came on 10 March 1843, when the Third Auchterarder and the Third Strathbogie cases were decided. In *The Earl of Kinnoull* v. *Ferguson* ((1843) 5 D. 1010), the court declared that the minority of the Presbytery of Auchterarder willing to obey the previous decisions in the series could constitute a valid Presbytery for the trials and induction of Mr. Young, and the majority of the Presbytery were interdicted from interfering with such procedure. In *Cruickshank* v. *Gordon* ((1843) 5 D. 909) the Court of Session asserted its jurisdiction to reduce the sentence of deposition passed on the majority of the Presbytery of Strathbogie by the General Assembly on account of their having disregarded the Veto Act, and on account of their contumacy in appealing to the civil courts.

Three things may be said about these cases: two distinctions and a comment. First, it may be noted that only the Stewarton case was concerned with the Chapel Act of 1834, the others all being occasioned by the question of patronage and the Veto Act. However, as said earlier when discussing the Acts, in a sense the Chapel Act was legally more fundamental, and therefore the Stewarton decision is the most important. In the Chapel Act the Church was really seeking to legislate *de novo* in setting up new administrative areas and in admitting a new category of membership to Presbyteries. By contrast it is arguable that the Veto Act was simply an attempt to modify existing ecclesiastical procedures. However, in terms of popular opinion, and impact, the Veto Act cases were of more immediate effect.

Secondly apart from the subject matter, a different and equally useful distinction between groups of the cases is to be found in the opinion of Lord Wood in the Stewarton case.[126] He suggested that the court had a two-fold duty: first to declare what the Church was bound to do, and to enforce its performance; and second, to declare what the Church was bound not to do, and to enforce the restriction. Using such a classification the whole law arrived at in the Ten Years' Conflict may be summed up. Positive obedience, what the Church is bound to do, is comprised in the three Auchterarder cases and the Second Strathbogie case. Negative obedience, what the Church is bound not to do, is comprised in the Lethendy and Culsalmond cases, the First and Third Strathbogie cases and the separate case of Stewarton. In both categories, positive and negative, the statements of the majority of the court indicate an increasing willingness to intervene in church affairs to rebuke, to indicate correct conduct, and then to require or facilitate that conduct.

The reference in the last sentence to 'the majority of the court' leads us on to the comment. The decisions in the cases were generally by a majority. Of course at later stages some judges, who earlier had dissented, had to work with the law as their brethren had decided it, and could no longer press their views. But the fact remains that in the decisions there was expressed a view sympathetic to the legislation which was struck down, and which was against interference by the civil authority in matters within the ecclesiastical preserve. We have not gone in to these opinions in any detail, as that would unnecessarily prolong matters, but in general they reflected the arguments put by the Church. What is important is that these dissents appeared in the judgements of the courts, and indicated that the arguments put to the court were not absolutely unfounded and unsupportable; the cases were not open and shut, and the judiciary was not entirely hostile either to what the Church had sought to do by its offending legislation, or to the view that the Church did have a jurisdiction into which the civil authority might not enter.

But what was to be done? In various of the opinions in the Disruption cases indications are given that only two avenues of escape existed. Either the law would have to be changed by parliamentary enactment, or the dissentients would have to leave the Church of Scotland as by law established. Indeed, reading the judgements with the benefit of hindsight, the second option begins to sound like a tocsin.

Three examples will suffice. The discussion of the appeal to the House of Lords, in the Second Auchterarder case above, quoted part of the opinion of Lord Campbell on the argument that the conscience of the majority of the Presbytery had compelled them to act as they had. Immediately after the quoted extract Lord Campbell went on to state that the kind of freedom which the Church sought was only available to the churches outside the establishment. They and they only could make up their own rules. 'Whilst the appellants remain members of the Establishment' they were bound by statute, and could amend statute only by seeking recourse to Parliament.[127]

In the Second Strathbogie case Lord Medwyn likened the establishment to a contract between church and state, in which there was an inherent condition that the state would be entitled to enforce that contract. The State would not have 'given an irresponsible power to a society that might become either a most useful and efficient ally, or a most tyrannical or oppressive opponent'. If the Church were the judge of its own jurisdiction, to the exclusion of the civil courts it would be so irresponsible. (His Lordship uses the term 'irresponsible' technically and not pejoratively). On the contrary, the Church had traded the enforcement of the contract for the benefits of establishment, and therefore:

'If the Church feels burdened with this condition, its remedy is not disobedience at its own hands, but a recission of the contract, and a *restitutio in integrum*, which is always within its power, however much to be deprecated.'[128]

Finally we may cite the judgement of Lord Hope in the Lethendy case. Like others he indicated the possibility of getting the law changed by Parliament, but until that was done the laws of the established church were those laid down by statute, and they had to be obeyed. Somewhat repetitively, Lord Hope was of the opinion that:

'As for those ministers of the Church whose conscience cannot submit to the law as long as it remains the law, I am afraid nothing remains for them but to retire from the Established Church.'[129]

All this is not to say that Parliament and government were inactive during the period. Following the Reform Act of 1832 the representation of the people in a variety of contexts was of interest, and the House of Commons *inter alia* set up a Select Committee on Church Patronage in Scotland. Before that

Committee reported the Veto Act was passed by the Assembly. It is therefore, to say the least, interesting that the Committee recommended the defence and preservation of an establishment which in their view was intimately interwoven with the general prosperity and moral welfare of Scotland. No recommendations were, however, made for change, and the Committee confined itself to rehearsing the evidence given to it. It does not appear to have considered that the 1834 legislation required either legislative or judicial correction.[130]

During the currency of the dispute the Melbourne government had indicated it would seek to remedy the situation. Thus in 1839 the Committee appointed by the Assembly after the First Auchterarder case did meet with government, but it appears that that government's political strength was not such as would have allowed satisfactory immediate action.[131] However, at the Commission of Assembly in August 1839 a letter was read indicating that the government intended to operate Crown rights of patronage in a manner congruent with the Veto Act, and it was implied that amendment of the law would follow. But, although the Crown did so do, for example in the Daviot case, its professed intention to act in a manner inconsistent with statute law was attacked both in the Commission by the Moderates and in the House of Lords by Lord Brougham. Finally, the position was further exacerbated by a long pamphlet published by the Dean of Faculty, John Hope.[132]

According to Buchanan,[133] one of the main reasons why the Church did not ask for the amendment of the Patronage Law by Parliament at the very beginning was its distrust of the 1834 Parliament's ability to appreciate the Presbyterian viewpoint. Whether this was justified does not now matter. The important fact was that the Assembly proceeded with its own legislation with the results we have seen. Naturally this demonstration of a will to independence reinforced whatever anti-evangelical feelings there were in Parliament, and, to borrow a metaphor from nuclear technology or warfare, the whole matter went critical.

Parliament did not come into the dispute again until things had gone far beyond questions of patronage and the internal constitution and self-regulatory powers of the Kirk. The fundamental problems of church-state relations were by then the subject of dispute. At that stage it offered a solution to the patronage problem, which eventually became the Scottish Benefices Act of 1843,[134] allowing members of a congregation to object to a presentee, or to give reasons why he was unsuitable for the charge. Presbytery was then to decide what effect was to be given to such objection. This was an improvement, but it did indicate that Parliament considered the *rationes* and *dicta* of the Disruption cases to be correct statements of the law. The State was the fount of all authority. Therefore, although the Benefices Bill would have gone some way to meet Veto Act procedure, it implied a supremacy of state enactment which by this time was repugnant to an important section of the Church of Scotland leadership.

What the evangelicals wanted was legislation by the state recognising and giving effect to the Church's claim to final powers of legislation and of judicial determination of spiritual matters, as matters within the province of the Church alone. This view was clearly stated in the Claim of Right, that remarkable document adopted by the General Assembly by a majority of 131 in the early hours of Wednesday, 25 May 1842.

The Claim of Right of 1842[135] narrated the theological and statutory basis on which the Church claimed independence from the State, and the opinion of the Church that the civil courts had entrenched upon the rights of the Church. It went on to claim that independence of the civil arm for which it contended; declared that the ministers of the Church could not continue within the establishment unless it were suitably reconstituted to give effect to that view; and protested the Acts of Parliament which had led to the current situation, while stating that these statutes would continue to be obeyed within the civil realm. The Claim ended by calling on members of the Church if necessary 'to endure resignedly the loss of the temporal benefits of the establishment, and the personal sufferings to which they [might] be called', were Parliament to refuse to give relief by altering civil legislation so as to secure the spiritual independence of the Church.

The Claim of Right was intimated to Parliament, and other steps were also taken to ensure that government could not be ignorant of the consequences if the Claim were not heeded and given effect to. In this time, however, the series of court actions continued. In August 1842 the Second Auchterarder decision came from the House of Lords. In January 1843 the Stewarton decision struck down the Chapel Act. In the meantime, on 4 January the new government under Sir Robert Peel replied, stating that the Claim was unreasonable, and that the government 'could not advise Her Majesty to acquiesce in these demands'. Despite this on 31 January the Commission of Assembly decided to make one further appeal to Parliament. This was made through the agency of Mr. Fox Maule in the House of Commons on 7 March 1843, who asked for a Committee of Enquiry, with perhaps an address to the Crown as its result, and for a declaratory Act in order better to define the jurisdiction of the Church, and confirming its jurisdiction within its own province. The motion was lost, though a majority of the Scottish members supported it.[136] Three days later, on 10 March, the decisions in the Third Auchterarder and Third Strathbogie cases were handed down.

Once it was clear that the Church was not to obtain the redress she sought from the State, preparation began for the formal separation from the Church of Scotland of those ministers adhering to the Claim of Right. A Protest was drawn up narrating their view of the matter, and laying the whole blame and responsibility for breaching the union of church and state upon the civil authorities.

When the General Assembly met on Thursday 18 March 1843, the Moderator, the Rev. Dr. David Welsh, opened with prayer. He then stated that

3

instead of the Assembly passing as normal to make up the Roll of Commissioners, certain matters had to be dealt with. As the liberties of the constitution of the Church had been infringed without redress, he protested against their proceeding further. He then read the Protest, laid a copy of it, signed by a body of the Commissioners to the Assembly,[137] on the table of the Assembly, and withdrew from the chamber followed by those of like opinion. These ministers and elders then walked to the Canonmills Hall, where they constituted themselves as the first Assembly of the Free Church of Scotland—a denomination having the legal status of a voluntary association.[138]

Was it all necessary? Could it all have happened differently? Should the Disruption have been avoided? There are no answers to such questions. It happened. And certainly it was part of a general change in Scottish life.[139] Yet we can see certain crucial elements and turning points in the story. For example, it seems clear that the successive governments of the day were either badly advised and unaware of the real seriousness of the situation (perhaps because their sources of information sympathised with the Moderate position), or that they misconstrued the facts for political reasons.[140] It may be that the success of their policy of inaction in coping with the problems of the Church of England misled them into applying a similar policy to the radically different Scottish Church. Alternatively the Scottish policy may have been deliberate, precisely to avoid stirring up the English situation again. At any rate the failure to see or permit that the will to participate in government which had manifested itself in the 1832 Reform Act should also affect ecclesiastical government is curious. Perhaps here, before his Lectures had received much publicity, we see in action the idea of John Austin's Sovereign, the ruler without equal or superior, from whose unfettered will all authority within his state is derived.[141] Such could not allow the spiritual independence of the Church.

On the other hand some would argue that the government did the best possible thing in refusing to heed a strident and divisive minority, whose instability was proved by its readiness theatrically to quit the establishment. It is likely that the 1843 Assembly would have contained a Moderate majority once more, which would have been willing to acquiesce in the Disruption judgements, and alter the ecclesiastical legislation accordingly. The Disruption can therefore be presented as a pre-emptive strike by the minority. But such an argument is not supportable in my view. The Church could ill afford the loss of those who 'went out', and the root of the matter goes deeper than that.

The Disruption was a tragedy for the Church of Scotland in that it absorbed so many energies at the time and subsequently when both sides (though especially the Free Church) sought to justify their stances. It is the cancer of schism that the parties rarely put it behind them and get on with their immediate tasks. Rather they fight the old battles over again. Both the Free and established Church were weakened in that way in the following decades, though the established Church did survive better in the long run.[142]

However, the Disruption was generally considered to be, and was, one of the finest acts of principle that had been seen,[143] as ministers, for their conscience sake, quitted the comforts and security of the establishment, and as members began the financial task of setting up a new Church, providing it with buildings, a college system and so on. It was a fine manifestation of an element of the Scottish character. But it was caused by other national characteristics. There were occasions early in the dispute when matters might have been solved by discussion and negotiation had first the Moderates, and then later the Evangelicals, been willing so to do. Too soon, perhaps, were stands taken on matters of principle, and the rights and wrongs of the situation, rather than its solution, contended for. The Moderates stood on the statute law, the Evangelicals on theological doctrine. Arguing from different premises, they could not reach an accommodation without seeming to surrender principle. The result of that failure to discuss and negotiate before positions became too entrenched is therefore a warning to the heirs of both sides in the modern Kirk.

CHAPTER IV

The Post-Disruption Period

Discussion of the legal developments between the established Church and the State in the period after the Disruption need not take as much space as that relating to the occurrence of that event. The general trend of the law is towards a greater recognition of the freedom and principles which the seceding ministers had contended for being granted by the State. The process was not immediate, nor without setbacks, but its general direction was towards the recognition of an independent jurisdiction vested in the Church greater than that contemplated by the dicta of the Disruption cases.

The Assembly which remained after the Disruption procession swiftly proceeded to revise the law of the Church to bring it into harmony with the statements on the effect of establishment which had been given by the various courts. The Veto Act and Chapel Act were repealed (Acts IX and X, 1843). The suspension of the majority of the ministers of the Presbytery of Strathbogie was treated as null and void. The only new development was that the Assembly welcomed the Bill which later became the Scottish Benefices Act, though that Act introduced an element of congregational opinion into the consideration by Presbyteries of whether a minister ought to be taken on trials, which went rather close to the Veto Act provisions, and certainly closer than many who had opposed the Veto Act would have wished.[144]

The effect of these legislative steps was to indicate clearly that any further development of the law of the Church would have to occur by the agency of the statute law. The Church itself now effectively disavowed its competence to revise its own constitution, just as in the previous ten years it had claimed that right. Accordingly we find that it is to statute law that we must look to see developments in the Church's constitution. This meant that at this particular point in time the State was theoretically supreme over the Church. How far this could have been pressed in practice is doubtful. It does not appear, for example, that the State could have interfered substantively with the Confession of the Church, though as we shall see in respect of education the State did no longer require that teachers should be subject to supervision by the Church, nor that they be required to subscribe the Confession. There are cases which make it plain that the relationship between the Church and State was conceived of as one in which the Church was supreme in its own sphere. These cases, however, do not contain the extravagant language to be found in the pre-1843 decisions, and fall to be distinguished from them as dealing with the judicial and not the legislative powers of the Church.

In 1849 two sets of cases discussed the legal position of the courts of the Church acting in a judicial capacity. In *Dunbar* v. *Stoddart*, (1849) 11 D. 587, issues were settled for trial of a case in which Dunbar, a parochial schoolmaster, sought damages for slander against the local minister. There, questions of malice were discussed, but it was decided that the facts did not raise questions of privilege. Later, however, an action for reduction on the grounds of irregularity of procedure was raised by the schoolmaster against the Presbytery, which, following upon complaint by the minister, had passed sentence of deposition against him. This was successful. Dunbar then sought damages against the Presbytery in respect of their actings. In *Dunbar* v. *Presbytery of Auchterarder*, (1849) 12 D. 284, issues were disallowed on this head as it was clear from the proceedings that the ground of complaint was one of error of judgement and not of malice.[145] But the question of the jurisdiction of the Church courts was not properly looked into in these cases, as they were performing a duty which had been given them under the statutes relating to the regulation of schools. Still more serious questions were raised by the normal disciplinary functions of the courts of the Church in respect of their members.

The point arose for determination in the case of *Sturrock* v. *Greig*, (1849) 11 D. 1220, where again a schoolmaster was involved, but in which the matter was clearly one of discipline. Peter Sturrock, assistant schoolmaster at Blairgowrie, sought damages against the minister and members of the Kirk Session of Blairgowrie, which had taken action against him in respect of a *fama* (a rumour of misconduct), and in respect of other faults. The case is complex, involving the failure of the Kirk Session to recognise the reversal of its decisions by the superior courts of the Church, and in respect of their failure to perform certain duties, but the point for which it is here cited concerned the privilege of the Church courts and the finality of their actings.

The first head note to the case summarises the decision succinctly:

'No action for damages will lie against a Church Court of the Established Church for any sentence or judgment pronounced by them in a proper case of discipline duly brought before them, regularly conducted, and within their competency and province as a Church Court, even although it be averred that the judgment was pronounced maliciously and without probable cause.'

The Opinion of Lord Justice-Clerk Hope made it clear that, in law within the scope of their proper duty, Church courts were an established part of the constitutional structure of the judicial arrangements of the country, and hence were not open to review, or to action in respect of their conduct. He said ((1849) 11 D. 1220 at 1231):

'. . . . in matters clearly within the cognisance of Church officers or Courts, as subject of Church censures . . . . when the Church judicatory is thus exercising the government so entrusted to it, (sc. by the State) its judicatories and its officers are not amenable to the civil courts for alleged wrong. They have been trusted as a separate government'.

The opinions of Lords Medwyn and Moncreiff were to like effect, the latter stating at p. 1238:

'. . . . the action and proposed issue are incompetent, in so far as they are founded on the sentences or resolutions of the Kirk Session regularly convened, and . . . . no addition of malice or want of probable cause can render them competent'.

Such statements were objected to by Lord Cockburn in his dissenting opinion (also at p. 1238), on the apparently reasonable grounds that they meant that a Kirk Session had an absolute licence of defamation. But it is not clear whether this is so. In the first place the opinions of the majority do speak in terms of 'proper' cases, 'regular' proceedings, and the 'province' and 'competence' of the appropriate Church court, and the language used might allow a later court suitably to interpret *Sturrock* if necessary.[146] Again other case law casts some doubt on the wider language of *Sturrock. Dunbar* v. *Presbytery of Auchterarder, (supra,* (1849) 12 D. 284), is one such case, and there are other later cases arising from the judicatories of the non-established churches which provide indications that the privilege of a Church court is only of a qualified nature, and may be displaced by proof of malice.[147] A court acting maliciously could be determined not to be a court acting within its province.[148] The question does not seem to have been argued in respect of the established Church since 1849, but I am inclined to doubt whether a wide interpretation of *Sturrock* would be followed.[149]

The importance of the *Sturrock* case for our present purposes, does not lie so much in its discussion of the privileges of the established Church courts, but in the view which it clearly states that in the judicial area, the area of discipline, the Church courts were final. Lord Cockburn pointed out that the decision in *Sturrock* seemed to run counter to the wide statements of the previous Disruption cases. He concluded his opinion by stating:

'It humbly appears to me that your Lordships' opinions amount to a reversal of the principle of these judgements. I am aware that this is not what your Lordships mean; but I suspect that it is the only construction that lawyers can put on what you are doing'.[150]

This dissent notwithstanding, the majority held that within its province the Church court was supreme, but (and this accommodates Lord Cockburn to a degree) it was a matter for a civil court to determine in the last analysis whether the Church court was within its exclusive jurisdiction. Lord Justice-Clerk Hope stated that the principle of supremacy in disciplinary matters 'will not surround these courts with protection if they exceed their jurisdiction', and he cited the Disruption cases as illustration. Further these cases showed that the Church courts were not protected if they 'refuse to perform a duty imposed upon them by statute, as part of the ecclesiastical constitution of the Church'.[151] But Lord Hope dealt with the Disruption material only in this oblique way. Lord Medwyn was in full agreement with Lord Hope, pointing to the separate jurisdiction of the Church courts so long as they acted within their sphere of competence. The only remedy for an unjust, as opposed to an illegal, sentence pronounced by a Church court lay within the appellate procedures of the Church in his opinion.[152] He went on expressly to distinguish the Disruption cases on points of patrimonial interest, but this does not seem valid. Previously the civil courts had been only too keen to right wrongs, and it does seem that on that basis Sturrock did have a relevant and competent case.

Despite the statements by the majority, one is left with the feeling that the Court of Session was no longer willing to make such extreme statements of the subordination of the Church to the State as they had for example in the Auchterarder and Strathbogie cases. The fact that an influential section of the Church had left the establishment because the Auchterarder and other statements reflected the view of the Church which they would not accept, seems to have cooled the ardour of the court a little. Of course, in so saying one is making an unsubstantiable interpretation of the facts, based simply upon the apparently more cautious attitudes of the judges, but it may be that there is other historical evidence for this opinion. At any rate their Lordships did state once more a principle which had in effect been mute in the Ten Years' Conflict; that there was an area within which the Church was final.

This principle was applied in *Lockhart* v. *Presbytery of Deer*, (1851) 13 D. 1296, where the First Division, without calling upon counsel for the respondents, refused a note of suspension brought by Dr. Lockhart against a sentence of deposition on the grounds of immoral conduct. Lockhart alleged various procedural deficiencies in the trial of the case which the General Assembly had refused to correct, but the court refused to consider the matter. Lord President Boyle stated:

'We are just driven to ask this question—does the Court of Session sit in review of the highest ecclesiastical court? We have just as little right to interfere with the procedure of the Church courts in matters of ecclesiastical discipline, as we have to interfere with the proceedings of the Court of Justiciary in a criminal question'.[153]

Lord Fullerton said:

'The deliverances . . . . on the irregularity or informality of which the present application is founded, are deliverances by a Church court, in the undoubted exercise of their own exclusive jurisdiction. . . . . I have always understood that a sentence of deposition pronounced by [the General Assembly] on an ecclesiastical offence, is beyond the reach of any interference by this Civil Court . . . .'[154]

Lord Cuninghame was equally emphatic that the ecclesiastical courts had an exclusive jurisdiction in proper ecclesiastical cases, and it would be 'altogether unprecedented and unconstitutional' to review their judgements.[155] This language is interesting and was commented on by Lord Ivory, noting that the important question was the extent of the 'proper ecclesiastical' nature of any given case, which allowed the court to distinguish the Auchterarder and Strathbogie cases.[156]

Further examples exist in which the Court of Session refused notes of suspension and interdict against proceedings in the Church courts on the grounds that these bodies were acting within their powers. The effect of this pattern was slowly to establish an area of judicial activity within which the Church was supreme, thus removing many of the doubts that the wider pronouncements of the Conflict cases had caused.

In *Paterson* v. *Presbytery of Dunbar*, (1861) 23 D. 720, the Court was asked to suspend a sentence of deposition of a minister on the grounds that a defence of insanity had not been properly dealt with in proceedings before the Church courts. Lord Ivory put the point most succinctly. He considered that for the Court of Session to grant the note

'. . . . would be going contrary to the whole principles of independent jurisdiction which separate the Ecclesiastical from the Civil courts. Each is independent of the other, and each has its own exclusive field of jurisdiction and within that field is paramount. No more can we interfere with the ecclesiastical jurisdiction, keeping it within its competency, than the ecclesiastical courts could interfere with us, keeping us within our competency'.[157]

Again in *Lang* v. *Presbytery of Irvine* (1864) 2 M. 823, the court refused to consider a note of reduction of a Presbytery minute on the grounds of irregularity, because the pursuer had not exhausted the remedies open to him in the hierarchy of Church courts. Until that had been done the civil courts would not even look at the matter to see whether they were excluded by reason of it being one within the exclusive competence of the ecclesiastical court.[158] In one of the best known statements of the principle, Lord Justice-Clerk Moncreiff, after reviewing the averments,[158a] stated in *Wight* v. *Presbytery of Dunkeld*, (1870) 8 M. 921 at 925:

'If, therefore, this were a case in which we were called upon to review the proceedings of an inferior Court, I should have thought that a strong case had been made out for our interference. But whatever inconsiderate dicta to that effect may have been thrown out, that is not the law of Scotland. The jurisdiction of the Church courts, as recognised judicatories of this realm, rests on a similar statutory foundation to that under which we administer justice within these walls. It is easy to suggest extravagant instances of excess of power, but quite as easy to do so in regard to the one jurisdiction as to the other. Within their spiritual province the Church Courts are as supreme as we are within the civil; and as this is a matter relating to the discipline of the Church, and solely within the cognisance of the Church Courts, I think that we have no power whatever to interfere'.

The rest of the Bench agreed in general terms with the Lord Justice-Clerk, though expressing some doubts whether the civil court could not under any circumstances interfere with a Church proceeding. Their restricted interpretation

THE POST-DISRUPTION PERIOD

seems to be a more correct statement of the present law. This would also accord with the possible restricted interpretation of *Sturrock* v. *Greig* (1849) 11 D. 1220, using the concepts of 'proper jurisdiction', 'regularity of proceeding' and so on to allow the court freedom of manoeuvre round that rather exceptional case. It is proper also on this point to refer to cases on the judicatories of the non-established churches as being of persuasive authority here, and in particular to the opinion of Lord Justice-Clerk Aitchison in *McDonald* v. *Burns*, 1940 S.C. 376.[159] So long as the courts of the Church do not act plainly *ultra vires*, or maliciously, or manifestly unjustly (not merely unjustly), or contrary to some civil enactment, no action will lie to reduce their proceedings, or to obtain redress for any injury they have caused. But this is not the same as a statement that the courts of the Church have absolute independence from review by the civil courts.

Notwithstanding, it is clear that by the time of *Wight*, the nature of the Church courts as constitutionally recognised courts of the realm was being emphasised in a way not present in the Disruption dicta. This is underlined in the famous observations of Lord President Inglis on the nature of the Presbytery as a court of the realm in *Presbytery of Lews* v. *Fraser*, (1874) 1 R. 888 at 892,

'We are dealing with a presbytery, an established judicature of the country, as much recognised by law as the Court of Session itself. Its jurisdiction, indeed, differs widely from that of the civil courts, but it is just as much the creation of law as that of any other court in the kingdom'.

As a court of the realm, the records of the court are of like status to the ordinary civil courts, belonging to and being held by the court inalienably for the benefit of the public. The records are therefore *extra commercium*, and cannot become private property by any means. Therefore lapse of time will not bar their recovery by the court, as was held in the *Presbytery of Edinburgh* v. *University of Edinburgh*, (1890) 28 S.L.R. 567, where the public character of the records overcame a defence of possession for almost two hundred years.

The subjection of the established Church to the State was shown during the post-Disruption period by four major statutory innovations. The first of these was the alteration of the law relating to the erection of new parishes *quoad sacra*; the second, an alteration of the powers of Church courts; the third, the abolition of patronage; and the fourth, the intervention of the legislature to liberalise the terms of subscription of the Westminster Confession by office-bearers.

The New Parishes (Scotland) Act 1844 modified the Act 1706 c. 10, making it more easy for the disjunction and erection of parishes *quoad sacra*. Although subject to the provision of satisfactory endowments (s.4), the Court of Teinds might proceed to the erection of the parish, usually with the consent of the heritors. However, s.1 abolished the requirement of the consent of three-quarters of the heritors under the 1706 Act. The Court was empowered to act with the consent of a majority, computed in terms of s.3 as all those not actively objecting, and, where there were 'good and sufficient reasons' for the disjunction and erection, s.4 provided that consent might simply be dispensed with. In the actual delineation of the new parochial boundaries the Church was to be the active force, but by s.8 it was clearly stated that the ministers and elders of such new churches were to have the full status of office-bearers of the Church. This meant that they could sit and vote in the courts of the Church in addition to exercising the usual ecclesiastical powers of their station.[160]

In this way the decision in the Stewarton case was avoided, and in effect many of the purposes for which the Chapel Act had been passed were achieved. However, as against that radical development, we may note that there is the requirement of endowment, and the intervention of the civil court in the proceedings. Further, the whole development, including the alteration of the constitution of the Church to allow the office-bearers of the *quoad sacra* churches to participate in the courts of the Church, was a matter of civil statute.[161] In other words, the development had occurred, but by the courtesy and action of the civil authority; an intervention which would have been rejected by those who by then had formed the Free Church.

The second development in the relations between the established Church and the State, which was opposed by a petition from the Assembly of the Free Church of Scotland, was the Church of Scotland Courts Act 1863. The purpose of this Act was to remove doubts as to the ability of the Church courts to suspend a minister from his parochial duties pending the determination of a libel against him. It was argued by the Free Church that, for the Church of Scotland to accept such clarification by the State clearly showed the erastian nature of the establishment. But the passing of the Act did indicate a willingness on the part of the government to afford a greater degree of liberty of action to the Church in its disciplinary function.[162]

The third step was the abolition of patronage, again by the act of the civil arm. The Church Patronage (Scotland) Act 1874[163] was the result of a petition by the Church itself following upon discussion in the 1860's.[164] Under the statute provision was made for compensation to be paid to private patrons only, if the patron so requested within six months of the passage of the Act. Such compensation was to be determined by the sheriff of the bounds (s.4), and was normally one year's stipend taken as the average of the preceding three years (s.5). Section 3 enacted that:

'the right of electing and appointing ministers to vacant churches and parishes in Scotland is hereby declared to be vested in the congregations of such vacant churches and parishes . . . . subject to such regulations . . . . as may from time to time be framed by the General Assembly of the Church of Scotland . . . .'

Further the Section declared that:

'. . . . the courts of the said Church are hereby declared to have the right to decide finally and exclusively upon the appointment, admission, and settlement in any church and parish of any person as minister thereof. The ministers . . . [so settled] . . . have in all respects the same rights, privileges and duties which now belong to or are incumbent on the ministers of the said Church'.

In the event of the congregation failing to act within six months the right to appoint a minister devolved in terms of s.7 upon the presbytery of the bounds.

The provision as to the devolution of the right of appointment soon gave rise to court action which clearly showed the extent of the concession made to Church autonomy by s.3. In *Stewart* v. *Presbytery of Paisley*, (1878) 6 R. 178, there was doubt whether the right to appoint a minister to the charge of Paisley Abbey had devolved on Presbytery. The time limit of six months had elapsed due to the minister selected by the congregation having declined the call to the parish. A note of suspension and interdict against the Presbytery acting, brought on the part of two parishioners, was refused as being out of time, and also because the Assembly and the Presbytery had in the meantime determined that no valid appointment had been made. This was final in terms of s.3 of the Act.

But apart from the merits of this decision, there are in the opinion of the Court, delivered by Lord President Inglis, observations as to the nature of the legislation and the relations of the civil and ecclesiastical courts constituted by it. The Presbytery had argued that under s.3 the courts of the Church were final, excluding any recourse to the civil judicatories. The Lord President stated clearly that the right to appoint under the Act is a statutory right, and not one of patronage. In such rights the jurisdiction to determine disputes rests with the civil courts of the country unless expressly excluded, and this had not been done. As he put it at p. 183:

'. . . . Being legal rights dependent upon stature their enforcement or a challenge of their validity in any particular case can only be tried in the tribunal which is appointed to interpret and enforce the statutes of the realm, that is, the supreme civil Court, unless the jurisdiction and duty have been conferred and imposed on some other tribunal. If the Legislature had thought fit they might have committed this jurisdiction to an inferior civil Court, or the Legislature, being omnipotent, might in like manner have conferred this jurisdiction upon the Courts of the Church, though an enactment conferring upon these Courts power to adjudicate in a competition of statutory rights would have been so entire a novelty that it would have required very clear words in such a case to oust the ordinary tribunals'.

It followed that the question whether a valid appointment had occurred was a matter for the Church courts to determine, but whether the consequence of that decision was that devolution to Presbytery also occurred was a matter for the civil court to decide. The Church courts might decide in the ordinary event, but where questions arose as to the collision of two statutory rights, the one that of the congregation under s.3 and the other that of the Presbytery under s.7, clearly the ordinary court might intervene, as it had not been excluded.

Within a fortnight the decision in *Stewart* was reinforced by that of the Second Division in *Cassie* v. *The General Assembly of the Church of Scotland*, (1878) 6 R. 221. There, Lord Justice Clerk Moncreiff explicitly adopted the opinion of the Lord President in *Stewart*, although he did not directly refer to that case.[165] The other judges similarly approved the decision in *Stewart*, while holding that the civil court was not excluded from taking jurisdiction in matters of a competition between interests under the Patronage Act 1874. In that case, however, the Division refused a note of suspension, where new members of a congregation sought to be placed on the electoral roll during a vacancy. The matter of the roll was for the Church courts to decide, and the civil courts would not interfere, no relevant case having been stated. But the Court of Session was careful to preserve its freedom of movement and action were the Church courts to abuse their powers. One judge put it thus:

'It is unnecessary, however, to hold, and I do not hold that there might not be such an abuse or excess of the powers of the Church Courts as to warrant the interference of this Court'.[166]

Following these decisions there were a series of cases in which the Court of Session showed that it was not unwilling both to take jurisdiction and to make determination of issues properly brought before them. In *McFarlane* v. *Presbytery of Coupar* (1879) 16 S.L.R. 480, Lord Young held that a right of appointment had not fallen to Presbytery *iure devoluto*, as the running of the six month period under the Act had been interrupted by an erroneous ruling by the moderator appointed by the Presbytery to moderate in the call. Again in *Dunbar* v. *Presbytery of Abernethy*, (1889) 26 S.L.R. 517, Lord Wellwood held that the right of appointment had not devolved as the Presbytery had misled the congregation in material particulars, resulting in the expiry of the calendar period without an appointment being made. These acts therefore interrupted the legal period in which the congregation had opportunity to appoint a minister.

Of course not all cases went against Presbytery,[167] but where the Presbytery acted in such a manner as to preclude the timeous exercise of the right of appointment by a congregation, the civil courts intervened to right the matter. Where the Presbytery was not at fault, in a competition between the right of the congregation to appoint under s.3 and the right *iure devoluto* of the Presbytery under s.7, the Court upheld the devolution when the six month period had so elapsed. In *Craig* v. *Anderson and the Presbytery of Deer*, (1893) 20 R. 941, the First Division passed a note of reduction on a minute of the congregation purporting to appoint the Rev. James D. Anderson as minister of the parish of Old Deer, on the grounds that by the date of the minute the right of appointment had passed to the Presbytery under s.7 of the 1874 Act. Mr.

Anderson had been 'appointed' during the six months but had then refused the appointment, so the Presbytery ruled this first appointment invalid. The subsequent appointment of Mr. Anderson had occurred more than six months from the date of the vacancy. It was held that the initial 'appointment' had not interrupted the running of the six months within which the congregation might act, and therefore their acting after that period was not competent. The point at issue was determined by the holding of the Presbytery that the first appointment was invalid due to Mr. Anderson's refusal of the appointment. That decision by the Presbytery was final under s.3, and the civil courts might only determine what the effect of that decision was. The rules of the Church debarred the civil court from holding that there had been a valid appointment followed by a resignation.

The intervention of the legislature to liberalise the terms of the subscription of the Westminster Confession required of ministers and office-bearers of the Church was the fourth way in which it was shown that the established Church remained bound to the terms of the statutes which were the ground of its privileges.

Subscription of the Confession was required under the Ministers Act 1693 c.38. The actual terms of the subscription were regulated by the Church itself, which required subscription by elders as well as ministers in 1694. In 1711 the Church had made the terms of subscription for ministers much stricter than was required by the 1693 Act.[168] With the change in theological opinion of the nineteenth century, particularly through the efforts of German theologians such as the Tübingen school, many aspects of the Confession came under fire, and the strict Calvinism of certain portions came to be disavowed by many. Accordingly the Church was faced with a demand to revise the terms of the subscription required.

One solution proposed was the return to the formula of the 1693 Act, and this was done in part by the Act 17, 1889, which was acquiesced in by the Church.[169] But this raised questions as to the propriety of the Church's acting, and whether, if the Church could so act, it could not go farther and enact a formula which would be even freer in its terms, and therefore more congenial to 'modern' theology. The Opinion of Mr. A. Asher, Q.C., Dean of Faculty, Professor John Rankine, Q.C. and A. H. B. Constable given to the 1900 Assembly on these points was that the Church was still bound by the 1693 Act, and that the 1711 formula could not be revived, not being sanctioned by that Act. On the assumption that the 1693 statute was still authoritative, the Church could not proceed to a more liberal formula; though if the Opinion were wrong on the vitality of the 1693 Act, the contrary decision would be possible.[170] The 1900 Assembly resolved to explore the matter further, and in 1901 the Assembly restricted itself by a narrow majority to receiving the Report of an enlarged Committee on the Powers of the Church with regard to the Confession, which stated that, statute obstante, the Church did not have power further to alter the terms of the subscription of the Confession. Against this, a large body of opinion led by Dr. Story and Sheriff R. Vary Campbell, argued that the Church had by reason of its spiritual independence, power to define the relation of its office-bearers to the Confession without the intervention of the State. That power was stated in the Confession which itself had been made part of the law of the land.[171]

Opportunity to deal with the matter came with the parliamentary proceedings in consequence of the Free Church cases of 1904. Section 5 of the Churches (Scotland) Act 1905 enacted that the formula of subscription to the Confession of Faith for ministers should be such as would be prescribed by the General Assembly following Barrier Act procedure.[172] Act XIII, 1910 was the response of the Assembly to this, enacting a formula of declaration of belief of the fundamental doctrines contained in the Westminster Confession, but without defining which doctrines were fundamental. In so doing the Church had approached to the 'liberty of opinion in matters not of the substance of the faith' which had been adopted as an escape from the strict totality of the Confession by other Scottish Churches.

In all the proceedings of the period 1843–1929 however, although there is a move towards the granting of greater freedom of action to the Church, yet that grant was always made by the intervention of the State. Patronage was abolished, but by the State, and the civil courts continued to have an important role in disputes under the Act. New parishes were more easily to be established, and their ministers were given full status, but only under statute. Even the requirements of the Church as to doctrinal profession of ministers was a matter in which the State had the last say. Although power was granted to the Assembly, yet 'what Caesar gives, Caesar may take away'. The established Church was therefore gaining freedom, but freedom, as it were, on a lead. Such powers as it had were given to it by the State, and were not inherent in it *ex natura.*

Amid such consistency of attitude in the case law and in the statutory interventions of the State it comes as no surprise to find that especially in the last quarter of the nineteenth century there was considerable agitation for the disestablishment of the Church of Scotland.[173] This was partly conditioned by similar moves in respect of the Irish and Welsh churches,[174] but was a well grounded native movement as well. Many Free Church figures, as well as the United Presbyterians, held that the only way for a true reconstruction of the Church of Christ in Scotland was for there to be a separation of Church and State. The continuance of an established Church, on the terms which that Church was established, meant that general union, which was also in the wind, was not possible.[175] The established Church, by far the largest church still, could not accommodate itself to the ideas of the lesser bodies, and they were unwilling to unite in its form. After all the ground of existence of many of the smaller denominations was disagreement with the then ruling principles of the establishment. The crusade against establishment was fierce, and of grave importance, affecting as it did the political life of the nation in addition to its church life, but in the end of the day the question faded from attention with the progress towards union. As will be seen elsewhere a major step was the union of the Free and the United Presbyterian churches in 1900, to form the United Free Church, and the discussion between that Church and the Church of Scotland eventually brought about the Union of 1929. In order to achieve this result, however, the whole question of the relationship between the Church and the State had to be resolved and restated.

CHAPTER V

The Settlement of 1921—The Declaratory Articles and the Church of Scotland Act, 1921

The present relationship between the established Church and the State is regulated by the Church of Scotland Act 1921 and the Articles Declaratory of the Constitution of the Church of Scotland in Matters Spiritual, declared to be lawful by, and scheduled to that Act.[176] The Church of Scotland (Property and Endowments) Act 1925 made provision for the financial reconstruction of the Church following the constitutional alterations of the 1921 Act. On the basis of these enactments and further negotiations the present Church of Scotland was formed by the union of the United Free Church and the Church of Scotland in May 1929.[177]

The Declaratory Articles which form the constitution of the Church in Matters Spiritual were formulated by the Church in consultation with the United Free Church in order to facilitate the union of the two churches. To narrate and discuss the actual negotiations would require a separate treatise,[178] but it will suffice here to summarise those points which are of interest for our present study.

Briefly, there were two points which the new settlement had to secure: the independence of the Church from State control, and the internal freedom of the Church's constitution in matters of doctrine, worship, government and discipline. Independence of the Church from State control was necessary in order to allow the former Free Church traditions of the United Free Church to be accommodated. Internal freedom was required to allow the new church to develop and change as might be thought good in future years, without the threat of action similar to the Free Church cases, and to include the constitutional freedom of the United Free Church, again to avoid a disruptive court action. This requires some elaboration.[179]

Proposals for the re-uniting of the several divisions of Presbyterianism were common during the latter part of the Nineteenth Century.[180] There was much to recommend the development. In doctrine there was little fundamental divergence between the denominations. Each subscribed the Westminster Confession of Faith, though with reservations caused by the then current theology. In government the churches were alike, and in their growing conviction of the duty of each church to seek corporate unity with each other there was also an element of sheer practicality, it being recognised that it was inefficient for these denominations to compete with each other when there was the whole of Scotland to be served.

The first major attempt to heal the divisions was between the United Presbyterian Church and the Free Church. This attempt foundered in 1869 on the opposition of a group led by Dr. James Begg. It was clear at that point that to have proceeded further would have led to a serious schism within the Free Church, and would not have had corresponding benefits. However, as discussed elsewhere, this union did come to fruition in 1900, though there was much bitterness, the new United Free Church seeking to expel from their charges those ministers who refused to enter the united church.

Unfortunately, in terms of politics, the minority of the Free Church which dissented from the Union, succeeded in the House of Lords in their claim to represent the Free Church, their lordships holding that the portion of the Free Church which had entered the Union had forfeited their right to the property and endowments of the Free Church by reason of their having departed from the principles on which that property was held.[181] The difficulties caused by this decision were solved by the Churches (Scotland) Act 1905, and the appointment of a Commission to divide the property between the two factions. In consequence of the decision of the House of Lords, the new United Free Church by the Act I 1906, anent the Spiritual Independence of the Church, stated, as a principle of the United Free Church, the right of that Church to independent and exclusive jurisdiction in spiritual matters, and the right,

'through her Courts to alter, change, add to or modify her constitution and her laws, subordinate standards, and formulas . . . .'[182]

In this way there was grafted in to the constitution of the United Free Church that freedom of action which the House of Lords had decided was not contained in the Free Church constitution. Such freedom of legislation and adjudication in matters of worship, doctrine, government and discipline had to be taken into the proposed union of the United Free Church and Church of Scotland, and made basic to the constitution of the new church, both to satisfy the United Free Church, and in order to ensure that the property of both churches would be carried into the union, for, though most of the Model Trust Deeds of the uniting churches and some individual titles made provision for union, the general constitution of the new Church of Scotland had to be flexible enough to accommodate all varieties.

Another element which had to be safeguarded in the constitution of the new Church of Scotland was its independence from the State. The United Free Church was in part the successor of the Free Church, which, though created in 1843 to avoid the 'erastian' establishment of the Church of Scotland, held a doctrine of establishment as had been made clear in the Free Church Case. In part the United Free Church was also the successor of the union of the Voluntary-ist churches in 1847 to form the United Presbyterian Church, and therefore had elements of opposition to any form of establishment within it.[183] Clearly independence of the Church from the State was to be sought, and certainly the establishment of the Church of Scotland at the time was not satisfactory from the viewpoint of the United Free Church. On the other hand, as indicated at the end of the preceding chapter, the Church of Scotland had survived a long campaign for its disestablishment and disendowment, and would not have entered a union requiring the dissolution of its ties with the State.

The result of the negotiations was a compromise, in which establishment of sorts was retained, involving a national recognition of religion, but without the odious appurtenances of the former system. In fact most of the prior faults of establishment had been elided by the development of the law relating to non-established churches, but in the stating of the compromise it proved possible formally to state that the position of the national Church in no way derogated from the standing of other denominations.

The idea that a suitable way of resolving the difficulties of the Church of Scotland might be the drawing up of a single simple constitutional document was not a new one. During the disestablishment controversy, a Bill to Declare the Constitution of the Church of Scotland had been introduced into the House of Commons by R. B. Finlay in 1886. This would have affirmed the spiritual independence of the Church, but it failed to satisfy either the Church itself or those who were at that time attacking its position. In 1912, on the initiative of the Procurator of the Church of Scotland, C. N. Johnston (later Lord Sands), the negotiations between the United Free Church and the Church of Scotland produced a Memorandum which was to be submitted to both churches suggesting that the proper procedure would be for the Church of Scotland to seek a reformulation of its constitution to be approved by the State which would meet all the difficulties in the way of union.[184] The topics of spiritual independence, continuity of traditions and identity and so on were all to be thus safeguarded. On the basis of the Memorandum and discussions it was found possible to proceed with plans for the union, and three sets of draft Articles for the Church's constitution were discussed over the next five years.[185] Eventually a bill was presented to Parliament, scheduling the agreed Articles, and this in due course became the 1921 Act.[186] The equally thorny question of the endowments of the Church was deferred for separate treatment.

The Articles Declaratory of the Constitution of the Church of Scotland in Matters Spiritual form a statement which seeks to balance and unify the different attitudes and traditions of the churches which were to unite on their basis. The freedom of the Church to govern itself in its institutional framework, and at a deeper level in its doctrinal formulations, was to be guaranteed. The Church was to be seen as an entity, deriving its authority and standing from God, recognised as such by the State, and no longer as the creature of the State as it had been depicted in opinions of the Ten Years' Conflict. At the same time the identity of the Church had to be preserved, yet without prejudicing the religious equality of other denominations. These points were dealt with in the nine separate Articles.

The main burden of Article I is, naturally, the general and fundamental doctrines of the Faith professed by the Church of Scotland, which lineally are the doctrines carried down through the centuries from the primitive Church. Narrated almost in credal form, orthodox Trinitarian doctrine is provided for. Legally the other provision made is for the reformed Protestant nature of the Church of Scotland, for reference is made to adherence to the Scottish

Reformation. The terms of the Article are therefore incompatible with an interpretation based upon un-reformed doctrine, or with non-trinitarian dogma. Doubt was cast upon whether this represented a restriction upon the freedom of the Church to formulate doctrine which was not present in the United Free Church Act anent Spiritual Independence, but the Opinion of Counsel was to the contrary. The ordinary principles of the law of trusts required that the property of the Church be held on an ascertainable trust purpose, and the restriction to Trinitarian and Protestant principle was already present in the United Free Church constitution.[187] Of all the Articles Declaratory only Article I is declared to be unalterable by the Church and adherence to that Article, as interpreted by the Church 'is essential to its continuity and corporate life'.[188] The ground of being of the Church of Scotland is therefore to be found in the First of the Declaratory Articles.

It is possible here to deal with some of the other Articles in a summary manner before turning to those which concern the relation of the two powers. Article II places the Westminster Confession of Faith in its position as a subordinate standard. It goes on to affirm the Presbyterian nature of the government of the Church, though reserving the right of the Church to alter by Acts of Assembly, or by custom, its system of government, principles of worship, orders and discipline. In that this Article is not fundamental in the way that the First Article is, it is clear that Presbyterianism is not considered essential to the identity of the Church, thus reflecting the establishment of the Church prior to the settlement of its polity in 1592. Nonetheless Article III affirms the historical continuity of the Church with that reformed in 1560, whose liberty was ratified in 1592 and for whose security provision was made in the Treaty of Union. Despite this affirmation of identity, however, Article VII recognises the duty of the Church to seek and promote union with other churches,

> 'in which it finds the Word [of God] purely preached, [and] the sacraments administered according to Christ's ordinance and discipline rightly exercised...'

Article IX once more ratifies and confirms the constitution of the Church.

Articles IV, V, VI and VIII contain the provisions which are of greatest importance in settling the alterations to the constitution of the Church and its relation to the civil power. Articles IV, V and VIII give doctrinal freedom, and Articles IV and VI independence.

As has been said, one objective of the United Free Church negotiators was to see a constitution for the new Church which would reflect their own stand on the question of the spiritual independence of the Church enunciated in 1906. The Church of Scotland on the other hand was bound by legislation to the Westminster Confession of Faith though, as seen in the previous chapter, some steps had been taken under the power granted by s.5 of the Churches (Scotland) Act 1905 to modify the terms of subscription of the Confession required of ministers. The cumulative effect of the Articles cited is to give that doctrinal freedom which was sought by the United Free Church negotiators. Article IV gives,

> 'the right and power subject to no civil authority to legislate, and to adjudicate finally, in all matters of doctrine, worship . . . .'

Article V states that,

> 'This Church has the inherent right, free from interference by civil authority, but under the safeguards for deliberate action provided by the Church itself, to frame or adopt its subordinate standards, to declare the sense in which it understands its Confession of Faith, to modify the forms of expression therein, or to formulate other doctrinal statements, and to define the relation thereto of its office-bearers and members, but always in agreement with the Word of God and the fundamental doctrines of the Christian Faith contained in the said Confession, of which agreement the Church shall be sole judge . . . .'

Article VIII allows the interpretation or modification of the Articles, with the exception of Article I, subject to modified Barrier Act procedures. In this way the sought after freedom of the Church from interference by the State in doctrinal matters was laid down.

In the same way the right of the Church to deal with its own organisation and structure independent of the State was established. Just after the portion quoted from Article IV there is set out the right to legislate and adjudicate finally,

> 'in all matters of . . . . government, and discipline in the Church, including the right to determine all questions concerning membership and office in the Church, the constitution and membership of its Courts, and the mode of election of its office-bearers, and to define the boundaries of the spheres of labour of its ministers and other office-bearers'.

The inclusion of this statement in that Article, and its being followed by a statement that the recognition of the separate and independent government and jurisdiction of the Church by the civil authority does not affect the character of that government and jurisdiction as derived from Christ alone, shows clearly that according to the Church's constitution, all such matters are spiritual matters. In normal matters of internal organisation and administration there is no place for the *rationes* of the Disruption cases.

Apart from the above affirmation of the spiritual independence of the Church, there is in Article VI a statement of the relation between the Church and the civil authority which deserves quotation in full. It reads,

> 'This Church acknowledges the divine appointment and authority of the civil magistrate within his own sphere, and maintains its historic testimony

to the duty of the nation acting in its corporate capacity to render homage to God, to acknowledge the Lord Jesus Christ to be King over the nations, to obey His laws, to reverence His ordinances, to honour His Church, and to promote in all appropriate ways the Kingdom of God. The Church and the State owe mutual duties to each other, and acting within their respective spheres may signally promote each other's welfare. The Church and the State have the right to determine each for itself all questions concerning the extent and the continuance of their mutual relations in the discharge of these duties and the obligations arising therefrom'.

The constitution of the Church of Scotland therefore asserts the coordinate jurisdiction of Church and of State, each supreme within its own sphere, but leaves the actual determination of that sphere to each. There is therefore room for conflict here. In the Disruption cases there was frequent affirmation by the civil court of the independence of the Church within its sphere, but the court considered that in all matters where there was the possibility of civil right being affected the civil court had jurisdiction. This difficulty might arise again on a construction of the plain words of the constitution, and there might be questions as to the proper forum for the determination of such disputes.

The body of the 1921 Act is very simple, but far-reaching in its provisions. Section 1 states that the scheduled Articles are lawful for the Church to hold, and the constitution of the Church of Scotland in matters spiritual is as there set forth. In all questions of construction the Declaratory Articles are to prevail, and all statutes and laws in force at the time of the passing of the Act are to be construed in subjection thereto, and in conformity therewith. In so far as statute and laws are inconsistent with the Articles they are repealed and declared to be of no effect. S.3 preserves some place for the civil court,

'Subject to the recognition of the matters dealt with in the Declaratory Articles as matters spiritual, nothing in this Act contained shall affect or prejudice the jurisdiction of the civil courts in relation to any matter of a civil nature'.

In so declaring the lawfulness of the Articles as providing for the constitution of the Church in matters spiritual, the State seems to have accepted the statements which had been negotiated between the churches concerned in the projected union, and did not act of its own initiative. From the point of view of the Church, what has been granted is *recognition* of the Church's constitution; the Church has not been given a constitution. Any remanent ideas of the Church being constituted by the State and deriving its powers and jurisdiction from the State, may therefore have been laid to rest by the declaratory formulae of the Act.

The settlement of the property question may be dealt with shortly. The principal legislation is the Church of Scotland (Property and Endowments) Act 1925, as amended, dealing with the tenure of the property of the Church and matters of teinds and stipends. Under the Act provision was made for the former burdens on heritable property for the upkeep of the Church to be valued in money at a standard value, with provision for their redemption[189], for all endowments to pass into the ownership of the Church, and for the provision and upkeep of churches to be taken over by the Church itself, and no longer to be the responsibility of heritors.[190] In addition the administration of the Church's financial affairs was to become a matter for the Church alone, property being dealt with through the Church of Scotland General Trustees. The civil courts are excluded from these matters.[191] This rendering of matters of property and endowments as domestic matters for the Church, makes them part of general internal Church law, and hence outside the scope of the present enquiry. Suffice it to say that this move makes the independence of the Church more complete.

Only one case has so far called in question the extent and nature of the settlement of 1921. In *Ballantyne* v. *Presbytery of Wigtown*, 1936 S.C. 625, it was urged that the right of a congregation to elect a minister was a civil right under the terms of the 1874 Patronage Act, and was not affected by the 1921 Act or the Articles. However, the Second Division, Lord Mackay dissenting, held that all the matters enumerated in the Declaratory Articles were declared by statute to be spiritual matters, under the jurisdiction of the Church, to the exclusion of the jurisdiction of the civil court. Accordingly an action for declarator and production and reduction of Kirk Session and Presbytery minutes failed.

It was clear, as both parties conceded, that the Court had power to determine whether the matter lay within the competence of the Court. But the construction of the Act clearly put the precise matter beyond the civil authority. At p. 654 Lord Justice-Clerk Aitchison drew attention to the comprehensive sweep of the first section of the Act, and stated the purpose of the Act as,

'to declare the right of the Church to self-government in all that concerned its own life and activity'.

It followed that the,

'question must therefore be—Is the particular matter complained of, ... a matter which, on a reasonable construction, falls within the Declaratory Articles. If so, the matter is at an end, and neither the statute nor the common law nor previous judicial decision, whether upon statute or upon the common law, can avail to bring the matter within the jurisdiction of the civil authority'.

This meant that the argument that the 1921 Act was merely declaratory and not innovative, fell. It could not be argued that all matters civil before the Act continued civil in character despite the Act, for s.1 'is the only and the final test'. Lord Aitchison observes of Article IV conferring the power of government, at p. 655, 'No more comprehensive words could have been devised'.

These arguments were not unchallenged by Lord Mackay's dissent, as he considered that the jurisdiction of the civil court was not excluded in the area under dispute. The Court had often in times past taken such jurisdiction, and to hold it now excluded by an extended interpretation of an Act which was expressed to be declaratory was erroneous. A declaratory purpose was merely to avoid doubts.

'Beyond that, reasonable interpretation must not go. If it had been intended by Parliament to make the Church independent (as some zealots had always claimed, but unsuccessfully) of all State control, other terms and other means must have been found. If it was intended to carve out a well-defined piece of what (with so much benefit) had been found to be civil jurisdiction and to give it over, it would have been easy to do so. Nothing of that kind is done.'[192]

Inconsistency with the Articles was the basis of the repeal of prior statutes, but a very restricted interpretation of 'inconsistency' amounting to a presumption against, ought to be applied.[193]

One would have wished this case to have gone further than the Second Division on such an important matter. It is to be regretted that the decision should stand simply on the basis of the opinions of two judges, with one dissenting. Lord Pitman, the Lord Ordinary, did not deal expressly with the point, basing his decision on relevancy, but he did observe that the form of the 1921 Act was unfortunate in that it left the matter for the decision of the civil courts.

'It is now said by the defenders that the right to elect a minister is a spiritual matter with which the Law Courts have nothing to do, and not a civil right at all. It is difficult to understand why, in view of the clear words of the [Abolition of Patronage] Act of 1874, the pundits responsible for the drafting of the 1921 Act did not have inserted into it a clause specifically repealing the 1874 Act, if, as counsel informed me, that was one of the most important things they had in mind when drawing up the Act . . . .'[194]

However, as there have been no subsequent cases since *Ballantyne*, there is a strong argument that there has been acquiescence in the majority opinions; but there are areas within which the matter could be re-opened.

For example, the General Assembly of 1972 passed an Act (1972 Act III) under which ministers inducted to a charge after the date of the Act are to retire at age seventy. Until this Act ministers were appointed *aut vitam aut culpam*[195], and it might be argued that the new Act interferes with their civil right, in respect that it truncates the period in which they have right to full stipend. Clearly this is a matter which bridges the question of civil right preserved for the civil courts under s.3, and the right of the Church to govern itself; the right of the Church to legislate in respect of government in the Church, and to define the spheres of labour of its ministers. On the argument of the majority in *Ballantyne*, this matter is ecclesiastical, although it has civil overtones. On Lord Mackay's argument it is civil, having been civil before the passing of the Act, and not being inconsistent with the provisions of the Articles, but only inconsistent with what the Church wishes to enact under those Articles. If for the sake of argument we disregard I Cor. 6:1–7, perhaps this is a matter which might be used to obtain further judicial opinions on the ambit of the 1921 Act. Is the 1921 declaration a charter of total freedom, within the limits of the First Article, in all enumerated matters, or is it to be interpreted within the context of its time? In a sense the question is whether we are dealing with a statute or a constitution, and so to phrase the question is perhaps to answer it.

Another current question, fraught with many dangers in ecclesiastical and political overtones, which might provide an opportunity for the civil courts to make a definitive statement on the relation of the Church to the State is that of the Westminster Confession of Faith. As has been indicated, over the last century there has been dissatisfaction expressed by some elements in the Church, who feel that the precision of the Westminster Confession is undue, having regard to its own admitted subordinate status. In addition there has been the growth of widely different theological viewpoints within the Church. The solution to this was the passing of Declaratory Acts by the various denominations, which in the Church of Scotland find expression by the recognition of 'liberty of opinion on such matters as do not enter into the substance of the Faith'[196] but without defining that substance. Over the years increasing use was made of this clause, until virtually any opinion might be classed as not of the substance of the Faith, and so not proscribed by reference to the Confession.

Dissatisfaction with this device grew, as it became more and more obviously a subterfuge and an escape clause, recognisably improper for a minister. The question therefore arose whether the Confession might be removed from its status. In 1968, following upon a request for guidance by two Presbyteries, the General Assembly asked the Panel on Doctrine to review the place of the Westminster Confession of Faith as the subordinate standard of faith of the Church, and the reference to it in the Preamble and Questions at the ordination of ministers and elders.

On the report of a working party the Panel suggested that the concept of a subordinate standard be departed from, that the Confession cease to hold its present place, and that instead a stricter formulation in the Preamble of the ordination service be substituted.

As finally proposed for legislation in 1974 the suggested Preamble enumerated certain doctrines as fundamental to the Faith, and arguably could have gone some way towards eliminating certain heresies. However, in 1974 the Assembly refused to take the final step of enacting such legislation. Problems however emerged from the way in which it was done. In particular the Assembly resolved to depart from the matter pending the adoption of a new statement of the faith. But the Panel on Doctrine found the formulation of an acceptable statement impossible. In 1978 the Assembly decided on a narrow vote to reconsider the whole question of the status of the Confession—which will take some time.

This is not the place to enter into a discussion of the detailed proposals of 1974, or their moral propriety and theological standing. Nor is this the place thoroughly to discuss possible solutions to the problem. It may, however, help to note certain points. First, the constitution of the Church of Scotland consists of the Articles Declaratory and the legislation of the General Assembly, along with the constitutional practices of the Church (i.e. in effect, its common law). The Articles, and in particular Article I, are fundamental, but not to the exclusion of all else. To argue that Article I is 'the constitution', and all else is secondary, is to argue nonsense. Article I is not self-executing, both because it is insufficiently clear, requiring further elaboration through other statements, and because it does not lay down the structures and ordinances of government of the Church.

Secondly, there is the utility of the Confession as it performs the necessary function of giving further detail as to the content of doctrines. Unless such a role is somehow fulfilled, it will be necessary for the General Assembly, at intervals, to address its mind to doctrinal questions, and determine whether or not certain beliefs are consonant with the holding of office in the Church. We have had a recent example of this, in the matter of second Baptism, which was before the Assembly in 1976, to serve as a warning. But, the fact remains that without a/the Confession, the doctrines of the Church of Scotland will require to be clarified by case law—an unattractive prospect, but the only other way in which confusion may be dispelled (see note 418).

Lastly, it may be noted that the commonest attack on the Confession is that it is too clear and rigid. That may have some force, though it has not been so applied. But it may also be observed that there is a much greater degree of rigour in the way in which the ephemeral fashions of modern theology are insisted upon.

But be all that as it may, for our purposes here the important legal point is the question of a displacement of the Westminster Confession as the principal subordinate standard of the Church and the elimination of subordinate standards as such. The legality of the Panel's proposals was put to the then Procurator of the Church in 1969, (W. R. Grieve, Q.C., raised to the bench in 1972 as Lord Grieve). Though the proposals were subsequently altered in detail, the changes were not sufficiently fundamental to render the Procurator's opinion irrelevant.[197] Has the Church of Scotland the power to remove its subordinate standard?

It was the opinion of the Procurator that the proposed alterations in status of the Confession fell within the terms of Article IV of the 1921 Act. Relying on Lord Justice-Clerk Aitchison's statements in *Ballantyne* quoted above, the Procurator considered that the Church does have power to act as was proposed. The Opinion is, however, rather uneasy in its treatment of the question; clear on the right of the Church to deal with subordinate standards, but less clear on the point of their elimination. 'Subordinate standards' is a phrase which at one point the Procurator uses as a term of art, and at another as a simple label capable of different meanings, for example the 'standard' which is flourished. It would have been a better argument to found on the power contained in Article V to define the relation of the office-bearers and members to the Confession.

Three arguments may be put against the Procurator's Opinion. In the first place the power of the Church is to modify or add to its subordinate standards, which is different from the proposed *elimination* of subordinate standards, while retaining the documents as historic affirmation of the Church's belief as was suggested. Secondly, the change involves a transition from a confessional to a credal church. Thirdly, the relation of the Act to previous statutes, notably the Treaty of Union legislation, can be called in question.[198]

The first argument involves a simple construction of the terms of the 1921 Act, which is within the remaining competence of the civil court. Does the displacement of the Westminster Confession from its position as a standard of belief, and the failure to replace it with another subordinate standard lie within the competence of the Church under the 1921 constitution? As indicated, the Opinion of the Procurator was that it does. But the Procurator did not really distinguish between the Westminster Confession as a statement of belief, and its use as a standard of belief to which office-bearers of the Church are to subscribe. Further the power stipulated under Article V is to modify or add to the subordinate standard. To eliminate the Confession as a standard, while retaining it as an historic statement does not lie within this language.

But the right to interpret the Articles is given to the Church under Article VIII, and it might be argued that the Church can therefore interpret the Articles and the power to alter or modify them, as it pleases.[199] During the passing of the 1921 Act doubt was cast in the House of Commons whether the Church could by a judicious use of its power to interpret avoid the provisions of the Articles. Although, there were statements in the House of Lords to the contrary, the observation of the Solicitor General in the House of Commons, that ultimately questions of such interpretation would require resolution by the civil courts, has force. It might be that on this ground alone any alteration of the status of the Confession would require court action. These divergent statements are as follows.

Solicitor General Murray, asked whether the phrase 'as interpreted by the Church' modifying the reference to Article I in Article VIII could be used to get round the provisions of the Articles, replied,

'My legal opinion has been asked whether that (phrase) means that the Church as a Free Church has a power of interpretation. In law, if my opinion was asked, I think there must be a limit. It must at least be 'interpretation', and in the long run, of course, you have to have recourse to judicial interpretation. Provided that the Church loyally and *bona fide* interprets its standard as there set forth, it has the right to determine that standard. That right is only limited by the right of the judiciary, where there has been mis-interpretation or absence of interpretation, to control'.[200]

In the House of Lords, Viscount Finlay, (who had introduced the Declaratory Bill of 1886) stated,

'The power of interpretation may be dangerous, and it has been asked: If the interpretation is in the eyes of lawyers erroneous, will not the Civil Courts interfere? I say without hesitation that on the terms of this Bill the Civil Courts could not interfere. The whole scope of the Bill is to oust any interference by the Civil Courts by way of suspension or anything of that kind'.[201]

Lord Parmoor, noted that the formula in the Bill did everything necessary to ensure the spiritual independence of the Church[202], and Viscount Haldane, who had been counsel for the United Free Church in 1904, stated, that there might under some circumstances be property difficulties, but spiritual independence was assured. He observed,

'When you get to property you cannot altogether oust the Civil Courts, and therefore to that extent, I think the Civil Courts always must come in. Whether it be the United Free Church or the Established Church of Scotland, they must have the right to see whether identity has been preserved.

If a number of burglars got into the Carlton Club . . . . ousted the committee and declared it an institution for the promulgation of Bolshevism, I think it would not be in vain that appeals would be made to the Courts, notwithstanding that there would be a new committee or majority of members to mould the constitution, and I think that the Courts would say that identity had ceased and continuity was non-existent, and at an end between the two bodies. So it may be if the Church of Scotland or even the United Free Church were to go over to the creed of Mahomet or even to adopt the jurisdiction of the Bishop of Rome, that the Civil Courts might intervene and say: "Are the people who have this property people who are continuous with those who have hitherto enjoyed the title?" That might be the case. But it is abundantly clear that so far as doctrine is concerned, so far as the spiritual side of the constitution is concerned, so far as doing everything which can appertain to its continuity of existence and is consistent with it is concerned, the Church of Scotland will have under this constitution the most unlimited power of determining in its own Courts, and free from intrusion from the Civil Court, the doctrine which will be taught. No Civil Court can intrude. That principle has been conceded in its fullest form, and, speaking for myself, I have no doubt that the misgivings which have been expressed are misgivings which amount to nothing'.[203]

The arguments as to the interpretation of the power to alter standards, of the transition from a confessional to a credal church, and as to the Treaty of Union have certain common features, which can be taken together at first. In these arguments the basic question is whether the 1921 Act gives power to the Church to alter the character expressed in its prior constitutional form as fixed under the Reformation and Revolution statutes, and confirmed under the Union Settlement of 1707. That character binds it to the Confession as a standard. Again on the argument of the majority in *Ballantyne*, the Church does have this power under the Act, so long as the First Article is not breached. In that Article I says nothing about the credal or confessional form, there would appear to be no difficulty. But it must be recognised that to say that on the basis of the 1921 Act the Church can alter its character from confession to creed is to go very far. It is to allow the Church in its option to 'repeal' the various statutes binding it to its Confession of Faith. One has sympathy with Lord Mackay's point that such a wide implied repeal by the 1921 Act is not to be presumed but must be proved. Wherever possible the 1921 Act should be interpreted not to conflict with prior statute: that changes of such magnitude are not to be implied is a well-known principle of statutory interpretation.[204]

If one considers that the power to modify or add to its subordinate standards does not include power to alter the status of that standard and that the civil courts are not excluded, then one is led into realms of the Law of Trusts. It would be entirely arguable that the Church of Scotland in departing from the concept of a subordinate standard would be breaking the terms under which it holds its property. An action might be raised by a section of the Church unwilling so to depart seeking control of the property and funds of the Church as representing the true Church of Scotland.[205] As we shall see in the next chapter, in the House of Lords decision in the Free Church case, *Bannatyne* v. *Lord Overtoun*, (1904) 7 F. (H.L.) 1 : [1904] A.C. 515, departure from the Confession was one ground on which the former members of the Free Church who had entered the United Free Church were held to have forfeited right to Free Church property.

Beyond this, a further question might now be raised. If it is accepted that a true interpretation of the Act is to over-set the pre-1707 legislation, it might be argued that the 1921 Act was *ultra vires* of the United Kingdom Parliament. In that the Act purported to repeal part of the Union settlement entrenched in the Treaty of Union it is arguably invalid. The polity of the Church of Scotland, including the position of the Confession of Faith, was declared by the Protestant Religion and Presbyterian Church Act 1706 c.6, to be 'held and observed in all time coming as a fundamental and essential condition of any Treaty or Union' between the two kingdoms. That Act was inserted in both the Scottish Union with England Act 1706 c.7, and the Union with Scotland Act 1706, of the English Parliament. If then there is any force in the argument that parts of the Union arrangements are enforceable limitations upon the power of Parliament, the question of the Westminster Confession could raise it.[206]

The possibility that an Act of Parliament might be held to be *ultra vires* inheres in the opinions of the First Division in *MacCormick* v. *Lord Advocate*, 1953 S.C. 396. In that case the Pursuers were held to have no *locus standi* in a matter of public right, but this defect could be avoided in a case on the 1921 Act and the Confession. It might be possible for the matter to be made justiciable by the 'secession' from the Church of a congregation holding its own property through local trustees and not through the Church of Scotland General Trustees, or for a congregation to raise an action against the General Trustees for transfer of their buildings and property or for the General Trustees themselves to present a special case. In all these instances the argument would be analogous to that of *Bannatyne* v. *Lord Overtoun* (1904) 7 F. (H.L.) 1 : [1904] A.C. 515, that the Church in altering the status of the Westminster Confession has broken the terms on which the property of the Church is held. Such argument would involve questions of private right, thus avoiding the flaw in *MacCormick*. Once the matter was so brought before the civil courts, a full discussion of the powers of the United Kingdom Parliament under Scots Law could take place.

On that basis the argument would start from the observation of Lord Cooper in *MacCormick*, 1953 S.C. 396 at 411, that,

'The principle of the unlimited sovereignty of Parliament is a distinctively English principle which has no counterpart in Scottish constitutional law'.

There are various dicta in Scottish cases which may be adduced to show that the terms of the Treaty of Union were intended to be fundamental, particularly in relation to the Church of Scotland. Thus in *Minister of Prestonkirk* v. *Earl of Wemyss*, 1808,[207] Lord Justice-Clerk Hope noted the hostility with which the Presbyterians viewed the Church of England at the time of the Union, and said,

'Accordingly, actuated by that jealousy, our ancestors, at the Union, provided that the regulations applicable to our national church, should be absolutely irrevocable, and that the Parliament of Great Britain should have no power to alter or repeal those provisions. An attempt to do so (such were the precautions then observed) would amount to a dissolution of the Union, and the consequence might be dreadful. Resistance on the part of Scotland could hardly be termed rebellion'.

The Lord President stated,

'The people of Scotland, at the period of the Union were most careful to preserve unalterably all the rights of their presbyterian church as by law established'.[208]

Both Professors Mitchell and Smith give other examples where the Scottish courts expressed similar opinions, but these do not seem quite so clear as the above.[209]

Further strands for the argument may be drawn from the columns of

Hansard, where, during the debates on the reconstruction of the judiciary last century, the Treaty of Union was expressly referred to as requiring the omission of the Scottish Courts from the proposals.[210] This was accepted by the government of the day. Another more equivocal point lies in the 1937 Regency Act, where, under s.4 (2) the Regent may not assent to the repeal of the 1706 Act of Security. This might be argued to indicate that the true Monarch may so assent. Finally account must be taken of the express concession by the Lord Advocate, and the assertion by the Court, in *MacCormick*, that Parliament cannot lawfully alter or repeal the fundamental conditions of the Union.[211] On this point Scottish and English law might usefully be held to diverge and the doctrine of parliamentary sovereignty, which we are told 'is almost entirely the work of Oxford men',[212] could be returned whence it came.

If such argument is accepted, the judicial oath of office would require the judges of the realm to give effect to the terms of the fundamental law limiting the power of parliament rather than any mere Act of Parliament.[213] But difficulty would arise as to the remedy to be sought, for Lord Cooper did express doubt upon the authority of the Court of Session to entertain such an action.[214] In the course of his judgement in *Gibson* v. *Lord Advocate*, 1975 S.L.T. 134 at 137, (a challenge based on the Treaty of Union to E.E.C. fishing regulations and their application through s.2(1) of the European Communities Act 1972) when dealing with the matter of holding an Act of Parliament void, Lord Keith reserved his opinion 'on what the question would be if the United Parliament passed an Act purporting to abolish . . . the Church of Scotland . . . .' He was, however, clear that where matters of private right were in issue, and the question was whether a change in the law was 'for the evident utility' of the subjects, as is permitted to the Union Parliament under art. XVIII of the Treaty of Union, that political question was not a matter justiciable in the Scottish courts. The status of the 1921 Act, the Treaty of Union and any alteration in the position of the Confession raised as a matter of private right as indicated, might therefore bring only the decision that the matter is not justiciable, and the point of limitation of the powers of the U.K. Parliament be decided by default. Again, it is noticeable that the English Courts refused to take cognisance of such a matter when the Irish Church was disestablished.[215]

On the other hand, the activities of prior courts, notably in the Disruption cases, seeking to give a remedy where there was considered to be a wrong, could provide a basis of action. It is not unknown for a court to take to itself the right of judicial review of legislation. That is the basis of the United States Supreme Court's actings since *Marbury* v. *Madison*, (1803) 1 Cranch 137, and has been followed by the Israel Supreme Court.[216] The development of such a power by the Court of Session would be useful, and might commence with the position of the adherents of the Confession.

But against this line of approach there lie strong arguments. The fact that there has been only the single case involving construction of the 1921 Act argues that there has been acquiescence in the propositions there stated.

However desirable it might be to introduce judicial review, the conduct of the Church and its members over the years has stemmed from the conviction that the 1921 Act was constitutive, sweeping aside the earlier restrictions upon action of the Church. It may therefore be argued that the Scottish Acts in the Union settlement have fallen into desuetude in their prohibitory aspect.[217] Other parts of the Union settlement have vanished without their unalterable nature being invoked.[218]

Most cogently, in *British Railways Board* v. *Pickin*, [1974] A.C. 765, [1974] 1 All E.R. 609, in the course of overruling a decision of the Court of Appeal, the House of Lords clearly indicated its opinion that the supremacy of Parliament is unassailable, according with the general English doctrine. Their Lordships refused a remedy in a case where an allegation was made that Parliament had been misled during the passing of a Private Act, and declined any reliance on a Scottish appeal, *M'Kenzie* v. *Stewart*, (1754) 1 Pat. 578, Mor. 7443 and 15459, (where this had been done), on the curious ground that there was no reported judgement of the House of Lords in that case sufficient to make the ground of decision clear. The 'traditional' doctrine of Parliamentary supremacy has therefore been re-asserted in *Pickin*, and the Lords have failed to take advantage of a useful opportunity to introduce judicial review of parliamentary legislation. Regrettably the possibility that the House would arrive at a different decision in a Scottish appeal must be considered remote.

In any event to return to the idea that the law is something which is to be fixed, and which may be fixed for all future generations, by express formulation is not something which is to be welcomed. It is perhaps better to recognise, as Dicey and Rait do, that the language of the Treaty of Union indicates that Parliament should proceed with caution in this area, and reflect rather than lead Scottish opinion.[219] But where change is desired, the stipulation of the Union cannot stand in the way. Thus Taylor Innes observes,

'So long, indeed, as Scotland appears to be unanimous, or nearly so, on the ground of the privileges secured by the Union, no attack could well be made upon them in the united Parliament of Great Britain. But in the event of either a need or a desire for a change on the part of Scotland being at any time demonstrated to the Legislature, it would be impossible for the Church of Scotland to oppose it on the ground of treaty made with it. In such a case the Legislature would come face to face with the great moral question which underlies all the legal and constitutional ones. Can one generation bind all those that succeed it in matters of conscience, religion, and faith? Can the solemn engagements of our ancestors tie up their descendants from their permanent allegiance to truth and to God? Can the supreme power of the State be bound, absolutely and unchangeably, by *any* engagements?'[220]

This goes to the root of the matter, both in respect of the State and in respect of the Church. If the Church is to be seen as an organism, developing and reformulating doctrine, then the right of the Church to act within the areas of the Declaratory Articles ought to be widely construed. This may be particularly argued since the procedures under Article VIII for alteration of the Articles, as is necessary for the Panel's proposals, requires that the Church be consulted through Barrier Act procedure in two successive years. It can be argued that this provision brings the 'evident utility of the subjects within Scotland' of Article XVIII of the Treaty of Union into play, and diminishes the plain words of the entrenchment of the religious settlement. Thus C. N. Johnston, the then Procurator of the Church, wrote that the provisions of the Treaty of Union deprived Parliament of all moral right to disestablish the Church without either,

> 'substantial unanimity, or else a distinct reference back to the people of Scotland, who only assented to that Treaty on the condition that Parliament should not interfere with the Church'.[221]

Such reasoning would also apply to the position of the Westminster Confession, the Barrier Act procedure constituting a 'reference back' to the people. Where the Church itself desires the change, that change ought not to be frustrated so long as the Church remains within its known identity.

Of course such sentiments settle nothing. The question still remains at what stage alterations to the Church's constitution are such that the Church has become something other than the Church with which the State dealt, and whose constitution in matters spiritual the State declared to be lawful as expressed in 1921? My own view is that, using Lord Haldane's graphic image, it is for the Church to say when the robbers have entered. It may have to be for the State to say when they are in control.[222]

Such a view is not accepted by all within the Kirk. Expression of it led to an addendum to the deliverance on the Report of the Committee of Forty being introduced in the 1974 General Assembly so that, apparently, the proposer might question the suggestion that the Kirk was or should be in any way still possibly controllable by the State. It was argued that such controls if they existed prevented the Kirk from truly preaching the gospel as it understood it—an argument which was not accepted by the Procurator. The motion was withdrawn.[223]

Whatever may be thought of the theological propositions involved and their desirability in an ideal world, it seems by contrast desirable that there should be an authority which has the ability to prevent a numerical majority in any church from changing the identity of that church, unless such possibility of change was present in the basic constitution of the church. It is not so present within the Church of Scotland. Given present theological uncertainty within the Church—an uncertainty at variance with the plain meaning of the subscription of the Confession and the promises taken on ordination—if such control does not exist, it seems likely that the assets of the Kirk could quite easily be taken and applied for purposes other than those intended by their donors.

But I suggest that one should not seek to push logic and the rigours of the law too far. The existing legal situation is satisfactory if only the Kirk would pay more attention to its own area of responsibility. The precise parameters of the independence of the Church of Scotland in spiritual matters may be legally indeterminate, but the balance between spiritual matters and civil matters provided for in the 1921 Act is workable. So long as that balance is not so badly distorted as obviously to do injustice, the right of the Church to this degree of self-government ought to persist. Indeed, it is interesting to find that the Church of England has only recently, and with some relief, been able to assume a similar control over its worship and doctrine.[224] In short we should pay heed to the warning explicit in these words of Lord Justice-Clerk Aitchison:

> 'The answer is, I think, as simple as this, that the right claimed by the Church of Scotland to legislate and adjudicate finally in all matters of government is now the law of the Church, declared by the Church itself, and recognised by Parliament. The General Assembly is not something alien to the Church; it is the Supreme Court of the Church, and the guardian of the Church's rights and liberties. . . . I have endeavoured to resist the temptation, in construing the Act, of being influenced by any preconception of what the law should be. But I may be allowed to make this observation. If the pursuers' construction of the Act were to prevail, the result, in my opinion, would be simply to open a new chapter of confusion in the history of the Church. It would involve once more interference by the civil magistrate in matters that properly belong to the Church itself. If past history affords any guidance for the future, such an interference could not be other than calamitous'.[225]

But if such an argument arose which did require these arguments to be settled, whichever way the result went the State would have to step in as it did in 1905 in the Free Church controversy, establishing a further Scottish Churches Commission to divide the property of the Church between those faithful to traditional doctrine and government of the Church, and those who seek the task of the Church in somewhat different terms.[226] Alternatively it would be more proper for any question of schism to be settled without court action as was done in 1929.[227]

Such then is the provision made by the Articles Declaratory of the Constitution of the Church of Scotland in Matters Spiritual, and the 1921 Church of Scotland Act. Assuming that the doubts expressed in previous pages are not pressed too far, their effect is to leave the Church of Scotland with a much greater degree of freedom of action, and freedom from State control, than it had under previous law. The contrast between the words of Lord Aitchison and those of the majority in any of the Disruption cases demonstrates this. The definition of the Church in Article I is sufficiently wide to allow full development within the Protestant reformed tradition. Yet despite this freedom, the Church of Scotland is the National Church recognised by the State, and is the

4

representative Church in Scotland. At the same time the position of other churches is not diminished, and they are also protected by law in the exercise of their functions.

That the Church of Scotland is the National Church is made plain in a variety of ways. Thus the Sovereign on accession to the Throne takes an oath to preserve the settlement of the true Protestant Religion and the Government, Worship, Discipline, Rights and Privileges of the Church of Scotland, (though its legal worth may be dubious),[228] and in Scotland the monarch is a member of the Church without special ecclesiastical standing. The Moderator of the General Assembly of the Church of Scotland takes precedence after the Lord Chancellor.[229]

Clear signs of the accommodation between Church and State are to be seen at the meetings of the General Assembly. Each Assembly is attended by a Lord High Commissioner appointed by the sovereign,[230] but he is not a member of the Assembly of his own right, and sits in a gallery which is not entered from the Assembly Hall, and which technically is not part of the Hall. Though the Lord High Commissioner is given opportunity to address the Commissioners, neither he nor the Crown has right to initiate business or to control the proceedings of the Assembly in any way. Even the former conflict as to the right of the Crown or the Assembly to fix the date and place of the next meeting of the Assembly has been elided since 1927, and the Lord High Commissioner undertakes to inform the monarch of the Assembly's own decision.[231] In such small formal and ceremonial ways the *modus vivendi* of the National Church and the civil authority is indicated.[232]

CHAPTER VI

The Church outside Establishment

As A. Taylor Innes observed, it is obvious and intelligible that the law has to do with Established Churches, but at first sight it is not clear that it has anything to do with churches which are not established. Indeed separation between the two might be welcomed by both ecclesiastics and lawyers. But this is not possible, and in fact the law relating to the non-established denominations is a topic of importance and difficulty.[233]

Three major problems arise in the law of Scotland relating to the non-established churches. First, the very legal existence of such bodies took time to be established. Secondly, the nature of the jurisdiction of these bodies over their members, and the circumstances under which the civil courts will consider themselves able to intervene, or to grant a remedy in respect of their actions, are a little uncertain. Thirdly, acute questions of property and of trust law have arisen out of church unions, and schisms, and from the very nature of churches as independently developing organisms.

I *The legal existence of the non-established church*

The legal position and standing of churches outside the established Church in Scotland has been arrived at over the course of four centuries of development, and is based upon the practice of these years rather than upon statutory enactment. The common law has come to recognise these bodies, and the old Scots Acts relating to the Church by law established are in desuetude in so far as they affirm that there is only one legally recognised Church in Scotland, as s.2 of the Church of Scotland Act 1921 shows.

As explained earlier, following the Reformation of the Church in 1560 various Acts ratified the Scots Confession as the faith of the reformed Church, annulled all prior acts inconsistent with that Confession,[234] and abolished the jurisdiction of the Roman Catholic hierarchy in Scotland,[235] idolatry,[236] and the Mass.[237] In the course of the general revision of the law the position of the Church of Scotland as the sole Church in the realm was clearly laid down in statute. In particular the Church Jurisdiction Act 1567 c.12,[238] stated:

> '. . . . thair is na uther face of Kirk nor uther face of Religion than is presentilie be the fauour of God establischeit within this Realme And that thair be na uther iurisdictioun ecclesiasticall acknawlegeit within this Realme uther than that quhilk [which] is and salbe within the same Kirk or that quhilk flowis thairfra concerning the premissis [which derives therefrom in conformity with its basis] . . . .'

The State went further in the Church Act 1579 c.6, affirming the people who professed the Scots Confession of 1560 'to be the only trew and haly Kirk of

Jesus christ within this realme'; those who disagreed, or refused the sacraments as they were ministered by the established Church:

> 'To be na membris of the said Kirk within this realme and trew religioune now presentlie professit sa lang as they keip thame selffis sa deuydit [themselves so divided] from the societie of christis body'.

Under the Deposition of Ministers Act 1592 c.9 provision was made that when the Church properly deprived a minister of his office, that also operated to strip him of the temporalities which had been his by virtue of that office. The way was therefore opened for a testing of the minister, and this was done. The Church was not willing that a man deposed from its ministry, or of his own volition, should set himself up as a minister, but not of the established Church. There ensued a struggle particularly between Episcopacy and Presbyterianism. The National Covenant strengthened feelings, and under the provisions of the Solemn League and Covenant Commissioners were sent from the General Assembly of the Church of Scotland, as observers, to help draft a Presbyterian scheme of Church government which would be applied throughout the two kingdoms. As is known, that enterprise failed, though it did produce the Westminster Confession of Faith, and other notable documents still of value. But the general enterprise failed, and for a period Episcopacy was imposed as the government of the then single Church in Scotland.[239]

On the accession of William and Mary there was another period of statutory enactment, including the Prelacy Act 1689 c.4 and the Claim of Right.[240] The Confession of Faith Ratification Act 1690 c.7 again repeated the favoured position of the established Church. For example, it enacted that only the Presbyterian ministers who had been ejected during the period of episcopacy, and those whom they approved, should:

> 'have and shall have rights to the maintenance, rights and other privileges by Law provyded to the ministers of Christs Church, within this kingdom, as they are or shall be legally admitted to particular Churches'.

The Ministers Act 1693 c.38, 'An Act for Settling the Quiet and Peace of the Church', further specified that ministers had to subscribe the Confession of Faith, and the Act 1695 c.35 provided against persons intruding into churches without a legal call.

In all these enactments it is clear that only the Church of Scotland as established in 1567, 1590 and 1692 was considered to be a church within the law. The only bodies which might have contended with this view were the Roman Catholics, who for historical reasons were in no position to make any protest, the Episcopal Church, which was under a similar cloud, and a body known as the Reformed Presbyterian Church, the Cameronians, who refused to enter the Church of Scotland as reconstituted, due to what they considered defects in its structure.[241] None of these churches held a view that other churches should and ought to be tolerated. The established Church was unwilling, for reasons of history as well as its own belief in its pre-eminence, that other churches should be given any official status. Accordingly, as the civil courts were faced with a large body of statute law stating the proposition that only the established Church had legal existence, development in the law took time.

The first real move towards the present position of tolerance was the passing of the Scottish Episcopalians Act 1711, often known as 'the Toleration Act', which forced the Scottish courts to recognise a church other than the established Church for the purpose of giving that church certain protection. But the Act (which was further extended by the Scottish Episcopalians Relief Act 1790) did not confer on the Episcopalian Church other standing in the law. As it was put by Lord President Boyle in *Dunbar* v. *Skinner* (1849) 11 D. 945 at 958:

'. . . . there exists in Scotland no Episcopal Church whatever except as a distinct sect, fully recognised and protected under the Toleration Act'.

The 1711 Act gave toleration and protection but did not give the Episcopal Church any standing such as that of the established Church, with independent jurisdiction exclusive of that of the Court of Session. The major principle in relation to non-established denominations in this country is therefore that such denominations are voluntary associations or societies, which the law may regard, but which do not by law necessarily have independence of the law.

The second step towards the recognition of such voluntary associations was the extension of tolerance in practice if not in law to non-established churches other than the Episcopalians. Thus when the Roman Catholic hierarchy was restored by the Bull *Ex Apostolatus Apice* of Leo XIII of 4 March 1878, the old statutes against Roman Catholicism were still on the statute book. It was the opinion of Patrick Fraser, Q.C., the Dean of Faculty, and A. T. Innes that while the action of the Pope was contrary to statute the new prelates would not incur any penalty.[242] Today, although most of the old statutes are still extant, their penal clauses have all been repealed.

As far as the law is concerned, it took the courts many years to establish that non-established congregations and churches had any legal existence even as associations. The first case raising the matter was that of *Bryson and others* v. *Wilson and others*,[243] 1752. Title to a meeting house of the Secession church had been taken in name of trustees, who granted a back bond obliging them to denude in favour of new trustees elected by the congregation. The congregation split on the question of the Burgess Oath, and the majority went with the minister against the Oath. The congregation voted to elect new trustees, and these called on their predecessors to denude in terms of their bond. However, on appeal it was held that the new trustees had no title to sue, 'their constituents being no legal congregation'.

Almost twenty years later, in the case of *Wilson* v. *Jobson* (1771) Mor.

14555, and followed in *Allan* v. *Macrae*, (1791) Mor. 14583, the case of *Bryson* was overruled. In *Wilson* the title to the meeting house of the Associate Congregation in Dundee had been taken in the individual name of David Jobson, a lawyer in Dundee, without acknowledgment of trust. The congregation at that time professed anti-burgher principles. The minister and, amongst others, Jobson had departed from these principles, and the minister was suspended by the Associate Presbytery. The remnant of the congregation thereupon brought an action against Jobson to compel him to give a valid disposition of the property. The plea was met by argument that the pursuers had no title to bring the action, being neither qualified as individuals or as representing a corporation. However, the pursuers argued that 'the Law of Toleration' made them a legal society, capable of enforcing the trust. Their title to sue was upheld, and Jobson ordered to denude as he had admitted that he held the property in trust. The Court therefore recognised the existence of the congregation as a society, but it did require the pursuers' designation as being 'subject to the Associate Synod' to be struck out as being without legal meaning. Similar attitudes were maintained as late as 1809 when in *Drummond* v. *Farquhar*, F.C. 6 July 1809, the designation of the pursuer as 'one of the bishops or senior clergymen of the superior order of the Episcopal communion in Scotland' was ordered to be struck out 'as not recognised by the Court'.

Progress in recognition was obtained mostly in relation to property cases. Thus in *The General Assembly of the General Baptist Churches and Evans* v. *Taylor* (1841) 3 D. 1030, it was held competent for an action to be raised in the name of that Assembly, and of certain persons delegated by it to carry on the action, and a plea that the action was brought improperly at the instance of an unincorporated association, and therefore without the individuals having title to sue, was repelled.

In 1850 a major development was the passing of the Titles of Religious Congregations Act allowing titles to property held for religious purposes to be taken in the names of the office-bearers and their successors in office, as trustees for the congregation or society, without the need for there to be a regular assumption of new trustees.[244] Despite this it was felt necessary, and was not challenged, in the first of the Free Church cases, *Bannatyne* v. *Overtoun*, (1902) 4 F. 1083; (1904) 7 F. (H.L.) 1, that the Third Defenders should include all the members of the United Free Church General Assembly of 1900, designated individually, the First Pursuers being the General Assembly of the Free Church acting through a special commission. The reason for this was that the property at stake was the whole funds of the former Free Church which had been purported to be taken into the United Free Church, formed by the union of the Free and United Presbyterian churches in 1900.

But while the identity of the non-established church and its organs may now be clear in the area of property, it took longer to establish their amenability to suit in other cases, and it may not be established in all instances. Thus in the Third Cardross case, *MacMillan* v. *The General Assembly of the*

Free Church of Scotland (1864) 24 D. 1282, it was held that the Assembly of the Free Church could not be sued as such for damages conjoined with an action for reduction of a deliverance deposing MacMillan from the ministry. The Assembly was a body of changing composition, and infrequent in its meeting, and the actual Assembly whose acts were complained of, that of 1858, had ceased to exist. In the Fourth Cardross case, *MacMillan* v. *The Free Church of Scotland*, (1864) 2 M. 1444, the Lord Ordinary decided that the Free Church itself could not be sued, due to want of specification of persons, the changing membership of the Church and so on, rendering it impossible to have held either that the body or its members had committed a delict, or (more dubiously) to have mulcted it or them in damages. Although the case did not go for decision to the First Division, MacMillan consenting to the refusal of his reclaiming note, it seems likely that the Lord Ordinary would have been sustained. It therefore appeared that it was impossible to sue in reparation the governing body of a non-established church with a presbyterian conciliar structure, or the church itself, though it would be possible to bring an action against the individuals themselves. But such bodies can raise actions, normally delegating the prosecution of the action to named individuals. In some peculiar way, therefore, these bodies were, and may perhaps still be, transparent to the law, unless they choose to be actors.

On the other hand it is clear that other forms of church structure do result in amenability to court action. Thus in *Skerret* v. *Oliver*, (1896) 23 R. 468 at 475, the Lord Ordinary held it proper to raise an action for declarator and reduction of a judgement against the Synod of the United Presbyterian Church through its officers, as being a permanent body, though not in permanent session.[245] And this is pre-eminently the position in relation to episcopal structures, where the members of the General Synod, for example, are known individuals, and the Synod is continuous in membership, as was the case in *Forbes* v. *Eden*, (1865) 4 M.143.

Whether the development of the law in *Skerret* can be taken to allow an action against the more traditionally structured presbyterian churches is moot. Certainly in *Bridge* v. *South Portland Street Synagogue*, 1907 S.C. 1351, a plea that it was incompetent to sue an unincorporated body for damages through its officials was repelled by Lord Salvesen. He considered that such cases as *Skerret*, and *Murdison* v. *Scottish Football Union*, (1896) 23 R. 449, showed a departure from the former law on grounds of expediency. Provided that the officials were also called as individuals, he was willing to allow the action. In the recent case of *McGonagle* v. *Glasgow Unitarian Church* 1955 S.L.T. (Sh.Ct.) 25, the congregation was sued through its office-bearers and committee of management. It would be unjust not to allow a similar development on the grounds of expediency against other forms of structure of voluntary associations. As Lord Kincairney said in *Skerret* v. *Oliver* (1896) 23 R. 468 at 474 (a United Presbyterian Church case);

'But if it be impossible to call [such a body] it cannot be necessary to call it . . . . It acts and is, I think, represented by its duly appointed tribunals and administrative and executive bodies'.

Lastly, it might be considered that a way out of the difficulty of lack of legal existence would have been for the non-established churches to seek incorporation, as many of the churches in the United States of America have. The short answer to this is that the churches see their existence as being founded upon Christ, and, therefore, to seek powers and constitution under or from the State would have been inconsistent with this view. In any event, once the question of title to property had been solved by the use of the trust device, there was little advantage to be obtained by incorporation as it existed at that time. Today the position of the non-established denomination has been worked out in the law in such a way that incorporation is unnecessary. The final step in this development was the enacting of s.2 of the Church of Scotland Act 1921, a solution first suggested by C. N. Johnston (Lord Sands) then Procurator of the Church of Scotland in his Memorandum on how the union negotiations between the Church of Scotland and the United Free Church might proceed and the union might be carried through.[246] This section provides that nothing in that Act, or the other Acts affecting the Church of Scotland, is to prejudice the recognition of any other church in Scotland as a Christian church protected by law in the exercise of its functions. With this provision, which reflected practice, any difficulties in the ecclesiastical legislation were resolved.

II *The legal nature of the non-established churches, and their jurisdiction*

The next question to be discussed is the nature of the authority of the non-established churches, and their jurisdiction; whether they are simply voluntary associations founded upon contract, or whether they form communities having, of their own nature, a jurisdiction over their members which is exclusive of that of the civil courts. This is most clearly to be seen if an action can lie against the judicatories of such bodies in respect of their acts, and in any restrictions upon such action. In fact this point was fairly easily established in practice, the question of relevancy of averment being a more complex theoretical problem.

The case law on the point begins with the refusal of Lord Braxfield in 1793 to review the findings of the Associate Synod 'so far as they regarded an ecclesiastical offence'. In *Auchinloss* v. *Black*, 6 March 1793, Hume, *Decisions*, 595, he did:

'not consider it competent for this court to review the proceedings of the Associated congregation, commonly called Burghers, when sentences are pronounced by them in their ecclesiastical character'.[247]

This was sustained on appeal, and the court refused to review the matter unless malice was alleged. On the other hand, it was quite competent for a connected action in respect of property to proceed, although the ecclesiastical sentence was excluded from review, thus underlining the Court's refusal to look into the ecclesiastical proceeding.[248]

The doctrinal basis of this attitude is seen to be that of Contract in the interlocutor and Note of Lord Moncreiff in 1831 in *Osborne* v. *Southern Reformed Presbytery*.[249] The principles of Contract require that where a person has submitted himself to the 'jurisdiction' of an association, he may not, as it were, tear up the contract, and then have recourse to the ordinary courts, except in exceptional circumstances. In practice the position is that civil action is competent, but may be barred if facts relevant to bring the action within the category of exceptional cases which the civil courts will entertain are not averred. This may be expressed by saying that, generally, actions arising out of the acts of non-established church judicatories are incompetent, but such expression misleads one into thinking that all such actions are barred.

The first case after the Disruption to consider the basis and limitations of the authority of a non-established church was *Dunbar* v. *Skinner*, (1849) 11 D. 945, and the judgments therein contain statements of general application as to the law relating to non-established churches. The facts were that the Rev. Sir William Dunbar of Durn, the minister of St. Paul's Chapel, Aberdeen, and a minister of the Episcopal Church of Scotland, had subscribed the canons of that church, and undertaken to submit to the authority of its bishops. He disputed with his Bishop, the Rev. Dr. William Skinner, on a variety of grounds, relating largely to the Bishop's using forms of worship not in accordance with the Book of Common Worship, and eventually withdrew his subscription to the canons. Sentence of deposition followed in strong terms, and Dunbar raised an action for declarator that the sentence had:

'been pronounced illegally, irregularly and without authority, and that the same was null and void'.

He also asked for monetary damages.

Skinner, the Bishop, pleaded, first, that the acts complained of were of regular ecclesiastical character and not subject to review in the civil courts; second, privilege; and third, the fact that the pursuer had voluntarily placed himself under the authority of the Scottish Episcopalian hierarchy. The Lord Ordinary, Lord Ivory, repelled objections to the competency of the action, and the matter went on appeal. The First Division unanimously rejected the argument that the Court of Session had no jurisdiction in the case. The Episcopal Church in Scotland did not have such jurisdiction as would exclude that of the civil court, as its power was not conferred by the State. Toleration under the 1711 Act did not confer the jurisdiction, the *'potestas judicandi et exsequendi causas jure magistratus competens'*.[250] The question of the voluntary submission of the pursuer to the 'jurisdiction' of the church was a matter requiring proof, which had not been met at that stage in the proceedings.

In view of the series of decisions in the Ten Years' Conflict, it was not possible to have come to a different decision, for that would have meant conceding to the non-established churches authority and power, not based on any statutory or common law authority, which by statute was reserved to the established Church, and a wider power and authority than was available to the established Church. *Dunbar* v. *Skinner* showed that the non-established churches did not have 'jurisdiction' within the legal meaning of the term. The extent to which such churches might have 'jurisdiction' based upon prorogation, the consent of the parties voluntarily to associate themselves in an association with certain rules, was dealt with more cautiously by the Court, and it was indicated that if prorogued jurisdiction were proved then a different result might be arrived at. Lord Fullerton stated:

> 'There is no doubt that all parties entering into an association for purposes not prohibited by law, may effectually bind themselves to submit without appeal to the determination of certain matters, and even to the infliction of certain censures, by the official authorities to whom such power is committed by the terms of the association; and if it could be instantly shown, . . . that, by the admitted or proved circumstances of this case, the defender had absolutely bound himself to submit to such a sentence as that for which he now seeks redress, the defence in the second plea in law might have been sustained [sc. submission by contract], and the case sent out of Court'.[251]

Further refinement upon the views expressed in *Dunbar* is to be found in the series of decisions which comprise what is known as the Cardross cases, *MacMillan* v. *The General Assembly of the Free Church of Scotland*, (1859) 22 D. 290; (1861) 23 D. 1314; (1862) 24 D. 1282; (1864) 2 M. 1444. But at the end of the series one is left with a question as to how far the law had been advanced.

The basic facts out of which the cases sprang were that the Rev. John MacMillan, the minister of the Free Church at Cardross was accused of misconduct before Presbytery, which found only part of the case against him proved. MacMillan appealed to Synod in respect of that part of the deliverance of Presbytery unfavourable to him, while the minority of the Presbytery acquiesced in the deliverance. Synod sustained the appeal, and the Presbytery appealed this decision to the General Assembly of the Free Church. When the matter went before the Assembly, that body, having a full print of the whole proceedings, re-opened the whole question, which they were not asked to do, and, against the argument of MacMillan, found a major portion of the original libel proven, suspended him from office *sine die,* and loosed him from his charge. As such a decision had effects upon MacMillan's civil interests, he presented a Note of suspension and interdict in the Court of Session. The interdict was refused but the Note was served on the Assembly. The Assembly cited MacMillan to appear to answer for his conduct. When he appeared he was required, without giving any further explanation, simply to state whether he had authorised the application in his name to the civil court. On receiving an affirmative answer the Assembly immediately deposed him from the Free Church ministry. MacMillan raised actions of reduction of the two sentences of the Assembly, and of damages in respect of the effects of both.

The First Cardross Case, *MacMillan* v. *The General Assembly of the Free Church of Scotland*, (1859) 22 D. 290, established that the Free Church of Scotland, as indeed every church other than the Church of Scotland, was in the eyes of the law simply a voluntary association. Where a member of that association claimed that his rights had been unlawfully and irregularly interfered with, a remedy in the civil courts was not necessarily excluded by the fact that the acts complained of were done by a 'court' of that Church. Lord Deas stated the point succinctly in his opinion, (1859) 22 D. 290 at 323:

'Now, if anything be clear in the case, it is that the defenders are invested with no jurisdiction whatever, ecclesiastical or civil. All jurisdiction flows from the supreme power of the State. The sanction of the same authority which enacted the laws is necessary to the erection of courts, and the appointment of judges and magistrates to administer the laws. The Established Church of Scotland had, and has, this sanction. The statute law of the land conferred upon it ecclesiastical jurisdiction . . . But there is no such statute law applicable to the association called the Free Church. When the defenders separated from the Establishment, they left all jurisdiction behind them.'

The Court of Session was therefore not barred and would examine the sentence complained of and the contract which was the basis of the defence, though the actual content of this element was reserved for future debate.

In the Second Cardross Case, *MacMillan* v. *The General Assembly of the Free Church of Scotland and Beith and Others* (1861) 23 D. 1314, the sentence of the Assembly having been produced, the Assembly claimed that its acts were spiritual acts, and as not affecting civil matters were not subject to review. These pleas were repelled without difficulty by the Court, though their opinions were less sweeping than in the First Cardross Case.[252] Other defences, however, were considered to be of more substance, notably the plea that the 'jurisdiction' of the Free Church judicatories depended upon contract between the Church and MacMillan as a minister of that Church. As part of that contract MacMillan had subjected himself to these judicatories, without appeal to the civil courts. Since the parties could not agree on the constitution of the Free Church, and the court was not willing to hear debate on the theological concept of a church, which was what the Free Church claimed to represent, the matter was remitted for proof.

At this stage the case came to a rather unsatisfactory end, at least in its legal aspect. In the Third Cardross Case, *MacMillan* v. *The General Assembly of the Free Church of Scotland and Beith and Others* (1862) 24 D. 1282, the court, *ex proprio motu*, raised the difficulty that the major defenders, the General Assembly of the Free Church, were not a body capable of being sued in the way sought. Being a body of changing composition, the General Assembly was not a proper defender, and any action for damages could not be insisted in. It followed that the action for reduction of the Assembly sentence could not be insisted in. Other questions as to malice were raised but were not essential to the case at this stage, and the action was dismissed.

In a final attempt to press his case MacMillan raised an action against the Free Church of Scotland itself for its interest, and various individuals, its Moderator and principal Clerks, as representing the association, and some of the members of the General Assembly of 1858 who had been most active in his deposition. The Lord Ordinary sustained the defence of the Free Church, and those called as representing it, observing that it would be impossible to determine that body. No decree could be given against the body, and the individuals could not be ascertained properly, nor could they be attacked through representatives.[253] For other purposes he was disposed to let the case proceed, and both sides reclaimed. However, by this time MacMillan was apparently weary of the conflict, and consented to his reclaiming note being refused, and the defenders assoilzied.[254]

Although the Cardross case was unsatisfactory because it collapsed when quite far advanced, yet it did clearly show the attitude of the civil courts towards voluntary associations. The Free Church, which had left establishment in order to find freedom, was discovered to be still amenable to the jurisdiction of the civil court. Indeed, it appeared that there was less independence outside establishment than inside, for at the time the cases of *Sturrock* v. *Greig* (1849) 11 D. 1220, and *Lockhart* v. *Presbytery of Deer*, (1851) 13 D. 1296, had reaffirmed the independence of the established Church courts within their own jurisdiction. It is a pity that the Cardross case did not proceed further so that there might have been determination of the basic contract between MacMillan and the Free Church, and decision as to whether it had been breached, or whether there was a term of contract excluding the civil courts which would have allowed the civil court to dismiss the case, as indicated by Lord Fullerton in *Dunbar* v. *Skinner*.[255] However, the position of the non-established church as open to the scrutiny of the court had been made clear, and this principle has been followed in such later cases as *Forbes* v. *Eden*, (1867) 4 M. 143, *Skerret* v. *Oliver*, (1896) 23 R. 468, and *McDonald* v. *Burns*, (1940) S.C. 376.

Having established that the Court of Session can take jurisdiction in ecclesiastical cases, and will consider the 'internal' workings of denominations, the next point is to consider the occasions on which the Court will intervene; what is required for a relevant case. The most recent opinion on this matter is that of L.J.C. Aitchison in *McDonald* v. *Burns*, (1940) S.C. 376. The action was brought by the Trustees of a convent, asking for a decree of removal against five Roman Catholic nuns, who had been expelled from their Order but refused to vacate the premises. The nuns' argument was that their expulsion was invalid, the investigation into their conduct having been a mere pretence. Allegations of prejudice and irregularity were also put forward. The Second Division remitted the matter for proof of averments, with limitations, and the case is important involving as it did statements of the right of the court to review the functioning of internal proceedings of the Roman Catholic Church.

In the course of his Opinion, the Lord Justice-Clerk said:

'. . . . the intervention of the Court in disputes arising out of the decisions of religious associations, and affecting the relations between them and their members, has always been regarded as subject to certain very clearly defined limitations. The judicatories of religious bodies in Scotland are not in the position of ordinary civil judicatories whose decisions are reviewable by appeal or suspension. They have their own exclusive jurisdictions, and their decisions, within their own sphere and in matters pertaining to their own life and discipline, are final and binding on their own members, and are not open to review unless in exceptional circumstances.

'It is true that the judicatories of dissenting bodies are not Courts in the technical sense in which the judicatories of the National Church, which had their foundation in statute, have always been regarded as Courts of the realm, but, whatever contrary views may at one time have been entertained and expressed, it can scarcely now be doubted that they have privative jurisdiction within the limits of their own constitution, in questions affecting their own members, who, by becoming members, have voluntarily undertaken to submit themselves to and abide by the constitution of the church to which they belong, although not entering into any express contract or convenant to do so'.[256]

Lord Aitchison goes on to summarise the other cases on this question, pointing out that these cases do establish limits to the occasions on which the court will intervene.

'In the case of Oliver v. Skerret, (1896) 23 R. 468, the right of the Courts to concern themselves with the resolutions of dissenting religious associations, where patrimonial interests are injuriously affected, was generally accepted, but subject, as I read the opinions, to recognition that there must be clear illegality, and not mere irregularity, in what is complained of.'

Further,

'The internal discipline of any such body [sc. a dissenting church] is a matter of domestic concern, notwithstanding that status, or civil rights, may be involved, and it is only in extraordinary circumstances that the Courts will regard it as within their competence to intervene'.[257]

These statements led Lord Aitchison on to a classic summary of the circumstances in which the civil courts of Scotland will now entertain actions arising out of the judgements of ecclesiastical bodies.

'Speaking generally, [these circumstances are] in either of two situations— (first) where the religious association through its agencies has acted clearly and demonstrably beyond its own constitution, and in a manner calculated to affect the civil rights and patrimonial interests of any of its members, and (secondly) where, although acting within its constitution, the procedure of its judicial or quasi-judicial tribunals has been marked by gross irregularity, such fundamental irregularity as would, in the case of an ordinary civil tribunal, be sufficient to vitiate the proceedings. But a mere irregularity in proceedings is not enough. It must be so fundamental an irregularity that it goes beyond a mere matter of procedure, and becomes something so prejudicial to a fair and impartial investigation as to amount to a denial of natural justice, as, for example, if a conviction of an ecclesiastical offence were to take place without an accusation being made, or without allowing the person accused to be heard in his defence. In short, the irregularity must not be simply a point of form, or a departure from prescribed regulation, but must go to the honesty and integrity of the proceedings complained of.

'Thus, if there has been "such a gross and wilful violation of the rules of the body, in order to effect a purpose which could not be attained without it, as shall amount to an entire breaking up of the contract, on the faith of which any jurisdiction was committed to these Courts" there may be a point "not undeserving of the consideration of the Court", *per* Lord Moncreiff (at p. 671) in *Smith* v. *Galbraith*, (1843) 5 D. 665. It is perhaps unnecessary that the violation should be wilful, but, at least, it must be fundamental. There must be some vital disconformity to the law and constitution of the religious association whose decision is being impugned, or some flagrant departure from elementary justice in the conduct of its proceedings, or some usurpation of jurisdiction, or, to put it generally, something against the essential faith of the contract by which the members of the body by entering into association have expressly or impliedly agreed that they shall be bound.'[258]

The statements in *McDonald* can be taken as a fair summation of the principles laid down in a long series of cases, beginning with the opinion of Lord Braxfield in *Auchinloss*.[259] The general principle is certainly that the civil courts will not intervene in the ordinary instance, but the dicta of the cases indicate that the Court reserves the right to intervene to do justice where this is very clearly necessary. But for this the Court will require that an effective remedy be possible, as the Court will not give an abstract decision. If it is not possible to sue for damages, then the whole claim will fail.[260] The Court will not force the voluntary association to receive back someone whom it has expelled. As Lord Deas stated in *MacMillan* v. *The General Assembly of the Free Church of Scotland* (1861) 23 D. 1314 at 1345–6:

'Nobody contemplates that the defenders are to be ordained to receive the pursuer back into their association; to allow him to sit and vote in their Presbyteries, Synods and General Assemblies; or that the Free Church Congregation at Cardross are to be compelled either to listen to his sermons or to absent themselves from the church, and leave him to preach in it to empty benches. The principle on which we should decline to take that course is a very ordinary principle. If a master unwarrantably dismisses his servant, we give pecuniary redress; but we do not compel the master to take the servant back into his service. If I engage a teacher in any department of science, literature, or art, the law will compel me to pay him, but the law will not compel me to be taught by him. It is not because the office of a clergyman is a holy office—it is not because those who ordained or deposed him did so by divine authority— . . . . that we decline to interfere further than I have indicated. It is simply because this Court deals only with civil or patrimonial interests and consequences, and, while vindicating or giving redress for these, refuses to go beyond them'.

It is therefore quite clear that patrimonial interest must be present for a pursuer to succeed in an action against a church judicatory. Thus in *Forbes* v. *Eden*, (1865) 4 M. 143; (1867) 5 M. (H.L.) 36, apart from the lack of irregularity of procedure, one reason for the failure of the Rev. Forbes' attempt to reduce certain canons enacted by the General Synod of the Scottish Episcopalian Church was that he could show no patrimonial interest.[261] Again *Skerret* v. *Oliver*, (1896) 23 R. 468, cited by Lord Aitchison in *McDonald*, is to like effect. There a minister of the United Presbyterian Church sought reduction of a decree of a Commission of the United Presbyterian Synod suspending him from the ministry. He did not plead, but expressly reserved, questions of damages. The First Division, and the Lord Ordinary, were unanimous in throwing the case out, on the ground that no patrimonial interest had been made out and no specific remedy other than reduction was asked for.

In order therefore for an action, or in the case of *McDonald*, a defence, to succeed by challenging the acts of a non-established church, patrimonial interest and gross irregularity of procedure are required to be averred for relevancy of plea, and proved in order to succeed. In this way alone will the Court consider that there has been a breach of the contract under which the person became a member of the association. But the terms of the contract will also have to be established, and if these are not properly condescended on the action will also fail.[262]

But although there are statements of the right of the civil court to intervene where there is gross irregularity, there are no cases in which this has been fully done—that is, which have led to final decision by the court. It is indicated in *McDonald* that in such cases the civil court will not itself review the sentence of the ecclesiastical judicatory, but, having determined that there has been what amounts to a breach of natural justice in the proceedings, the church court is expected to re-hear the matter.[263] This observation did depend upon the pleadings of that case, where the irregularity was raised as a defence against a civil action of ejection, but where the matter arises pleaded by a pursuer the civil court may well have to consider how to proceed. One remembers the confident statements of Lord Brougham in the First Auchterarder case that he considered it inconceivable that a church court would defy the civil law, and the result.[264]. It might be that damages would be the only effective remedy, and that could be a difficult remedy to arrive at. The Cardross cases show that some church structures make it difficult, if not impossible, to call proper parties who may be liable in damages to a pursuer. If a church judicatory refused to re-hear a case, or were directed so to refuse, by a superior court of inconstant membership and existence, against whom would an action lie? One would hope that such questions will never have to be determined, and can only suggest that the appropriate procedure would be to sue the several individuals constituting the body which has wrongfully acted, leaving them to seek such remedy as they may have from the funds of the association.[265]

In any event, apart from the defensive position inherent in the *McDonald* situation, it is not clearly decided, though it is adumbrated, that the courts would automatically entertain any action which properly sought damages. It might be held in a given case that the submission by membership to the courts of a church is final, barring any appeal to the civil authorities. Lord Justice Clerk Hope after narrating the statutory and doctrinal basis of the Church of Scotland in *Sturrock* v. *Greig*, (1849) 11 D. 1220, stated at 1231:

'From this, I think it necessarily follows that in matters clearly within the cognisance of the Church officers or courts . . . .its judicatories and officers are not amenable to the civil courts of the country in damages for alleged wrong. . . . .

'The inquiry into their motives . . . . is absolutely repugnant to the freedom which must belong to the Church in matters of discipline.

. . . .

'The view that may be taken of this matter by independent religious bodies, unless their constitution is very express, may go much further; and it may be that their Church courts may have, as against their own ministers, the sole right to decide what is a competent matter for Church government and ecclesiastical discipline'.

Lord Justice-Clerk Hope went on to indicate that in the case of the established Church there might be limits to the protection afforded to the Church courts if they acted *ultra vires*, and a similar limit would apply in the case of dissenting churches, but the general point might be drawn, that in submitting to the jurisdiction of the courts of the dissenting church, a person gave up his right to recourse to the civil courts.[266] The opinion of Lord Fullerton in *Dunbar* v.

Skinner[267] indicated that a plea of prorogued jurisdiction might be determinative of a case, though there is a question whether he had in view the situation where the church court had acted in an irregular and oppressive manner or out of malice, and that point is clearly left open in Lord Aitchison's opinion in *McDonald* v. *Burns*.[268]

But even if it is held that the church court is not final in an absolute sense, it may be that when it acts the occasion is qualifiedly privileged as being a *quasi*-judicial occasion, and that malice must be both averred and proved for a successful case to be brought in the civil court. It was so averred in *Edwards* v. *Begbie*, (1850) 12 D. 1134, and the Court approved of the issues. But in the various stages of the Cardross case malice was averred only against the individual members of the Free Church Assembly who had been active in MacMillan's deposition. However the action terminated before it was fully discussed if malice ought to have been generally averred. It is clear that malice must be averred for proceedings to be competent against a judicatory of the established Church, but in one of the cases which clearly shows that point, *Lang* v. *Presbytery of Irvine*, (1864) 2 M. 823, Lord Deas went out of his way to comment on *MacMillan* and the position of the dissenting church. After noting the requirement that malice be alleged in an action against a court of the established Church, he went on at 836–7:

> 'The only other observation I have to make is this, that as we are dealing with the procedure of a constituted court of this country, the principle is different from the principle applicable to a voluntary association—different as respects their right to regulate their own procedure and power of process, and as respects the principles of their constitution. In the case of a voluntary association, the question resolves itself into a breach of a civil contract, and I know no law for holding that malice is necessary to render parties liable for a breach of a civil contract. That was the sort of question that occurred in the case of MacMillan against the Free Church'.

This opinion was immediately challenged by Lord Ardmillan at the end of his judgement, at p. 838:

> 'In consequence of what has fallen from Lord Deas, I feel it to be my duty to state my deliberate opinion that, in this matter of privilege in judicial proceedings, there is no difference between . . . . the church court of the Established Church, and the church courts of non-conforming bodies, provided there is jurisdiction which by law or by contract the parties are bound to recognise, and a judgement pronounced by Judges whom by law or by contract the parties are bound to obey. In both cases I think that the judgement is privileged and that malice must be alleged. . . . . Whether the grossness of the irregularity of a judicial proceeding might or might not be held as sufficient to infer the malice which the law requires, is a question which is not now before us; . . . . But I think it right to add, that, as at

present advised, I am not satisfied that any mere irregularity would be sufficient; and I am disposed to think that it would be necessary to instruct special malice, apart from the irregularity of the procedure. . . .'

Lord Deas responded:

'I must explain that I did not give any opinion as to what would be the law in the case of a civil contract with a voluntary association acting within the contract. The case to which I referred was one in which it was distinctly alleged, and offered to be proved, that the parties had acted not according to, but in violation of the contract. It was of that case alone that I spoke'.

Lord Ardmillan noted that he himself referred to no particular case, but had expressed his view that the broadly stated dictum of Lord Deas was not one in which he concurred.

The problem inherent in these two attitudes is that of the nature of the ecclesiastical court. Lord Deas had at various times stated that the courts of the non-established churches did not have 'jurisdiction', and his view follows from this.[269] Only courts established by the State have jurisdiction and therefore immunity. Other informal bodies could not on his view claim immunity or privilege. But the developed law has not followed this view, preferring that of Lord Ardmillan. The Opinion of Lord Curriehill in *MacMillan* v. *The Free Church of Scotland*, (1862) 24 D. 1282 at 1295, states the point succinctly:

'Parties upon whom judicial functions are lawfully conferred and who in the *bona fide* exercise of these functions over parties subject to their authority, fall into errors in judgment, are not liable in damages to those parties in consequence of such errors. *Humanum est errare* . . . . But such functionaries have immunity from liability for errors in judgment, unless their errors arise from corruption or malice. The law unquestionably confers such immunity upon judges officiating in the public judicial institutions of the country, whether civil, criminal or ecclesiastical, upon whom jurisdiction is conferred by the State. It also extends such immunity to private persons, upon whom the parties, by voluntary agreement, confer authority to adjudicate in certain matters among themselves; it being the policy of our law to encourage and support the settlement of disputes by such private arrangements. . . . . In like manner, when voluntary associations, constituted for religious purposes, confer upon some of their own members authority to adjudicate among them in certain matters, the law extends to the persons so appointed immunity from claims of damages, on the part of members of their respective associations, for errors into which these functionaries may fall in the *bona fide* exercise of the authority so entrusted to them. They enjoy such immunity, ... because these members by voluntarily conferring such judicial authority upon them are held to confer upon them likewise the privilege which the law itself attaches to the *bona fide* exercise of judicial functions. This is a principle which is of great importance in this country, as, in my opinion, it enters into the constitution of most, if not all, of the voluntary religious associations which have been formed in Scotland under the protection of the Toleration Acts'.

From these statements, and the already quoted statements of Lord Aitchison in *McDonald*,[270] it is clear that, in the ordinary instance, malice must be pleaded in order to attack the regular proceedings of a duly constituted court of a non-established church. It is also now clear from *McDonald* and from the development of the concept of natural justice in other contexts, that a plea of privilege would not now be sustained in the face of gross or fundamental irregularity. However, the exact limits of irregularity, the point at which irregularity becomes fundamental, breaking up the contract of association and allowing recourse to the civil court, is something which has not required, and I would hope will not require, decision in relation to the non-established churches of Scotland.

III Property

One main area in which the Courts have had to consider the question of the constitution of non-established churches, and indeed their tenets and beliefs, has been in relation to matters of property. The churches have in the main adhered to the view of the Church of Scotland, expressed in the Auchterarder cases, that they were not opposed to the civil courts regulating property matters, however much they might object to the intervention of the courts in what they considered to be matters of spiritual jurisdiction. The line of cases is long, and comes to a climax in the House of Lords decision in the Free Church cases of 1904, the *General Assembly of the Free Church of Scotland, Bannatyne and Others* v. *Lord Overtoun and Others* : *MacAlister and Others* v. *Young and Another* (1904) 7 F. (H.L.) 1; [1904] A.C. 515.

The matter of the disposition of and rights to property is one which has concerned, perhaps over-concerned, a variety of the non-established churches over the years (cf. Matt. 5:40; Luke 6:29; I Cor 6:1–8). As the churches in this country have not sought incorporation either under Crown charter or under the appropriate statutory provisions it has been necessary for their property to be held in trust. Accordingly the basic principle which the civil courts apply in the case of the property relations and problems of non-established churches is that of the general Law of Trust. Since the property of such bodies is not tied to them by statute as in the case of the established Church, but rather is given to them by members and adherents for the purposes of the Church, the court merely applies the terms of the trust upon which the non-established churches accept the property. The court does not create the trust, but it will enforce that trust which it finds to exist on the evidence before it. This has raised problems over the years, but problems which have been largely elided by the drafting of suitable model trust deeds, and by appropriate statement of principle by the governing bodies of the churches. The problems referred to are seen most acutely in the Free Church case of 1904, and may be simply stated. Where a church has in its basic constitution no inherent right of doctrinal deviation—the right to alter its doctrines and their statements over the years—then the civil court will hold that that church forfeits its property if it does deviate from its original principles. Any minority which continues to adhere to the former principles, doctrine and constitution, will be adjudged entitled to the property held in trust for the church. As said above, there are ways around this difficulty, and one may hope that such problems do not arise in acute forms in the future, but the law clearly lays down the results of failure to avoid the problem.

The early cases already quoted with regard to the recognition of the non-established churches as associations, were almost all raised in order to settle questions of property. In most of them the root cause was a disruption or schism in the original body composing the congregation, and the unwillingness of trustees to convey the property to one or other of the factions.[271]

The first major case reported which deals with the precise question of property, arguing the matter on the facts, is that of *Dunn* v. *Brunton*, (1801) Mor. App. Soc. 10, involving the Burgher Seceders and the 'New Light' controversy. However, the Court sidestepped the issue put before them. They were invited to consider the terms on which the minister of a church in Aberdeen held tenure, and his conduct in replacing the locks on the church when a majority of the congregation failed to follow him into the 'New Light' on the matter of the duty of the civil magistrate stated in Ch.XXIII of the Westminster Confession of Faith. But the Court being 'much divided in the opinion' simply stated that:

> 'The Court can enter into no investigation as to the religious grounds of the schism here, and if they did, they must presume the majority in the right.'[272]

Apparently in the other cases of the time the Court of Session considered that questions arising from change of objects by the majority of the church involved, were not matters for the Court to concern itself.[273] But the Court was not really satisfied with such a position and selected the Craigdallie case 'to try the general point again more deliberately'.[274]

The Craigdallie case, *Craigdallie* v. *Aikman*,[275] 'was taken up and determined with the very view of fixing and settling a general question'.[276] The process took twenty years. It is unnecessary here to enter into a full discussion of its several parts,[277] but the general principle enunciated in the House of Lords by Lord Chancellor Eldon was simple in concept, if difficult of application. Property is held in trust for the principles of the Church.[278] The concept of the prior cases, that the will of the majority should prevail, was swept aside, without apparent difficulty, in the House of Lords, though not in the Court of Session.

The case clearly established for the first time that questions of property were to be decided according to the ordinary rules of the law of trusts, and meant that a minority could, if they so wished, block a union, and refuse to transmit a property, as against the wishes of the majority. As it was explained in the Campbeltown case by Lord Meadowbank, what was important was not numerical superiority, or a greater sum contributed by parties, but:

'their adherence to the original principles which it was their professed object to maintain in the constitution of the trust'.[279]

Lord Meadowbank indicated that he considered that there might be limits to the extent of this statement, considering that it was possible that a church might have the power to reform its doctrines through its governing body, and this has provided a way out of the difficulties inherent in the too strict application of the 'original principle' concept.

The principles of *Craigdallie* were applied in other later cases. *Galbraith* v. *Smith*, the Campbeltown case, (1837) 15 S. 808; (1843) 5 D. 665, adds little to the law, in that the Court relied on the 'original principles' test, but in fact decided that it had not been proved that the Relief Church had departed from its original principles. The case is of main interest in the observations of Lord Meadowbank in the earlier report, referred to above, since he had been counsel for the Synod in the Craigdallie case. His opinion on the Campbeltown case was, however, roughly treated by Lord Justice-Clerk Hope in *Craigie* v. *Marshall*, the Kirkintilloch case, (1850) 12 D. 523, on the grounds that it confused adherence to a governing body of a church with adherence to original principles.[280] Lord Meadowbank must, therefore, be treated with extreme caution, as later cases have followed the Justice-Clerk.

In *Craigie* v. *Marshall*, which, it must be noted, is subsequent to the Disruption cases, there was a point of difference with the earlier cases, for the title which was under construction was clearly one which placed main emphasis upon the congregation. It was held by:

'trustees and fiduciaries for behoof of the members of the Associated congregation in Kirkintilloch, commonly called Seceders, and presently in connection with the United Secession Church'.[281]

But the weight of opinion in the case took the matter beyond that question, and indicated that in any case, the question at issue was the adherence of the congregation to the original principles, and not questions of its adherence to a formal church structure, or the judicatures of a given church.[282] This goes rather far, as it would be difficult to conceive of a situation of a church, on the Presbyterian model at any rate, in which the form of government and the obedience of the congregation to higher authority could be argued to be an essential doctrinal base.

The case has more important elements yet, for part of the question at issue was the propriety of church union, and the Lord Justice-Clerk gave it as his opinion that:

'. . . . any congregation in the circumstances of this one, is entitled to refuse to submit themselves to any such changed government, or to concur in any such union. This is, in my opinion, the leading and most fundamental principle of all such congregations . . . .

'The desire to keep separate—to keep one sect apart from all others—as in itself a good way strictly to maintain certain peculiar opinions, especially if of a severe and stern character— . . . may be unreasonable—it may be to many unintelligible—it may appear idle caprice: But it is the first privilege of every congregation of such a body.'[283]

Lord Moncreiff's opinion also was to the effect that the property remained with those who adhered to the original principles. They might refuse to concur in any union of churches, and might stay out, without penalty of losing their buildings and assets. The proposed union in the case would clearly have involved a departure from original principles, but even so the congregation was not bound even to make enquiry into the differences between the sects. The fact that the two were separate was proof enough of their difference, and justified their refusal to go with the ruling judicatories of their own sect into union.[284]

A further step in this trend of decision was taken in the Thurso case, *Couper* v. *Burn*, (1850) 22 D. 120, where again questions of church union were at stake. But again principle was expanded, so that the minority of a church were not bound to union even with a separate body whose principles were the same as their own, and this by the unanimous decision of the Inner House. In such instances it is, however, necessary that the dissentients should act timeously, otherwise they will be presumed to have acquiesced in the change.[285]

It is of course possible to consider all these cases from a different viewpoint. The question at issue was on one plane that of trust and change of trust purposes, but there is another sense, viewing the church as a developing organism, in which the question at issue was the identity of the church. Before we turn to consider the Free Church cases, it is perhaps better to bring this out by looking at cases in which churches have been regarded as keeping or losing their individual identities in relation to 'third party' property.

The point arose most clearly in relation to the Ferguson Bequest Fund, but unfortunately was not fully decided. The Ferguson Bequest was a sum of money left to Trustees for certain purposes in 1856. Two of the purposes gave rise to conflict before the Courts. In *Wallace* v. *The Ferguson Bequest Fund*, (1879) 6 R. 486, a question arose over the share of the Fund appropriate to the Reformed Presbyterian Church. In 1863 that church had split on questions of taking part in civil functions, and the Trustees of the Fund had recognised the majority as the Church for the purpose of the Trust. In 1865 and 1876 the minority who had been refused access to the trust funds sought participation in their benefits, but this was refused. However, in 1876 the majority had united *quoad sacra*, though not *quoad civilia*, with the Free Church, and the minority brought a declarator to have it declared that they were entitled to participate in the Fund to the exclusion of the majority. At the same time the Trustees applied for directions.

The Court eventually decided, on a construction of the trust deed, that the principles of the Reformed Presbyterian Church should not be narrowly construed, and that both forms of that church, the majority and minority ought to participate in the Fund, proportionately to their respective numbers. Although there had been schism, there had not been such a departure from identity as took either part of the former church out of the purposes of the trust.

Later, in *The Ferguson Bequest Fund* v. *The Congregational Union*, (1899) 1 F. 1224, there was investigation into the tenets of would-be participants in the Fund, and it was decided that irrespective of name, and of entry into the federal union of the Congregational Union of Scotland, only those congregations which held principles in accordance with the principles of the Congregational Church designated in the trust deed, ought to participate in the Fund. Again the question was one of identity, and in this case there had been added to the 'Congregational Union' congregations which held different beliefs from those designated by the testator. These did not come within the scope of his provision.

The decision in the Free Church cases, the *General Assembly of the Free Church, Bannatyne and Others* v. *Lord Overtoun and Others : MacAlister and Others* v. *Young and Another* (1904) 7 F. (H.L.) 1, [1904] A.C. 515,[286] was a major decision in the area of Church and State relationships, and in the law relating to the property of religious associations. It did not itself amend or alter the law, and may be taken more as an application of the principles of the opinion of Lord Eldon in the *Craigdallie* case. Its main historical importance lies in the effect which it had upon the development of the United Free Church, and upon the eventual union negotiations between that church and the Church of Scotland, the Basis and Plan of Union of 1929, and the Articles Declaratory of the Constitution of the Church of Scotland in Matters Spiritual, scheduled to the Church of Scotland Act 1921. But also, as demonstrating the application of the 'original principles' test in relation to property held in trust for church purposes, the case has an important legal function.

The facts of the cases derive from history, and require a short treatment. The ground of the dispute was the Union in 1900 of the United Presbyterian Church with the major part of the Free Church, forming the United Free Church of Scotland. The Free Church was the body which was created at the Disruption of the Church of Scotland in 1843. The United Presbyterian Church had come into existence in 1847, being the union of the Relief Church and the New Light elements of the Burgher and Anti-Burgher Seceders, or more properly the Associated Synod and the General Associated Synod, which had united in 1820 to form the United Secession Church.[287] As such, the United

Presbyterian Church contained within it almost all the former churches which were opposed to the principle of connection with the State. This position, known as Voluntaryism, not only implied that the Church was to be supported by itself without State connection, but also involved active hostility to the principle of an establishment of religion for any church.

The controversy between establishment and a voluntary system was one of long standing. It was involved to some extent in the positions taken up by not a few of those active in the general discussions at the time of the Ten Years' Conflict, but the Free Church had at the Disruption set its face against Voluntaryism as a principle, though it had separated itself from the establishment of the time. Over the years, however, under Principal Rainy, the Free Church had come to recognise that the schism of the Church was something to be avoided, and annulled wherever possible. The Presbyterian duty to unite with all who preach the Gospel purely was reasserted, and discussion began with the United Presbyterian Church as to the possibilities of union.[288] These discussions came to a halt in 1871 after it became clear that a large element in the Free Church, led by the Rev. Dr. James Begg, were opposed to union, but they re-started in 1896, leading to the union of 1900. A minority of the Free Church Assembly dissented from the union, and ministers adhering to this body were deposed, actions being raised by the majority to evict them from their churches. The minority constituted themselves as the Assembly of the Free Church, to continue the work of that church, and raised actions against the Trustees of the Free Church, claiming the property of the Church, or a proportion of it.

The two actions involved in these proceedings were as follows. The case of *Bannatyne* v. *Overtoun*, (1902) 4 F. 1083 was an action raised by the continuing Free Church Assembly, and officials delegated to prosecute the action, against the General Trustees of the Free Church as individuals, and as holding office within the United Free Church, for payment or transfer of the whole assets of the property held in trust for the Free Church. *Young* v. *MacAlister*, as it began, was an action raised by the Trustees for the United Free Church and its officials against the trustees of the Free Church in whose name title to the Free Buccleuch and Greyfriars Church stood, in terms of the Model Trust Deed of the Free Church.[289] These two cases between them, therefore, dealt with virtually the whole assets of the Free Church; the property held by its General Trustees, and the property held by local trustees in terms of the Model Trust Deed of that Church. Beyond that area there were some churches whose title was taken in special terms, but these were not the subject of action at this time.

The two actions were conjoined, as they proceeded substantially upon the same ground. The Free Church argued that the United Free Church had no title to the property as the property of the Free Church had been held by the Trustees in trust requiring in terms of the Summons, 'In the First Place', that:

'no part of the said lands, properties or funds so vested might lawfully be
diverted to the use of any other association or body of Christians, or at least
of any other association or body of Christians not professing, adhering to,
and maintaining the whole fundamental principles embodied in the
constitution of the said Free Church of Scotland, without the consent of the
said Free Church of Scotland, or at least without the unanimous assent of
the members of a lawfully convened General Assembly of the said Free
Church; . . . .'

Since:

'. . . . the association or body of Christians calling itself the United Free
Church of Scotland is an association or body of Christians associated under a
constitution which does not embody, adopt, and provide for maintaining
intact the whole principles which are fundamental in the constitution of the
said Free Church of Scotland; . . . .'

it followed that:

'. . . . the said United Free Church of Scotland has no right, title or
interest in any part of the said lands, property or funds . . . .'

and former members of the Free Church adhering to the new church had lost
their beneficial interest in the funds and property.

Other claims were made, both in the General Trustees case and in the
Model Trust Deed case, but the whole issue boiled down to the question
whether the United Free Church did in fact hold to the whole original
principles of the Free Church of Scotland as constituted in 1843. If it did not,
then it had no right to the property which it had purported to take over from
that Church along with the bulk of its members and ministers.

The question of the original principles of the Free Church had two grounds.
In the first place, the Free Church contended that the principle of a National
Establishment of Religion was a fundamental tenet of the Free Church, based
on the Twenty-third Chapter of the Westminster Confession. Since it was a
fundamental, essential and distinctive principle, the General Assembly had
had no power to unite with a church which did not hold to that principle, or to
admit persons who did not hold such principle to share in the trust funds of the
Free Church. Nor could it deprive the dissentient minority of the right to share
in the funds. On the contrary, entry into the union with the United
Presbyterians necessarily involved the forfeiture of all right, title and interest in
and to the funds, by reason of breach of trust.

In the second place, the Free Church drew attention to the terms in which
subscription of the Westminster Confession of Faith was required by the
United Presbyterian Church. At its inception in 1847, by its Basis of Union,
Head 2, that Church declared that the Westminster Confession of Faith and
the two catechisms were the authorised faith of that church, and 'contain the

authorised exhibition of the sense in which we understand the Holy Scriptures'. No approval was given to anything in these documents which taught intolerant principles in religion.[290] In 1879 there had been a further modification, which was made compulsory in the formula of subscription.[291] In particular this Act departed from the doctrine of predestination as set out in the Westminster Confession, in favour of an Arminian view.[292] In 1892 the Free Church Declaratory Act (No. 8 of Class II) had recognised liberty of opinion on matters in the Confession which did not enter into the substance of the faith, the Church having the power to determine what points fell within such category.[293] These contradictory elements from the United Presbyterian and Free Churches were included in the constitution of the United Free Church, members being able to choose their own standpoints. This allowed doubt to be cast upon the whole relation of the new church to the Westminster Confession itself, adherence to which was stated to be a fundamental principle of the Free Church.

The United Free Church argued that the establishment principle had not been a fundamental, essential and distinctive principle of the Free Church, and that even if it had been, the General Assembly had had power, which it had exercised, to depart from that principle. The change in the Declaratory Acts had not altered the Confession, being not inconsistent with it, and declaratory of its meaning as understood by the United Presbyterian Church. The proper procedures for union had gone through in the two churches, and the minority of the Free Church were bound, either to accede to the union, or to forfeit their right to the property involved.

The Lord Ordinary, Lord Low, and the Second Division of the Court of Session, Lord Moncreiff being absent, decided in favour of the United Free Church.[294] Lords Trayner and Low, and the Lord Justice-Clerk, Lord Kingsburgh, considered that the question of the establishment principle was not one which was fundamental to the Free Church, and might therefore be departed from. Lord Young went further, giving his opinion as being that there was nothing in law:

'to prevent a dissenting church from abandoning a religious doctrine or principle, however essential and fundamental, or from returning to it again without qualification or modification'.[295]

There might indeed be property effects on occasion, but where the property was given *ex facie* absolutely to a Church, the Court ought not to import an implied condition that the property was to be held in trust for original principles. Lord Trayner considered that the principle of establishment had been existent at the beginning of the Free Church, but that it was not fundamental to that Church and had been departed from.[296]

The appeal to the House of Lords in both cases was heard twice, due to the death of Lord Shand. It appears that there was some evidence that at the end of the first hearing before six Lords of Appeal their Lordships were equally divided, in which case the decision of the Court of Session would have stood. But the death of Lord Shand, who was said to be in favour of the United Free Church, before he had signed his judgement, caused a re-hearing, at which the Free Church succeeded by five to two. The re-hearing and 'altered result' are common grounds of criticism of the decision among church writers. But whatever the facts as to the change, I would suggest that the 'second' decision was both right and legally correct. In the House of Lords, Lord Robertson stated specifically that the re-hearing left the House in a much better position to deal with the question, because at the re-hearing the judges had been given copies of all the historical documents relied on in argument. Incredibly, it appears that this had not happened during the first hearing, though it seems elementary that a decision on a complex matter—which the case was—is better taken if one sees the text of the documents involved.[297]

The *ratio* of the decision was clearly a holding that the establishment principle was an original principle of the Free Church, from which, by its constitution, it did not have power to depart against the wishes of a minority. This fundamental and essential principle of establishment had been breached by the purported union, and it followed in the opinion of the five judges in the majority in the House of Lords, that the United Free Church, and those former members of the Free Church who had joined it, had lost their right title and interest in and to the whole funds and properties held in trust for the Free Church. Lords James and Alverstone did not feel it necessary or desirable to go beyond the question of establishment for the decision. Lords Davey and Robertson stated it as their opinion that the case might have been disposed of not only on the matter of establishment but also on the question of the modified relationship of the office-bearers of the United Free Church to the Westminster Confession. The change from owning the Confession as the confession of the faith of the office-bearer, to acknowledging it as expressing the sense of Scripture as acknowledged by the Church, was a fundamental change, removing the Westminster Confession from its place of authority as a standard.

The Lord Chancellor, Lord Halsbury, gave the widest ranging judgement, favouring the Free Church on the question of establishment like his colleagues. He also took up the departure from the Calvinist doctrine of predestination under the Declaratory Acts of the United Presbyterian Church of 1877 and of the Free Church in 1892, holding this to be incompatible with the Free Church principles. Again he went out of his way to state that the opinion of Lord Young indicating that the Court ought not to read in an implied term of principle into a transfer of property in trust, could not stand in the instant case. There was no proof of the point made before the House, following Lord Young, that the Free Church had had an inherent right to change its doctrines or principles and yet retain its property. Lastly, he considered on the reading of the Basis of Union of 1900, that the provision in that Basis, that the former members of the Free and United Presbyterian Churches were free within the

new United Free Church to retain their original views, made the union a
'colourable union'. The Trustees of the Free Church were not at liberty to
admit to the use and benefit of the trust funds and property persons who did
not hold to the principles of the Free Church.[298]

The decision in the Free Church cases was of considerable political importance, and as has been shown in the previous chapter, affects the settlement of
1929. As far as the law is concerned, one may agree with the observation of
Ferguson, that '[t]he recent judgement applies but does not alter or amplify
the existing law'.[299] Lord Eldon's statement in the *Craigdallie* case, that a trust
will be enforced for the benefit of those adhering to the original principles of
the trust, irrespective of their number, was applied. In the Free Church case it
was applied in the case of a church rather than a congregation for the first time,
but there was really no hint in the earlier cases that a different result would
attach to church property as opposed to congregational property, and the words
of Lord Eldon could not easily be forced to bear such a meaning. The principle,
therefore, was and is clear. The terms of a trust will be enforced, though it is
obvious that in any given case it may be arguable of what the original purposes
and principles involved may consist.

Following the decision in the Free Church cases, many of the churches have
been careful to write into their constitution, either in a plan and basis of union,
where there has been union, or by way of Declaratory Act, the right of the
church to modify its doctrinal standards and fundamental principles. In so
doing the church does not necessarily affect property held at the time of the
change—and the change itself might be challenged as a breach of the principles
of the original trust—but lapse of time settles the question for prior property,
and newly acquired property is held on the new form of constitution.[300] It
follows that in such cases it would be much more difficult to set up an
argument of fundamental breach of trust than in the Free Church case. The
best example of this evasion of future difficulty is the United Free Church
itself, which in 1906 passed a Declaratory Act, the Act anent the Spiritual
Independence of the Church (1906 Act I), which stated *inter alia* that the
United Free Church:

> 'has the sole and exclusive right and power from time to time as duty may
> require, through her courts to alter, change, add to, or modify her con-
> stitution and laws, subordinate standards and formulas, and to determine
> and declare what these are, and to unite with other Christian
> Churches . . . .'[301]

It may be noted in passing that this form of language has influenced that of the
Articles Declaratory of the Constitution of the Church of Scotland in Matters
Spiritual, the effect of which is discussed elsewhere. But where no such steps
have been taken and been acquiesced in by the whole church concerned, the
courts continue to apply the clear statements of the *Craigdallie* case, as
reiterated by the House of Lords in 1904.[302]

The decision in the Free Church cases naturally gave rise to much controversy as it appeared that a small minority were to have property which had been contributed to by many persons, the descendants of whom had joined the United Free Church. Nothing daunted the Free Church asked for the judgement of the House of Lords to be applied, and this was allowed.[303] In addition other actions were raised on the model of the successful ones, for the transfer of the assets of the former Free Church.[304] But it was quite apparent that the thirty remaining congregations of the Free Church could not either support or administer the property which they had just successfully claimed, and parliamentary action was the only way out. Only the United Free Church was in any position to fulfil the real purposes of the trust.[305] In 1905 the Churches (Scotland) Act set up a Commission to allocate property between the Free and United Free Churches on a fair and equitable basis. In general where one third of the former Free Church remained in that denomination the property was to go to the Free Church, but s.1(2) gave power to vary this norm where the presence of numerous buildings or other circumstances made this sensible. Under s.2 orders of the Commission were registrable in the appropriate Sasine Register and operated as transfers of property to the United Free Church, or as confirmation of the title of trustees for the Free Church as required. The proceedings of the Commission took ten years to cover all the properties in dispute, but eventually the Free Church was left with a manageable property, adequately financed, and with college property sufficient to train the required numbers of ministers for its size.[306] As a postscript to this settlement it may be noted that at the union in 1929 between the United Free Church and the Church of Scotland, there was no question of court action, provision being made for the minority of the United Free Church which decided to stay out of the union.[307]

Finally, consideration must be given to the question of failure of the trust purposes for which the property of a church might be held. It does not appear that there would be any difference between it and the case of property held for a congregation. In both cases property held for a church or congregation would be considered to be held for a general charitable purpose, and in the ordinary case a *cy près* scheme would be possible, by application to the *nobile officium* of the Court of Session,[308] that is that court would order the trust fund to be applied to another charitable purpose, closely related to the original trust purpose. Thus in *Burnett* v. *St. Andrew's Episcopal Church*, (1888) 15 R. 723, a charitable trust in favour of an episcopal church in Brechin had failed. The United Presbyterian church in Brechin claimed the trust fund in the *cy près* proceeding, as, it averred, the majority of the members of the former episcopal church had joined the Relief Church, one of the constituent elements of the United Presbyterian Church in the 1847 union. The newer episcopalian church in Brechin also claimed the fund *cy près*, and a scheme in its favour was sanctioned by the Court, without allowing the United Presbyterian church a proof of its averments, in what seems an eminently fair decision.

On the other hand the Court is not anxious to step in and make a *cy près* scheme in church cases. For example in *Thomson* v. *Anderson*, (1887) 14 R. 1026, it refused to act on the application of the Original Secession Church, holding that the trust purposes had not failed in respect of a particular church, although no services had been held in the buildings for some years, and it did not appear likely that services would be resumed. Again in *The Pringle Trust Petitioners*, 1946 S.C. 353, the Court refused to rewrite the terms of a trust deed, which could continue to operate, although it was argued that a change in church law had reduced the benefit which the testator had intended to confer.

But a *cy près* scheme is not always possible. As far as the minor sects and denominations are concerned it might be found by the Court that the terms of the trust were so restrictive of charitable intention that the *cy près* doctrine could not be applied. In that event the fund would fall either to the original donors, or their representatives, by way of resulting trust,[309] or if they were not ascertainable the property would so fall to the Crown.[310] It is, however, unlikely that property would so fall where there is a connection with an existing denominational body. Thus, eventually, in the case of the property at stake in *Thomson* v. *Anderson, supra*, a multiple poinding was raised, and the Court repelled the claim of the Crown as *ultimus haeres*, and allowed the United Original Seceders to try to establish their claim, which failing, a *cy près* scheme might be sanctioned.[311] One would hope that competent lawyers and memories of I Cor. 6:1–8 will ensure that no similar problems trouble the courts in future.

CHAPTER VII
The Interaction of Religion and Law

So far we have been dealing with the relationships between institutions, between the Church of Scotland and the non-established churches on the one hand, and the State on the other. However, this is only part of the true purview of church and state, because law applies to all the population and not merely church members. The effect of religious ideas upon the ordinary municipal law is as important as the matter of institutional relationships. In some areas that impact is traceable to the interaction of institutions, but in others general religious principles and ideas enter in on a more inchoate basis, forming the climate of expectation and conviction which the law must reflect. Of course the process is untidy. In some instances religion has been a source of law. In others it moulds law which has other valid justification. In yet other instances the law has been distorted, as religious and secular purposes within the same body of law have diverged and become inconsistent, often because the religious element has become out-moded or unfashionable.

To cover this arm of church and state in Scotland fully would require a further book. The history both explicit and implicit in the previous chapters has coloured the law in a variety of ways, but we have been dealing only with legal development. There have been other changes in religious ideas and practices, beliefs and expectations, to say nothing of theology itself, which have affected the law, and I have neither the space nor the competence properly to discuss them. It follows that in this chapter we are forced to be selective and, to an extent, dogmatic. The selection of those areas of interaction of religion and law which are to be covered is, in marginal cases, a matter of opinion. The evaluation of those areas depends even more upon opinion, in this case my own.

There is a rough sort of order among the subjects which have been selected for treatment. We begin with matters where the element of state involvement is great and proceed through to those topics which are more of individual conduct and belief. Thus we move from questions of education and broadcasting to other questions of control before we turn to such things as marriage and divorce, crimes and oaths. Another possible arrangement would have been to group those laws which foster certain religious views and acts attributable to religious belief, then deal with those which restrict practice based on beliefs, and finally to have grouped laws which may be considered as neutral. However, as the arrangement chosen allows us to begin with a discussion of institutional arrangements not dissimilar to those we have dealt with in previous chapters, I have preferred it.

First, however, a preliminary word should be said about the present role of the churches in the creation and maintenance of the sort of laws we are to look at. I shall deal only with the present, as, where necessary, the past can be considered in connection with particular areas of the law. Further, I deal mainly with the Church of Scotland, owing to its historic importance and its habit of voicing opinions ranging so widely over legal and political matters.

The rôles of the churches

The churches play two rôles in the interaction of religion and law. The first, and conceivably the more important, lies in the general effect which their teaching has in forming and maintaining the ethos of the community. Notions of right and wrong, and of correct practice, including matters of tolerance, are rooted both in past religious teaching and in present activity. In that the Kirk has moulded the Scots by its action and by reaction to it, ideas which are fundamentally religious have been built in to our assessment and hence our acceptance of certain legal provisions.

The second rôle of the churches is more active or direct, in helping preserve and in helping bring about change in the law. Churches are by no means diffident in submitting memoranda and comments to working parties, Royal Commissions, and the like. Indeed, traditionally, the Presbyterian churches, and especially the Church of Scotland, go beyond that. Apart from the frequent publicity given to the views of individual churchmen, the Report of the Church and Nation Committee of the General Assembly of the Church of Scotland is debated annually in that Assembly. Opinions and recommendations on a variety of topics emerge not only from that Committee but from many others. Social, economic and political matters are dealt with, in addition to more precise questions of legislation. While other churches, notably the Free Church of Scotland, similarly make opinion known, the Auld Kirk maintains the largest output, and, being the established church, may claim an effectiveness for its pronouncements which is not shared by the other denominations. The facts are more difficult to prove.

Certainly, since the Union of the Parliaments in 1707, the General Assembly of the Church of Scotland is the nearest thing Scots have had to a domestic parliament. The Commissioners are drawn from all over the country, each parish being represented at least every four years. The elders are being drawn from a broad spectrum of the community, and they, and the ministerial commissioners, may therefore be said to represent a voice of Scotland which might otherwise be unheard.

But questions can be raised. Is the opinion expressed as representative as one might imagine? The reports of the Committees of the Assembly, including that of Church and Nation, are written by a few, who are not drawn uniformly from round Scotland, nor across the spectrum. Those interested get appointed, and, especially once they have become known, their names recur. There is also the treadmill of the annuality of the Assembly, which produces doubt as to the depth of research and discussion which precedes many reports. Drafts have to be well advanced early in the church year to meet the printer's deadline of mid-February for most matters. In the Assembly itself Committees have a vested interest in getting their report carried. Again few commissioners have the time or interest to study all the reports, and, though there are vocal exceptions, my feeling is that most of the elders shy clear of the social, political and legal matters for a variety of reasons. It is easier just to let a group have its way on such questions, precisely because we do not think they have too much effect. Further, it seems to me that the weight of the opinion of the Assembly has been dissipated by its being spread selectively across a variety of topics on which it is clearly lawful for Christians to disagree. I would therefore hope that if a Scottish Assembly were ever to come into being—a pity they would not use the name Parliament—the General Assembly would lay down a burden it should not have taken up in the first place. And, even if devolution does not happen fairly soon, perhaps practice will change.

One useful development would be to cease to present a voting majority of the Assembly as the mind of the Church in any matter where there is a reasonable division of opinion. Rather it should simply report that, after debate, so many of its members were of one opinion and so many were of another. That would be more honest, and avoid the implication that the minority were wrong, or in some ways less in tune with the mind of God on the matter.

But whatever may happen, it is arguable that the views of the Kirk, in Assembly or otherwise, carry no greater weight than any other minority pressure group, and perhaps much less. The Kirk is known to be weaker than its formal statistics of membership might indicate, and its internal organisation is not such as to permit it to reflect broad opinion within Scotland any more.[312] The unedifying spectacles of the debate on the World Council of Churches' Fund for Combating Racism at the October 1978 Commission of Assembly, and that on the Church and Nation statement about the Scotland Act and devolution at the February 1979 Commission, are merely examples of the perils this leads to. For these reasons I believe that the Kirk's 'views' are discounted, probably more than they deserve. The final paradox is, surely, that a reasonable opinion which is sought to be enhanced by origination from a 'Christian' body may be discounted by the very reason of that origin. *Tempora mutantur.*

1. *Education*

In the realm of education[313] the main areas of interest are the presence of denominational schools within the state system, the provision of religious instruction in secular schools, and the relationship between the Universities and the church.

Scots are proud of their educational history, with justification. The *First Book of Discipline*[314] contained provision for the country-wide establishment of parochial schools financed by the heritors of each parish, with a bursary system for the financing of the 'clever poor' through the universities which had been taken over from the Catholic Church. Although the Book was not accepted by Parliament, in practice many such schools were created, and fed a thriving

5

educational system. In later years further schools were established in many of the burghs, though these were also subject to Church inspection, supervision and control through the Presbytery, and through the teachers having to subscribe the Westminster Confession of Faith.[315]

State interest on a wide scale begins with the Parochial Schools (Scotland) Act of 1803, settling the salaries of teachers, and dealing with their accommodation and maintenance. Increasing provision was thereafter made for the state subsidy of parochial and burgh school education, with a parallel provision for inspection by state officials. Throughout this period, however, the interest of the Church in standards and the content of education remained paramount in law, though declining in practice. A major factor was the establishment of many Free Church schools after the Disruption,[316] schools which resented the attempts of the presbyteries of the established Church to supervise them and try the qualifications of appointees, although such was their legal right. The first case after the Disruption involved the headmaster of Campbeltown School, who was deposed from office by the Church of Scotland Presbytery of Cantyre, as he had joined the Free Church. He asked the civil courts to suspend the sentence of deposition (i.e. effectively to quash it) and applied for interdict, but the Lord Ordinary held that by statute the matter fell under the jurisdiction of the established Church Presbytery.[317] The Elgin case was the last straw.

The case of Elgin Academy, *The Presbytery of Elgin* v. *The Magistrates and Town Council of Elgin,* (1861) 23 D.287, is of crucial importance in the development of the relations of Church and State in Scottish education. The facts were that a grammar school had existed in Elgin at least since 1585 and perhaps earlier than that. In 1620 a Sang School was established in connection with it, and this was later converted into an English school. In 1800 the two schools were united and moved into new buildings. Over the years the Academy so created was expanded, always under the control of the Town Council, and existed as the burgh school for Elgin. In 1844 and 1849 the Town Council appointed teachers to the school without reference to the Presbytery for trial of their qualifications, and without requiring these gentlemen to go before the Presbytery to sign the Confession of Faith and Formula of Worship, although the Presbytery made frequent and express protest of this conduct. In addition in 1846 the Town Council effectively breached the Presbytery's right to examine the conduct of the school, by arranging to have the school inspected by State inspectors two days before the date for the usual Presbytery inspection and by also arranging for the school to be shut up and the children on holiday when the Presbytery commissioners arrived.

Ultimately the Presbytery of Elgin raised an action in the Court of Session on 20 December 1850 asking for a declarator that the Academy fell within the jurisdiction, superintendence and control of the Presbytery, particularly under the Acts 1633, c.5, 1690 c.25, 1693 c.38, 1706 c.6, and 43 Geo.III c.54. In addition they asked for declarator that the magistrates were bound to appoint as masters in the school only those found qualified, that the judicatories of the established Church had rights to try qualifications, to supervise and to dismiss, and that the masters were under a duty to appear before the Presbytery of Elgin—

> 'and respectively to acknowledge and profess, and to subscribe the Confession of Faith, as the confession of their faith, and to practise and conform themselves to the worship of the Established Church of Scotland, and to submit themselves to the government and discipline thereof, and never, directly or indirectly, to endeavour the prejudice or subversion of the same . . . .'[318]

The claim of the Presbytery was therefore, important. If successful it meant that the established Church of Scotland had very extensive rights of supervision and of interference in the working of almost all educational establishments, even in the face of the opposition of the local authorities. It also meant that teachers who were unable or unwilling to subscribe the Westminster Confession of Faith could not be employed. Indeed the declarator asked for went even further, for all Free Church members could sign the Confession (some with clearer consciences than many established Church members), but the declarator would require them to give up their denomination, the whole basis of which was dissent from the constitution of the church as then established.

It is unnecessary to trace the progress of this case before the Courts. The process took ten years, with many judgements on the different questions that arose in the course of the argument. In the end of the day the Court found in favour of the Presbytery, holding that the Academy formed a public burgh school, and that, in terms of the statutory law, the masters in the school were subject to the jurisdiction, superintendence and control of the Presbytery: but this was a pyrrhic victory.

The effect of the Elgin Academy case was almost immediate and wide-ranging, for the government introduced what became the Parochial and Burgh Schoolmasters (Scotland) Act of 1861, radically transforming the law. Section 9 abolished the right of Presbytery to examine teachers, and gave the function to Boards of Examiners appointed by the Courts of the Scottish Universities. Section 12 abolished the requirement of subscription of the Confession, and replaced it with a simple declaration to be made by the parochial school teacher that he would never attempt to subvert the Westminster doctrines or the Church of Scotland. Burgh schoolmasters did not even have to undertake such an obligation.

Shortly after this, however, the whole of education was transformed by the passing of the 1872 Education (Scotland) Act, in the train of a series of reports on education by a Royal Commission under the chairmanship of the Duke of Argyle,[319] and in the wake of the corresponding 1870 English Education Act.[320]

The 1872 Act took from the Church the remaining control of education, vesting it in school boards of elected membership. Of course members of the

Church served on such boards, but the formal control of previous centuries was gone. In addition education was, at the elementary level (five to thirteen years), compulsory (s.69) and in the state system, undenominational. The requirement of the declaration under s.12 of the 1861 Act vanished. Under s.68 the so-called 'conscience clause' which had operated as a matter of custom in the church schools,[321] was incorporated into law, and this was referred to in the Preamble to the Act. Section 68 provided:

> 'Every public school and every school subject to inspection and in receipt of public money . . . shall be open to children of all denominations, and any child may be withdrawn by his parents from any instruction in religious subjects and from any religious observation in any such school; and no child shall in any such school be placed at any disadvantage with respect to the secular education given therein by reason of the denomination to which such child or his parents belong, or by reason of his being withdrawn from any instruction in religious subjects. . . .'

Concomitant with such provision it was also made law by ss.66 and 67(2) that there should be no inspection in religious knowledge in state schools and that no grants of public funds should be made for religious instructions.

As outlined in Chapter VI, throughout all this development the Roman Catholic church had been emerging from the disfavour of previous centuries, and it is not surprising to find that, in areas where there were sufficient Catholic children, a system of private Catholic schools was developing in parallel to the state system. Other denominations had also established some schools. The basis of such education was denominational, doctrine playing a part even in 'secular' subjects, and these churches were loathe to see 'their' children go into the state system. At the same time they found that their financial problems were growing, and that teachers were leaving the denominational schools for the state system which was better paid and more secure. Educational standards in the denominational schools therefore fell, aggravating the problems. The 1872 Act therefore made provision for the accepting into the state system of denominational schools whose managers so agreed, but the transfer had to be in effect by gift. This was unsatisfactory.

It took almost fifty years for the matter to be resolved. In 1918, as part of the major revision of educational structures, provision was made for the inclusion of denominational schools in the state system in terms which are virtually those current today.[322] By s.18 of the 1918 Education (Scotland) Act the newly constituted Education Authorities running the existing state system were placed under a duty to accept the transfer of voluntary schools, with powers to make payment in consideration. This allowed the churches owning schools to re-coup in part at least their building outlays.

The local Education Authority was required by s.18(3) to hold all schools taken over under the provisions of s.18 as public schools of the same character and status as at the date of transfer and to retain the staff in post at the date of transfer. Further, provisos (ii) and (iii) to s.18(3) required that teachers appointed thereafter by the Authority had to be approved by the church or denominational body which used to manage the school, that the time allocated for religious instruction (subject to the conscience clause) was not to be reduced from former practice, and that a supervisor of religious instruction, appointed by the church or body concerned, had to be given access to the school and facilities for the conduct of such religious instruction.

Provision was made for the termination of the religious character of a school after the expiry of ten years, where the facts showed that the denominational alignment of the children had changed. On the other hand, and this was crucial to the 1918 settlement, by s.18(7) there was provision for the conversion of existing schools into 'denominational' schools, or for the creation of new 'denominational' schools where the local facts warranted such a development.

The 'religious' provisions of current legislation are to be found in the Education (Scotland) Act 1962, a consolidating statute, as amended. In broad, they repeat the provisions of earlier Acts without major change. Under them the State provides through local government 'denominational' schools at the request of interested churches where the character of the local population justifies this (s.17(2)), and existing 'denominational' schools continue to exist. In this way the religious beliefs of a significant proportion of parts of Scotland are catered for within the school system. This solution to a very real problem is unique to Scotland.

But the Scottish system is not without challenge. It does appear that the concept of the denominational school in the publicly financed system is running into difficulty. Attacks have been made on it in political conferences and in the General Assembly of the Church of Scotland, to say nothing of newspaper articles, letters and other media. The most general attack, reinforced by developments in Northern Ireland, is based on the dangers inherent in the separation of one group. Within the denominational schools there is also difficulty. The Archbishop of Glasgow in 1975–6 strongly advised Catholics to send their children to a 'Catholic' school, advice made necessary by falling numbers as parents preferred to put their children into the non-denominational system. The grounds of their action are obscure. Allegations are made that the 'denominational' schools are not in practice as well looked after financially as the ordinary schools, and certainly teachers seem to prefer the greater promotion prospects in the general system. But the whole area is murky. It may here suffice to say that in Scotland we have developed this curious yet useful concept of the denominational school within a secular system. Whether it will continue to work remains to be seen.

The other area of major concern which should be mentioned is that of religious education in schools. As stated earlier, the practice from early times, and law from 1872, has been for religious education to be offered in schools, but with a right of withdrawal and without financial provision being made for it. This has proved unsatisfactory in many eyes, many teachers being unwilling to teach the subject, and many, though willing, being less than competent at it.

In 1968, the Scottish Education Department set up a Committee under the chairmanship of Professor Malcolm Millar of Aberdeen University, to review the current practice of non-denominational schools with regard to moral and religious education. Its Report[323], published in 1972, construed its terms of reference closely and simply made recommendations for the improvement of the present situation. The appointment of specialised teachers, alteration in course content and orientation, the setting aside of one period a week for the subject, and methods for arriving at a syllabus were all suggested. In 1977, a new agreed syllabus was published for the subject, and it will be an examinable subject in the Higher and Ordinary level exams in the near future. These developments have all, however, taken place within the current legal framework. But perhaps the provision of such education in schools should not be taken for granted.

Whether there ought to be any religious instruction in the general curriculum in schools is a matter of enormous difficulty, and has been productive of much argument and strife. Broadly, one's theology determines one's attitude to this question of policy. It seems clear that the independent denominational schools must be allowed to give religious instruction—that is a major reason for their very existence. Within the State system a modification of that argument would allow instruction in the denominational schools operating under the 1918 concept. But the ordinary non-denominational schools pose different problems. Though the Millar Report states that a large majority of parents want their children to receive religious education, the Report may be right in asking whether the parents really want 'moral education', which is a rather different matter.[324]

There are those who argue vehemently the duty to rear the young in the truth, even if parents are rather hazy as to what that might be.[325] However, such people usually are somewhat inconsistent, abhorring the dissemination of Marxism in the schools beyond the Iron Curtain, and objecting for example, to members of the Hari Krishna movement being allowed to talk to senior pupils in some Edinburgh schools (1972). Others argue for a general 'moral and social' education, not necessarily attached to Christian doctrine. Yet others have their own variety of truth. The divergence of opinion, attitudes and ignorance of teachers are other factors to be considered. In our pluralist society there is not sufficient agreement on the content of a course in religious education to make it a compulsory part of the school curriculum. But, as said earlier, can education omit consideration of a basic formative influence on our present society? Surely not. However, need that consideration move over into religious instruction? Can that be kept separate?

What I am feeling after is some sort of separation of education in the rôle played by religion in the growth of our culture, and instruction directed towards belief in religious propositions. This may involve a difference in presentation rather than in content. Even allowing for the doctrine of predestination, the present system seems to 'inoculate' many against Christianity, which is a pity.[326] Everyone knows of teachers who go through the form, yet their own position or beliefs result in depreciation of what is taught. Therefore I wonder whether it might not be better to eliminate the present religious education as a subject even with the conscience clause, perhaps allowing some place for 'religion' considered as a formative influence (though this ought to be implicit in the existing subjects), and to allow and encourage local churches—not necessarily ministers—and concerned teachers, to provide voluntary religious instruction in schools, either out of school hours or in non-compulsory special periods. This raises the problem of sects, and the non-Christian religions, and would involve negotiations with the headmaster. But, where a school has, say a high proportion of Muslim children, it would allow some instruction within the scholastic framework, yet without the formal pressure of curriculum. As a corollary, examination in religious education as a non-compulsory subject might be introduced.[327]

So far we have been dealing with schools, but to round off the picture the position of the universities must be looked at. Like the schools they were subject to church control, the main Acts being those of 1567 c.11 and 1690 c.25, made part of the Union Settlement by the Union with England Act 1706 c.7. Under these provisions it was required that professors and others holding office in the universities had to subscribe the Westminster Confession of Faith and conform themselves to the Church, including the government exercised by the Presbytery of the bounds. Needless to say this was irksome, but matters simmered until Professor J. S. Blackie, on his induction in 1839 as Professor of Humanity (Latin) at the Marischal College, Aberdeen, signed the Confession, but with expressed reservation. Eventually a court case was needed to permit Professor Blackie's settlement.[328] Discussions then ensued, but similar to the Presbytery of Elgin case for schools, the final trigger was an attempt to return to the letter of the law. Though the statutory requirements had not been generally enforced for years, some Moderates sought to use the legal provisions requiring subscription of the Confession and submission to the Church of Scotland to debar members of other churches, and non-believers, from professorial positions. This may seem incredible now, but preferment to any university chair was a matter of great interest a hundred years ago.[329]

As in the Elgin case, the effect of the use of the law was its cancellation. By the Universities (Scotland) Act 1853, subscription of the Confession was required only for theological chairs, defined as chairs of Divinity, Church History, Biblical Criticism, and Hebrew. The holders of all other chairs were required simply to make a Declaration, akin to that later introduced for school teachers by the 1861 Act, that they would not seek to subvert the doctrines of the Church, or the Church itself. However, 'laicising' was in the wind, and by the Universities (Scotland) Act 1859, subscription of the Confession was retained only for the Principalship of St Mary's College, St Andrews.

The final step in this church control over universities in general was the abolition of the Declaration procedure for 'Lay' chairs by s.17 of the Universities (Scotland) Act 1889. By s.18 the University Commissioners were empowered to take evidence as to the propriety and necessity for tests for university officers, and in a special report in 1892 they recommended (by 7 to 9) that the Declaration procedure remain in abeyance.[330]

General church control of universities has, therefore, been broken, but there remains an interest in the position of divinity faculties. Some would argue that nowadays there is no difference between the Church interest and that of any professional body which accepts a university degree or examination as exempting from its own professional requirements. Churches, like the Law Society or accountancy bodies, or the Royal Institute of Chartered Surveyors, should restrict their interest to one of recognition or non-recognition of the university product, with perhaps some recommendation as to the general kind of qualification they would like university teachers to possess. But for historical reasons the link between the Church of Scotland and the divinity faculties is closer.

As a result of the union of the United Free Church and the Church of Scotland in 1929, the United Free Church colleges in Aberdeen, Glasgow and Edinburgh were taken into the local universities. Further, in the next few years agreements were worked out between the four divinity faculties and the Church of Scotland, under which the power to make recommendations to each University Court for appointments to divinity chairs and some other posts in each of the four universities was entrusted to a Board of Nomination for Theological Chairs. These arrangements were revised in 1950–51, and the current provision is that each university has a Board of Nomination for Theological Chairs, consisting of twelve or other even number of members, of whom one half are appointed by the General Assembly of the Church of Scotland. (Of course it should be noted that some of the university appointees are likely also to be of that denomination).

The current regulations are very comprehensive, requiring an appointee to have the support of at least two thirds of the membership of the Board. Only if no valid recommendation is made to the University Court within twelve months can the university act on its own, except in the case of certain enumerated chairs. These latter are chairs which the Church in part supports, and, if there is no valid appointment recommended in them, they remain vacant, and the Church is relieved of liability during the vacancy.[331]

But what of the appointment in May 1979, of Professor Mackey, a Roman Catholic, to the Thomas Chalmers Chair of Theology in the University of Edinburgh? I have no wish here to enter into that dispute. Suffice it to say that the appropriate procedures were followed. It may be, therefore, that the General Assembly will wish to review the appointment mechanisms, though that will be very awkward. Alternatively it might replace its representatives on the four Boards of Nomination. But, if that results in the Boards being unable to make valid recommendations under the present rules, the work of the divinity faculties would be impeded, to the detriment of the Church, and the strengthening of the arm of those who would wish the demise of the divinity faculties. Thought and caution are indicated.

Finally, each university's Board of Nomination has advisory functions. Scrutiny of divinity courses and curricula, and negotiations and discussions of them are, however, matters for the General Assembly's Committee on Education for the Ministry, which functions rather like the equivalent committees of other professional bodies which recognise university degrees. Obviously, as long as the Church of Scotland is still the main goal for the majority of divinity students, its views are of great importance for the universities and the continuance of this link is reasonable.

2. *Broadcasting*

The propagation of beliefs in education leads naturally to the question of religion and the radio and television media.[332] Here there are problems in that the British Broadcasting Corporation and the Independent Broadcasting Authority are semi-autonomous organisations, and that they are in a monopoly position. Their practices are therefore important, though the legal skeleton which sustains these practices is minimal.

The constitutional documents of the B.B.C. are the Royal Charter of 1964 (Cmnd. 2385) as amended and subsequently extended, and the Licence and Agreement of 1969 (Cmnd. 4095) (also amended and extended) between the Corporation and the Post-master General (whose responsibilities now lie with the Home Secretary) under which the Corporation is permitted to broadcast under the Wireless Telegraphy Acts. None of these contains specific provision regarding religion, though Clause 9 of the current Charter allows the appointment of advisory bodies, and is the legal basis *inter alia* of the Central Religious Advisory Committee (the C.R.A.C.), which was the earliest advisory committee in broadcasting. The first C.R.A.C. was set up in 1923 by John Reith, as he then was, within the British Broadcasting Company, and taken over into the structure of the British Broadcasting Corporation when it was created in 1927 (1926, Cmd. 2756). Another usable power within the constitutional documents is Clause 13(4) of the Licence and Agreement, under which the Secretary of State 'may from time to time by notice in writing require the Corporation to refrain at any specified time or at all times from sending any matter or matters of any class specified in such notice.' This has never been used in regard to matters of religion. However, the power given by Clause 14(1) regarding transmission times was used to establish the 'closed period' on Sundays, as discussed below.

By contrast, specific provision is made for religion both in the constitution of the Independent Broadcasting Authority, and in its internal codes. This is because the I.B.A. is concerned with commercial broadcasting, and financed by advertising. There was therefore a possibility that religious groups might either purchase programme time or advertising slots in order to press their messages.

Accordingly by s.4(5) of the 1973 Independent Broadcasting Act[333] no transmission by the independent network may include any religious service, or
propaganda relating to religious matters without the prior approval of the
Authority. Further by Rule 8 of Schedule 2 to the Act: 'No advertisement shall
be permitted which is inserted by or on behalf of any body the objects whereof
are wholly or mainly of a religious . . . nature, and no advertisement shall be
permitted which is directed towards any religious . . . end . . .' That provision
is repeated, *mutatis mutandis*, by Rule 10 of the I.B.A. Code of Advertising
Standards and Practice[334] and seems both sensible and necessary although it has
caused some discussion.[335] In addition to such general provision, the I.B.A. is
required by s.10(1) and (2)(a) of the 1973 Act to have a religious advisory
committee, although it is now no longer bound to comply with its advice as was
the position under s.8(2) of the Television Act 1954. In fact what has happened
is that the C.R.A.C. set up originally by the B.B.C. acts also for the I.B.A.,
though it now usually meets the Corporation and the Authority separately.

Within these structures religious broadcasting seems rather a matter of
usage and practice. Under Reith the early B.B.C. slowly developed its practice,
so slowly that the Ullswater Committee which reported before the renewal of
the first Charter in 1936 was constrained to suggest that Sunday programming
might be a little lighter, and more 'popular' at least in one of the B.B.C.'s
alternative services.[336] During the Second World War there was some concern
lest the increased military and political concern which had crept in to religious
broadcasts in relation to foreign events might spill over into discussions of
municipal affairs, and in August 1941, what was known as the 'Concordat'
embodied the principle that ministers of religion could expound only the moral
and religious principles and criteria on which political decisions ought to be
taken. Detail and criticism did not lie within their purview.[337]

Thereafter for many years the development of religious broadcasting lay
within the so-called 'main-stream' concept, though a progression can be seen
in the two major Reports on broadcasting. The Beveridge Committee of
1949–51 recommended that the object of religious broadcasting should not be
to seek converts to one particular church, but to maintain the common element
in all religious bodies. However, the body of the Report went somewhat
beyond this and referred to maintaining the common element 'as against those
who deny spiritual values', which is somewhat different.[338] The Pilkington
Committee of 1960–62 accepted the summary of the B.B.C.'s attitude in its
Handbook for 1960 as being applicable both to the B.B.C. and I.T.A. (as it
then was). This stated that the B.B.C. was not required to be neutral or
impartial on the subject of religion, and gave the aims of religious broadcasting
under three heads:

'The first is that it should reflect the worship, thought, and action of those
churches which represent the main stream of the Christian tradition in the
country. The second is that religious broadcasting should bring before

listeners and viewers what is most significant in the relationship between the Christian faith and the modern world. The third aim is that religious broadcasting should seek to reach those on the fringe of the organised life of the churches, or quite outside it.'[339]

Broadcast religion was not a vehicle for any one group, though this did not dilute religion beyond utility. Explicit doctrinal exposition was allowable, but not undue emphasis on difference nor the disparagement of other faiths.[340]

By the 1970's the C.R.A.C. was advising the Annan Committee that while the 1960 objectives were 'still valid as a rough working guide, they needed revision and re-interpretation.' New guidelines had been evolved in discussions with the B.B.C. and I.B.A. and were:

(i) To seek to reflect the worship, thought and action of the principal religious traditions represented in Britain, recognising that those traditions are mainly, though not exclusively, Christian;
(ii) To seek to present to viewers and listeners those beliefs, ideas, issues and experiences in the contemporary world which are evidently related to a religious interpretation or dimension of life;
(iii) To seek also to meet the religious interest, concerns and needs of those on the fringe of, or outside, the organised life of the Churches.'[341]

The Annan Committee recognised that this statement represents a fundamental departure from previous objectives, and abandons the mainstream concept tied to varieties of Christianity. It is a recognition that 'religious broadcasting should not be the religious equivalent of party political broadcasts'.[342] However, Annan also recognised that this was more a recognition of what religious broadcasting departments have been doing for some few years. Nonetheless the Committee thought the Christian denominations should retain their primary place in religious broadcasting [343]

Two things follow from such a view of the objectives of religious broadcasting. In the first place it is sensible that the so called 'closed period' in the television programming on Sunday evenings should be shortened, though the argument really justifies its abolition. The closed period was the 70 minutes after 6.15 p.m. and was established by ministerial direction in 1955 following consultations with the churches and the broadcasting authorities. The direction was given in terms of Clause 14(1) of the B.B.C. Licence and s.17 of the Television Act 1954 which relate to the hours of broadcasting, the closed period not being counted so long as the programmes within it were of religious material.[344] When this control of broadcasting hours was lifted in 1972[345] the Authorities continued the practice for some years. Recently, however a change has been agreed. While there continues to be at least 70 minutes of religious programming on Sunday evenings the actual closed period has been reduced to the 35 minute period following 6.40 p.m. on Sundays.[346] But the justification for the closed period is tenuous. It used to be thought that there should be no counter-attractions available in time of evening service. But this cannot be the justification with present timing. In any event the argument could be inverted—the closed period may keep folk at home, while if the programmes were non-religious they might go to church. Again there are not that many churches holding evening services in Scotland. Lastly, there is a massive inconsistency in that there is no closed period in radio broadcasting. Perhaps the truth is simply that despite allegations, it is not television which empties churches.

The second matter raised by the changing view of religious broadcasting is its emphasis and bias. Naturally access to religious broadcasting time has caused dispute over the years, as various groups, both minority religions and atheists and humanists, have attacked the privilege given to the main denominations, and have sought access for their own views. The Annan Committee, like its predecessors, thought that this was something for the broadcasting Authorities to work out, and that the principal denominations should have primary place in religious broadcasting.[347] One change over the years has, however, been the broadening of the membership of the Central Religious Advisory Committee within its 29 member number which has permitted justice more clearly to be done in this matter.[348] Consequent to its proposals for the future of broadcasting the Annan Committee was in favour of separate Religious Advisory Committees for the several Authorities which it recommended, with the same character as the existing C.R.A.C., but this has been left by Government to the Authorities themselves to negotiate.[349]

Finally a word should be said about certain Scottish peculiarities, which are responses to the different requirements faced by Scottish broadcasting. Within the B.B.C., Scotland forms a separate region, and has retained that status through the development of local radio which resulted in the dismemberment of the other B.B.C. regional radio services in the early 1970's. The Scottish region has its own Broadcasting Council, and is represented on the national body. A similar arrangement obtains within the structures of the I.B.A. In religious broadcasting there is a special B.B.C. Scottish Religious Advisory Committee of 14 members, and the several independent television companies have their own advisory committees.

Prior to the re-organisation of 1978, Scotland as a separate entity originated some of its own programming, though it did suffer from an undue reliance on programmes networked from the south mainly for financial reasons.[350] Under the new arrangements Scotland does not seem to contribute much to Radios 1–4, and the Scottish 'element' in these services appears to be reduced. This has a special impact in religious broadcasting, where the different requirements of England and Wales affect programming. Even so it seems curious, for example, that there is so much of 'liturgical' styles of service, which seems disproportionate to the episcopal element in the U.K. As for 'religion' in Radio Scotland, its problems are shared by the rest of that service, and we can but pray for improvement. More can be said for B.B.C. Scotland television, which has pioneered some interesting programmes. Given time perhaps radio will catch up.

Of course, none of this deals with actual content, which is really outside my field of inquiry here, but it may be noted that the Annan Committee was critical of standards, and was very cutting about some clerics. It suggested that more finance be allocated to religious programming, and 'a different sort of producer' might be one cure. But the Committee also made the fascinating suggestion that perhaps the religious broadcasting departments should be disbanded, and their personnel deployed throughout the broader field of programming, with a consequent effect there.[351] Religious programming would then cease to be a specialist interest, with consequent dangers, but would be a known expertise of certain producers and presenters working across the field of broadcasting. The experiment deserves to be tried.

3. Charities

As a matter of law, by s.22 of the Valuation and Rating (Scotland) Act 1956, churches and halls are exempt from local rates other than water rate, and this was extended by s.4(8) of the Local Government (Financial Provisions etc.) (Scotland) Act 1962 to the residences of full-time ministers, where the property is owned by his church.[352] By s.4(2) of that Act partial rating exemption was also given to property held for charitable purposes, though precisely what comes within that category has produced legal dispute.[353]

Apart from such property tax matters charities are now exempt from direct taxation under *inter alia* s.360 of the Income and Corporation Taxes Act 1970, and s.35(1) of the Finance Act 1965[354], though they may be liable to V.A.T. under the Finance Act 1972. This clearly applies to the traditional churches and denominations, but with other bodies it may be a question whether the body is a charity for tax purposes. In England what is currently required is registration with the Charity Commission in terms of the Charities Act 1960. The Commissioners are responsible for ensuring that the body does have charitable objects, and that during its existence it continues to fulfil these objects properly.

In Scotland, the establishment of a trust for public benefit is easier than in England, but the gaining of charitable status for tax purposes requires conformity to English law and a different procedure. In the *Inland Revenue Commissioners* v. *Glasgow Police Athletic Association* 1953 S.C. (H.L.) 13, the House of Lords decided that taxation statutes are U.K. statutes framed on the basis of English law and definitions. A Scottish trust therefore has charitable status only if it comes within the third category of charitable trust laid down by Lord Macnaughton in *Commissioners for Special Purposes of Income Tax* v. *Pemsel* 1891 A.C. 531 at 583, that is 'trusts for the advancement of religion', as that category has been elaborated.[355] Whether this condition is met depends in practice upon negotiation with a special section of the Inland Revenue, who may be willing to give informal guidance on the matter in advance. A question therefore arises whether a more generalised system of registration and of scrutiny of the operation of 'charities' in Scotland would not be a good thing, especially if such were general and not confined only to religious charities.[356] The problem is, of course, that bodies apparently existing for charitable purposes can gather large sums of money, and allow their officials to live well, while the nominal object of the charity receives less than might be considered proper. This would appear to be a major danger in the religious area, where the impetus to give is bound up with very powerful motivating factors. Religious language and concepts contain very effective 'triggers'.

Such points are made in the concluding paragraphs of Sir John G. Foster's enquiry into the practice and effects of Scientology. He noted that religious bodies are privileged, and that the bases of these privileges were 'the remoter parts of our history'. It appeared to him 'debatable what correlative benefit our society today derives from their continued existence'. Even if that benefit were in general conceded, precautions were necessary to prevent abuse of the privileges granted, and Sir John suggested that a full review of the topic is now required.[357] That was in 1971.

Without accepting that all privileges should cease, I think the cases for a review, and for safeguards, stand. The tax concessions are attractive, and there is the problem of the possible abuse of a relationship (a point to which we will return in considering the control of sects). One way to cope with the problems would be to abolish the tax concessions, but this is draconian and stupid, probably crippling many useful endeavours. However, were the tax concessions less easy to come by that might help. Privileges could be restricted to religions with a substantial following, and might be conditional on a 'church' satisfying the tests for registration for marriage purposes. It should also engage in genuine and overt acts of religious worship, defined on the lines indicated in *R. v. Registrar General ex parte Segerdal* [1970] 2 Q.B. 697.[358] Whether other existing religious charities should continue to enjoy their existing privileges is a matter of doubt, though some would qualify as trusts for the advancement of education or under other heads.

On the other hand it may be that the scope of the work and responsibility for registration, and the continued scrutiny and review of charities, would be too large and too costly in terms of its return. Perhaps the only reasonable check would be a slight alteration in the definition of the crime of obtaining money by false pretences, to be automatically brought into play when the costs of a charity rise above a small fixed percentage of its turnover. This could be policed by a small body of inspectors, who would be given power to inspect where they felt there was need, but without laying on them a general duty to oversee the whole operation of the charitable trusts of Scotland. But these are difficult matters of policy, and I would hope they would be thoroughly explored if, as is to be hoped, the present dissatisfaction with the law relating to charities leads to its general review.

In such a review attention should also be given to the question of Deeds of

Covenant, under which a charity can recover from the Inland Revenue the tax paid on a sum covenanted to be paid to the charity out of taxed income. While this is reasonable where the state is encouraging charitable activity—for example educational charities, hospitals and poor relief—it seems entirely inappropriate that churches, which are really nowadays private clubs, should so be subsidised. Where a denomination engages in activities falling under other categories of 'charity' that could be coped with under those other heads.

4. Control of new sects and churches

Cognate with the question of charitable status for religious bodies and trusts is the matter of the control of new religions and quasi-religions. Two questions arise; first, the possible exploitation of the relationship between leaders and the convert, and second, the social consequences involved in the practice of beliefs.

As to the first it seems clear that in most religions a 'pastoral' relationship is likely to be created between an instructor and convert, which may amount to a dependency. Indeed the situation may require such. That relationship is open to abuse, and it would seem wise to establish some sort of scrutinising and licensing body where the relationship is constituted for hire or reward. This would of course go beyond the category of religion and include all psychotherapy practices.[359]

But where the relationship is not constituted for hire and no financial burdens are imposed, where there are mystical elements or overtones, and the basic doctrine involved is religious or quasi-religious, problems of personal freedom arise. If a man wishes to join a sect, and give away all his worldly wealth, this can not be attacked in law, unless undue influence or deception be proved. It would be an improvement to require him first to provide for his dependents to the satisfaction of a court, but this raises all sorts of problems.

However where there is evidence that children are being attracted and held by psychological pressures and techniques, and families are being broken up, different concerns arise. I have sympathy with the person who will be a true Christian despite the pressures of parents, but find it difficult in law to differentiate such a case from that of some minority groups.

Such a problem therefore raises the fundamental question whether the law ought to be brought into play in such a case at all.[360] Certainly the laws relating to the right of a parent to recover his child from a detainer should continue to operate, but when we are dealing with an adult, different considerations arise. The basic question is one of freedom, and freedom is a basic value of our society. Suffering, hurt and distortion of personality (viewed from one standpoint) may occur as a result of a person joining a sect. But where that is the will of the individual, and there is no element of coercion involved, nor is the sanity of the individual such as would ground an application for a guardian to be appointed over him, it is more in the ultimate interests of our society that the law should not intervene.

There are limits, of course. These are the slowly evolving limits of the presuppositions of our society, which are still of the Christian ethos. Such limits should be set as far back as possible without the abandonment of that ethos. It may be that in the future the ethos may change—that is a different matter: but that change should spring from within society, and not be brought about within society by the use of law. Similarly the law should not be used to stifle change, and it follows that, so far as is reasonable, freedom should be allowed.

The alternative to such an approach is to set up a state system of scrutiny and interference to review and correct what are seen as undesirable developments under the guise of religion. Such a system is as capable of abuse as that which it seeks to control. It would then be too easy for 'acceptable' beliefs and practices to be codified, and for others to be 'restricted' in accordance with 'official' views. Too many existing statutes allow the intervention of a state official for the 'good' of the individual. We need to depart from that road, not tread it further, and resist the perverted humanism it can embody.[361]

It makes no difference which side you fall off a tight-rope. If machinery is set up to allow the detailed scrutiny and suppression of 'undesirable religious and quasi-religious movements', we will be back in the most unwelcome manifestations of an 'ecclesiastical' control of society, without even the assurance that the controllers have a true base to work from. The history of many nations shows that when beliefs and practices are curbed more than the minimum necessary for the existence of a free society, that free society ceases to exist. If we set up a machinery of control, even for the best of motives, the dangers of abuse are too great, for if the power is there it will be first used, and then will degenerate.[362] Indeed there is an interesting palindromic quality present. We have moved from the all-pervasive control of the Kirk to the possible all-pervasive control of the State.

5. *Marriage and Divorce*

1. *Marriage*

Marriage and Divorce are areas where the interaction of religion and law has produced distortion.[363] The fundamental problem in marriage has been the lack of a single coherent doctrine of marriage either in law or theology. This has been aggravated by the well-intentioned interventions of the State to correct and amend the law from time to time, but without regard to the basic concepts. Thus it is not now clear whether in law marriage is constituted by the consent of the parties alone, or whether the presence or even intervention of a third party as 'celebrant' is necessary. Nor has it been clear what qualifications are required in a celebrant.

In former centuries marriage and marriage law were the province of the Church. Two forms of marriage were recognised; regular marriage, which involved a church ceremony, and irregular marriage, which was a matter for the parties alone. Irregular marriage was constituted in three modes: first by consent of the parties before witnesses (*per verba de praesenti*), secondly, by promise followed by intercourse on the faith of that promise (promise *subsequente copula*), and thirdly by habit and repute, where a court presumed the marriage to have occurred where the parties had cohabited for a period, and there was a general belief that they were in fact married.[364]

As the Scottish Reformation took place in 1560, the abolition of irregular marriages by the Council of Trent in 1563 was without effect in Scots Law, which continued to recognise these marriages until 1940, when by the coming into force of the Marriage (Scotland) Act 1939, *de praesenti* and promise *subsequente copula* ceased to be legal methods of constituting marriage. Marriage by habit and repute remains possible.

Habit and repute, and the two forms of regular marriage, civil marriage before a registrar, and a religious marriage in a religious service, are the remaining modes of marriage recognised in Scots Law, and this marks one of the ways in which religion and law have produced distortion. If, as seems right theologically, marriage is a matter for the consent of the parties, the old Scots law which gave wide scope for the evidencing of that consent is doctrinally proper. The Catholic abolition of the irregular modes in 1563 seems designed both to encourage priestly intervention in the constitution of marriage, and to facilitate the state interest in the making known of the occurrence of marriages. This latter interest also explains the introduction of registration of marriages. By the requirement of formal ceremonial and registration, the State knows who has entered marital status, and who has marital rights and duties. This is certainly important now that modern arrangements make taxation, social security, pensions and many other benefits contingent on marital status. The legitimacy of children is also involved. But the effect has been to deprive marriage of its central emphasis on the consent of the parties. Forms, requirements and ceremonial designed for these important but secondary social purposes are now more important than a coherent concept of marriage. Consent has been surrounded and hedged around, so that in most cases consent evidenced only in a certain context will now create marriage. It is true that a court declaration of marriage by habit and repute is a competent procedure, though it is not a welcome one for many people. To that extent the older writers' opinions remain valid. Thus we may still quote Stair (Inst. I.4.6.):

> 'The public solemnity is a matter of order, justly introduced by positive law, for the certainty of so important a contract; but not essential to marriage.'

And there are the words of Lord Deas:

> '. . . consent makes marriage. No form or ceremony, civil or religious, no notice before nor publication after, no consummation or cohabitation, no writing, no witnesses even are essential to the constitution of . . . (the contract of marriage).'[365]

Given the existence of the habit and repute procedure these words are not wrong, but it remains that the legislation dealing with the constitution of regular marriage is now so tight that one wonders whether the simple concept of consent is a true theory of marriage nowadays. It does not adequately explain the facts.

At the same time there is a certain incoherence between that fact and the growing numbers of statutes which pay attention not to a formal marriage bond, but to a *de facto* 'marital' situation—known usually as cohabitation. The definition of 'family' and of 'household' in various of the social welfare statutes operate on such a *de facto* basis, quite separate and distinct from any question of marriage.[366] It would therefore appear that a cleavage is developing between 'marital' practice for such matters, and marriage requirements laid down by the State.

These are broad criticisms, but there are also problems caused by the detailed requirements of the law. Historically only ministers of the Church of Scotland were entitled to perform marriages which were recognised as valid marriages *in facie ecclesia* (i.e. with religious ceremonial) by the State. Other marriages with religious ceremonial were technically irregular marriages *de preaesenti*. As such these marriages were subject to criminal penalty by the Act 1661 c.246 and 1698 c.6, though they were valid marriages, and the practice developed of arranging to have the parties found guilty of the offence of contracting an irregular marriage. The conviction 'proved' the marriage.

But various statutory provisions came to be made for special groups. Quakers and Jews were permitted to celebrate regular marriages by their own forms by s.5 of the Marriage Notice (Scotland) Act 1878, and general powers were given to celebrate regular marriages to 'priests and ministers not of the Established Church' by s.2 of the Marriage (Scotland) Act 1834. However, the extent of such provision for non-established church dignitaries was not specific, nor were 'priests and ministers' defined. The case law did not help definition[367] and resulted in confusion as to the regularity of some marriages. The only advance was the administrative action of the Registrar General for Scotland in accepting for registration, marriage schedules in terms of the Marriage Acts, completed by persons whom he had previously authorised for the purposes. Unfortunately there was no true legal basis for his action.

Accordingly, it was a matter for relief that the Kilbrandon Committee on the Marriage Law of Scotland 1969 (Cmnd. 4011) recommended the establishment of a formal register of approved celebrants, and this has been made law by ss.9–12 of the Marriage (Scotland) Act 1977. Those provisions, taken along with s.8, give an unwonted clarity in the definition of the persons authorised to celebrate a marriage. Under s.8, apart from civil registrars, these are ministers of the Church of Scotland, ministers or pastors of religious bodies designated by statutory instrument,[368] persons recognised by bodies so designated as entitled to solemnise marriages, and celebrants registered under s.9. Such provision means, for example, that senior members of such bodies as the Plymouth Brethren, which abhor the concept of a regular paid ministry, can celebrate regular marriages.

By s.9(1), religious bodies other than those listed in s.8, can nominate to the Registrar General, members to be registered as empowered to solemnise marriages. By s.9(2), the Registrar must reject such a nomination if the nominating body is not a religious body, the marriage ceremony is not appropriate in terms of s.9(3), the nominee is not a fit and proper person for the function, or there are already sufficient members of the body already registered for the purpose. I envisage many interesting actions based on such provision. The boundaries of the Registrar's powers are wide enough to remove many current difficulties, but will still need judicial definition.[369]

However, the new legislation has somewhat complicated matters. Whereas previously there was doubt as to the need for anything other than the exchange of consent of the parties in the marriage ceremony, now in some cases it apparently must contain a declaration by the celebrant that the parties are man and wife. This is necessary in terms of s.9(3)(a) for the 'marriage' ceremony of a body not listed in terms of s.8, to be proper for the purpose of s.9. The inference is that s.8 churches and denominations already contain such a declaration in their ceremonials, and that it is legally necessary and effective—propositions dubious in fact and under previous law. Indeed I would go so far as to say that the legal effect of the declaration of the celebrant was a ceremonial frill, adding nothing to the legal act. I suspect that it has now been included in the legislation by error. This curious provision is explicable only on the grounds of the presence of the declaration in many current ceremonies, and the curious but mistaken belief of many ministers (and perhaps even registrars) that they 'marry' the couple. In fact the minister or registrar merely conducts a ceremony at which the parties mutually consent to marriage and therefore marry each other—at least that is the analysis a simple doctrine of marriage leads to. The new provision is odd. Suppose the parties consent, and the celebrant has a coronary thrombosis before he gets his declaration made. Are we to hold that the marriage has not occurred? Surely not.

2. Divorce

Prior to the Reformation divorce *a vinculo* (i.e. release from the marriage bond) was unknown in Scotland, though separation *a mensa et thoro* (i.e. from table and bed) was competent. In addition it was also possible for use to be made in appropriate cases of the various grounds of nullity of marriage which had been elaborated by the Roman Catholic Church. Consistorial jurisdiction was vested in the bishops, though normally there was a more formal system of commissary courts, whose jurisdiction in part was composed of questions of the 'dissolution' of marriage.

After the Reformation the Church courts continued to exercise jurisdiction over family matters until 1563 when at the request of the Church[370] their powers were given to civil commissary courts. The Court of Session Act 1830 transferred that jurisdiction to the Court of Session, where it has remained. Divorce on the ground of adultery was introduced in the church courts in 1559, the concept being taken over and thereafter developed by the civil commissaries.[371] Divorce for desertion, or perhaps the regulation of that ground of divorce, was introduced by the Act 1573 c.1, though it may be traced in the teaching of the continental reformers, particularly Calvin,[372] and both grounds appear in ch. 24.5 and 24.6 of the Westminster Confession of 1645. One can therefore see the Church's doctrine as formative of early divorce law.

Thereafter, however, the Church of Scotland and the other churches have not played a truly significant part in the development of divorce law. The Roman Catholic church (a main possible protagonist) was in no position to express a view effectively, and the Church of Scotland had surrendered its jurisdiction to the civil judicatories in 1563. Development has therefore been solely in the hands of the courts and Parliament, which proceeded to elaborate a series of grounds of divorce without a fully coherent doctrinal base. Thus, at the fullest extent of the list, divorce was available on the grounds of adultery, wilful desertion for three years, cruelty, incurable insanity, habitual drunkenness, sodomy and bestiality. The absurdities of that system have been mitigated by the adoption of the concept of 'breakdown of marriage' in the Divorce (Scotland) Act 1976, but the main older grounds remain as evidence of breakdown. The most interesting development in the Act is the inclusion of 'desertion' in the form that a divorce may be granted with the consent of both parties to the marriage after they have lived apart for two years, or without the consent of the defender after a separation of five years. This is an attempt to balance interests to which we will return.

Although the Church of Scotland discussed the question of divorce law reform at the Assemblies of 1937, 1957 and 1958 when proposals for change were in the wind, its deliberations do not seem to have had much intrinsic weight in the reform of the law. This must be contrasted with the activity south of the Border, where the 1966 report *Putting Asunder*, written by a group appointed by the then Archbishop of Canterbury, began the discussion of breakdown of marriage as a basis for divorce, which eventually came into law with the Divorce Reform Act 1969. The Scottish legislation of 1976 really followed in that train, and, though there was wide discussion within the Kirk and views expressed, the initiative in the matter lay elsewhere.

Of course, the developments in divorce have produced problems for ministers, which vary in their intensity with the doctrinal views held by each individual. The remarriage of divorced persons is a matter left to ministerial conscience, though with some guidelines from the church. The new divorce law will be awkward for some in that context if they are of the view that only the grounds of adultery and desertion carry a permission to re-marry for the 'innocent party'.[373] Again, as divorce and re-marriage become increasingly common some ministers could have problems with office-bearers, or potential office-bearers. A broad spectrum of opinion is evident, ranging from a prohibition of all re-marriage after divorce, to what is said to be an 'unwillingness to condemn', and from a pragmatic approach to 'people where they are' to the suggestion that the time is approaching for the Church to separate its procedures and requirements from that of the State, but this last takes us in to another area—the future.

3. *The future of marriage law*
   What the future holds in the law of husband and wife is moot. Many accept that marriage as an institution is undergoing profound change, and that divorce and re-marriage will become easier and easier. How the churches may react to this is dubious, and given the current state of the churches I am inclined to predict that, with exceptions, the trend of that reaction may well be benign (not to say weak), since historically there has not been an attempt by the Church of Scotland at any rate to enforce a doctrinal line. Thus, although in law by the Act 1600 c.20 a decree of divorce for adultery was supposed to state the name of the paramour, and the marriage of the 'guilty party' and the paramour thereafter was barred, the practice developed of omitting the name from the decree precisely in order to permit that marriage. Again, though in England an applicant for a divorce had to come before the court with clean hands, (the institution of the King's (or Queen's) Proctor existed to ensure this point and divorce would be refused to those unable to meet that standard), such was never the position in Scotland. It was always possible for cross-actions to occur, in which each party simultaneously divorced the other. The effect of that procedure was as much to do justice in the property settlement of the divorce as to seek the truth of the matter. Again, although promise *subsequente copula* was frowned on, the irregular forms of marriage were permitted and allowed for within both the Church and State.
   In short we can say that the Scottish law and practice of marriage and divorce in the past combined to regulate and deal with the fact that people are less than perfect. When there were only the two grounds of divorce it seems to have been deemed better, and in accordance with Scripture, that those situations be dealt with and terminated. The use of the irregular forms of marriage, alongside the regular, allowed the other side of the problem to be dealt with. But the extension of the grounds of divorce introduced different factors both into divorce and into marriage. The State has more clearly come to deal with its own interests in regulating the relationships between individuals, and in knowing what those relationships were since more and more social legislation and tax and other benefits depend upon them. Further, the State has begun once more to take an interest in the factual situation where a 'marriage' exists, but not formally[374] and it may be observed in passing that such is a form of limited marriage for a period less than the mutual lifetime of the parties. In these ways the interests of the State and the Church have diverged.
   In England the substantive law and proposals for further change in the law have gone further in dealing with the rights and duties of couples cohabiting without marriage. By s.1 of the Domestic Violence and Matrimonial Proceedings Act 1976, as construed by the House of Lords in *Davis* v. *Johnson* [1978] 1 All E.R. 841, a mistress can obtain protection, and exclude a man from a house which they have shared, even though he possessed a proprietary interest in the house. Further, the court indicated that this was possible even

136 OF PRESBYTERS AND KINGS

where the man had the sole interest in the property. The Scottish Law Commission has invited views on this matter, but has otherwise clearly come down against any revision of the law to equate property consequences on cohabitation with those on marriage. The arguments against are first, that it is unduly paternalistic for the state to intervene legislatively to impose a 'marital' property law when the parties have chosen to avoid such, and second, that the equation of unmarried cohabitation and marriage as far as property is concerned would sooner or later mean the end of marriage itself.[375]

But the 'state' concept of marriage is slowly becoming different from the traditional. The question must therefore be asked whether the Church or churches can continue to go along with such developments. For example, can it be accepted that a promise taken in the face of a congregation 'till death us do part' means 'until one or both of us thinks the marriage has broken down'? Certainly, churches other than the Roman Catholic have traditionally accepted divorce on the limited grounds of adultery and desertion, for which an argument can be made from the Bible. But can they honestly go beyond that? Doubts have been expressed. I would not want to see a system set up whereby the Church might in certain instances, and in a narrower compass than the State, declare that an 'ecclesiastical' marriage has come to an end. But what else might be done? I can think only of an arrangement whereby kirk sessions supervise and advise in the case where a party has and wishes to retain membership of a congregation, or where a divorced and re-married person wishes to join a fellowship.

On the other hand I think there is less problem with the 'irregular' marriage. Such associations could be fostered into permanency by properly caring church members. It should not be assumed that there is no 'marital' intention present merely because of the lack of a ceremony in church or registry office.

It would therefore be possible, and in my view desirable, that the divergence of interest between the State and the Church in the matter of marriage and divorce should become quite clear and marked. The change would have to occur within the Church, not necessarily by the establishing of separate procedures within Church and State, but by the churches being more deliberate and clear in their doctrinal position. Were there some assurance that church marriages were between persons properly instructed and genuine believers in the Christian faith, that might also help. This would involve a return to a system of church discipline which is of course open to abuse, but the pendulum seems to have swung rather far the other way at present. Marriage vows seem very frangible. There should be some greater assurance that those taken in church are meant, and will be kept.

6. Medical Practice

Religious questions arise in a number of areas of medical practice. Can a practitioner refuse to give treatment which offends against his religion? Can treatment be given to children in the face of religious objections by parents or guardians? Can treatment be given in the face of the patient's own religious objections? What about euthanasia? These are but types of the questions which arise.

By s.4 of the Abortion Act 1967 conscientious objection to the giving of treatment has been allowed for personnel in the case of abortion, unless the abortion is necessary to save life. The working of that section has, however, been criticised, as has the whole structure and functioning of the Act itself, but the fact remains that there is provision made here for a medical person, whether nurse or doctor, to refuse to participate in a medical procedure. Of course behind that there is the legalising of abortion itself. It should be noted that Scottish practice prior to the passing of the Act was not to prosecute in respect of an abortion carried out for medical reasons in a hospital. Whether that practice was preferable to the present legislation is moot.[376]

As noted, the general duty to save life overrides the conscience provision, but it is a question how far that duty extends to override the objections of parents and guardians to the medical treatment of their charges. Here it is clear that the interest of the child is paramount, as in other areas of the law, but it is unclear at what point parental objection is overset by the child's best interests. A possible solution would be for the local Children's Panel to seek court permission for an operation, or for the local authority to assume parental rights under the Social Work (Scotland) Act 1967 for the express purpose of giving such consent.

As far as patients who are themselves capable of giving or withholding consent to treatment is concerned, in theory treatment without consent is an assault in law, and for both civil and criminal reasons consents are normally obtained. However, urgency may come into the question. Awkwardness can only really arise where the consent of a patient is refused, as can happen on religious grounds. It would seem unlikely, however, that there would be a criminal prosecution for assault, as one would expect the patient's wishes would be ignored only in very serious cases, or possibly where the patient is mentally unbalanced. The patient would also have difficulty in succeeding in a civil action for damages. He has suffered no loss, and punitive damages are unlikely. In less serious cases it is doubtful whether a doctor would override a patient's wishes. To do so would involve both legal questions, and professional ethics. But the point at which the duty to save life overrides the duty to observe the wishes of the patient is difficult, and has not yet been fully considered in Scots Law.

What if the patient wishes to die and refuses treatment for that reason? It is accepted that in terminal cases doctors need not 'officiously and unnecessarily' prolong the agonies of the dying. Life support machines are turned off when 'brain death' has occurred,[377] and pneumonia is sometimes called the Old Man's Friend. In these instances permitting death seems natural and reasonable, and the duty to save life is modified.

But what of euthanasia? It would seem to be a logical progression from the last paragraph, but I am not satisfied that somewhere between allowing death and bringing about death a great chasm has not quietly been passed over and ignored.[378] I am also not satisfied that the law can draw the neat lines which the legalisation of euthanasia would require. I should therefore be content that euthanasia should continue to be but a cosmetic term for murder, and yet allow that there may be circumstances under which Crown Office (the prosecuting authority in Scotland) would not seek to bring a charge of murder in a 'mercy-killing'. It is noticeable that when such cases come to court the tendency is towards leniency.

7. Miscellaneous obsolete crimes

There were many attempts, mostly by the Scottish Parliament, to place the sanction of the secular law behind biblical prohibitions.[379] In some cases these statutes were later repealed: in others the statutes fell into desuetude, that is they were declared to be in disuse by a court, or have been so generally considered so to be that no prosecution would be brought under them. Desuetude is an interesting and valuable Scottish manifestation of good sense, taking the view that if it can be shown not only that a statute is 'inactive' and no longer obeyed, but that a contrary practice has developed, the community at large has repealed it, and courts should act on that basis.[380] (In passing I would comment that it is a pity the doctrine of desuetude does not apply to post-Union Acts, owing to the English principle that an Act remains vital until formally repealed).

Various statutes attempted to deal with sexual matters. By the Act 1567 c.14, fornication could be punished by imprisonment, the pillory, a fine and ducking, but in the case of *Donaldson* (8 July 1768)[381], that act was found in desuetude, and a fine of £10 imposed in terms of the later Act 1661 c.338. Simple adultery was punished at common law by the forfeiture of goods, while notour adultery (i.e. flagrant and persistent adultery) also produced such forfeiture by the Act 1551 c.12. However, the latter crime was declared capital by the Act 1563 c.10. Notour adultery was further defined by the Act 1581 c.7, in itself an indication that the 1563 Act was not being enforced because of its severity, opportunity being taken to convict on the lesser charge. The Fornication Act and the three Acts against adultery received their formal quietus from the Statute Law Revision (Scotland) Act 1906. Parts of the Incest Act 1567 c.15, incorporating Lev. 18,[382] and the Parricide Act 1594 c.30 remain with us, but other family law statutes have vanished. Of these the oddest was the Act anent Cursing and Beating of Parents, 1661 c.215, which imposed the death penalty for this offence, unless the child was insane, thus enacting Deut. 21: 18–21. That act had been inactive long before it was formally repealed by the 1964 Statute Law Revision (Scotland) Act.[383]

The Acts 1649 c.28, 1661 c.216 and 1695 c.14 authorised the imposing of the death penalty on any person who 'not being distracted in his wits, shall rail

THE INTERACTION OF RELIGION AND LAW

upon, or curse God, or any of the persons of the blessed Trinity'. The Act 1695 c.14 further extended that area of trespass to include the denial of the authority of Scripture. Prosecutions under the Acts were few, according to Hume, and the death penalty was rendered only once, when it was carried into effect in the case of Aitkenhead in 1697 under circumstances which do not reflect well on those involved.[384] The statutes were repealed by The Doctrine of the Trinity Act 1812, which gave relief from penalty to those who impugned a variety of doctrines, though the offence continued criminal. Additional regulation came in the Criminal Libel Act 1819, which was really directed towards questions of sedition, and unlawfully attempting to change and subvert the constitution of the country, including in the relationship of Church and State. The Leasing Making (Scotland) Act 1825 reduced the penalty for blasphemy to a fine, and thereafter the crime became obsolete.[385]

Spoken blasphemy is not now dealt with as a separate crime. Where necessary proceedings are taken as an ordinary charge of breach of the peace. The last prosecutions in Scotland for written blasphemy were in 1843,[386] and it is doubtful whether the Crown Office would bring such a charge, or the Scottish courts would permit a private prosecution. This is not to say a charge of obscene publication might not be relevant, but that is different from blasphemy. The Gay News trial of 1977–8 for blasphemy by publication of the poem about Christ on the Cross and the homosexual centurion could not occur north of the Border.[387]

Another area which has been freed from explicit legal intervention is the practice of witchcraft. The proscription of witchcraft dates back into Roman and biblical times, but it was only following the Bull of Innocent VIII, *Summis desiderentes affectibus* of 9 December 1484, appointing Heinrich Kramer and Jacob Sprenger as inquisitors of the phenomenon, that co-ordinated opposition to witchcraft got under way.[388]

Prior to the Scottish Reformation there does not seem to have been the same interest in the matter that there was on the Continent. Then the Act 1563 c.9 enacted the injunction of Exodus 22 : 18 'Thou shalt not suffer a witch to live.' Thereafter Scotland followed the normal pattern of the time, even the Crown contributing when in 1597 James VI published his *Daemonologie*.

The Witchcraft Act 1735 repealed the 1563 Act, and prohibited the prosecution of persons for witchcraft, sorcery, enchantment or conjuration, or for charging any other person with such offences and this made an end of a rather sorry chapter of Scottish jurisprudence.[389] However, the pretended use of witchcraft and similar arts for fortune-telling, the recovery of goods and similar practices remained an offence, and is now dealt with under the Fraudulent Mediums Act 1951.

The effect of the legislation is that the practice of witchcraft is not now a criminal offence, *per se*. This is not to say that the manifestation of some forms of its rituals and practices may not lead to prosecution under other ordinary laws of the land.

8. *Oaths*

The vitality of oath taking belies that we are living in the much vaunted pluralistic society. Or it may indicate either that we are fond of quaint traditional practices, or that people are very superstitious. Whatever the foundation, oaths are still prevalent, serving their original functions of imposing, subject to religious penalty, duties to obey, to serve, to act faithfully in the exercise of office or discharge of duties, and in marking ceremonially some transition in life.[390] Such oaths are largely now governed by the Promissory Oaths Act 1868 as amended. Most other oaths are connected with the administration of justice, and of these that of the witness is most interesting as he asserts the truth of what he is to say. Another peculiarly Scottish procedure is the 'oath on reference', where in a civil case a party may refer a question of fact to the oath of his opponent. The precise forms by which this is done vary by the circumstances in which it is required, but essentially it is an appeal from the more usual court procedures for the determination of fact to the conscience of the party involved.[391]

Oaths of witnesses, and the oath on reference, together with all other similar oaths affirming truth have a religious basis, and it may be noted that Green's *Encyclopedia of the Law of Scotland* suggests that:

'It is found that a witness giving his testimony on oath will tell the truth more exactly than if he were making a statement without such sanction.'[392]

On the other hand, more recently, in *Cuthbertson* v. *Patterson* 1968 S.L.T. (Sh. Ct.) 21, Sheriff I. A. Dickson noted that:

'. . . in the not too distant past, the certainty of perpetual condemnation to condign darkness (or worse) in perpetuity, was, to large numbers, an assured consequence of all swearing and so provided a real and strong deterring sanction. It is questionable whether such considerations loom so large in modern thought.'

It would seem elementary that oaths can be required only from persons holding a religious belief. That certainly was the older Scottish position, though interestingly it was not required that that belief should be Christian. Thus Alison states in words which go beyond their immediate context: 'All persons who believe in God and a future state are admissible, of whatever creed or religion they may be.'[393] The formalities used are such as the religion requires, if these are reasonably practicable. If they are not, then the individual may be required to affirm.

The development of affirmation was not first directed towards the person excluded from oath-taking by lack of religious belief. The problem attacked was the person whose religious belief was such that he could not in conscience take an oath under any circumstances. This was dealt with in one special case for England by the Quaker Oaths Act 1695. Parallel legislation for Scotland, and only then in criminal cases, did not come until the Justiciary Courts Act

1828. Thereafter other legislation broadened the scope of the permission to other groups and to other courts these Acts being consolidated by the Affirmations (Scotland) Act 1855. Atheists and agnostics were, however, still barred since their consciences could not be thought as strong as those who would affirm through religious conviction, and therefore atheists and agnostics had nothing wherewith to indicate the reliability of their word.

The opening of affirmation procedures (and therefore of the remaining public offices where an oath was required on entry) to atheists and agnostics came with the passing of the Oaths Act 1888. The break in the reliance on the religious sanction of an oath is attributable largely to the pressure exerted by Charles Bradlaugh and his associates. Using the English legislation permitting affirmation on grounds of conscience by Quakers and others, Bradlaugh, an atheist, attempted to enter Parliament by being elected to the House of Commons. He was refused opportunity to take the oath required of Members of that House, and a short series of interesting constitutional cases ensued on the powers and privileges of the House.[394] These need not detain us. Suffice it to say that, as a result of the publicity, Bradlaugh was successful in this object of one of his many campaigns. The law was altered and affirmation is now acceptable by an agnostic or atheist as an alternative to taking an oath.

The present law on oaths and affirmations is consolidated in the Oaths Act 1978 c.19, which by s.3 now permits use of the Scottish form of swearing oath with an uplifted hand throughout the U.K. That novelty apart the Act provides that an oath binds a person to whom it is administered, if it is administered in a form which he declares is binding on him (s.4(1), from s.1 Oaths Act 1838); and that the validity of an oath is not vitiated by the actual absence of religious belief in the person taking it (s.4(2), from s.3 of the Oaths Act 1888). By s.5 (formerly s.1 of the Oaths Act 1888) affirmation is permitted, and where permitted may be required. Section 6 (also from s.2 of the 1888 Act) prescribes the form of affirmation, and stipulates for the omission of 'any words of imprecation or calling to witness.' Naturally perjury after oath or affirmation is criminal, and that general proposition is backed up by the False Oaths (Scotland) Act 1933, another consolidating statute, though perjury and false swearing are also crimes at common law beyond the instances dealt with in that Act.

In such ways the oath procedure has been opened up, allowing account to be taken of all religious stances, but this now raises the question of the desirability of maintaining the religious oath as the normal procedure. If Sheriff Dickson's opinion cited above is correct then it would seem desirable to guard against the depreciation of religious ideas by the too easy taking of oaths. Where the principal function of the oath is ceremonial, as in the case of most promissory oaths, it would be quite possible to replace the religious element or omit it, without affecting the solemnity which is sought. Where the function of the oath is in 'guaranteeing' truth, there is also an element of ceremonial which is not integral to the words spoken. However, in such 'guaranteeing' procedures, the law has developed a second sanctioning system, that of the law of perjury, which is arguably more important nowadays than the religious sanction. That second sanction could well be made more explicit by being couched as a formal statement that the person acknowledges that from the outset he recognises that if he does not speak the truth he is exposed to the penalty for perjury.[395]

I consider that such changes in the normal procedures for oaths would make the whole more honest, and would help guard against the debasement of religious concepts. However, the oath should be retained as an option for those who would out of religious conviction wish to use such a procedure. The change would rather be in the normality of the practice. Affirmation, together with a warning where appropriate, would be the usual ceremony, and the oath the optional procedure, thus usefully inverting the present relationship of the two procedures.

9.   *Sunday Observance*

The Scottish Sunday is an institution which has gathered many tales, and it is therefore interesting to find that in many ways the present position is one of practice rather than law. The strict sabbatarianism of last century[396] has in the main been departed from, though Scotland has still not wholly adopted the 'Continental' Sunday, which is based upon a different religious tradition. Development has occurred as a social change, the old Scots Acts on the profanation of the Sabbath simply falling into desuetude (a concept explained above in dealing with miscellaneous crimes). The legislature has not replaced these Acts, nor has it itself taken any major initiative in the process.

The Scots Parliament before the Union passed fourteen Acts between 1503 and 1701 dealing with Sabbath Observance, and prohibiting and punishing such things as fishing, gaming and passing to a tavern or alehouse, trading and labouring if they were done on Sunday or in time of church services. The bulk of these Acts were held to be in desuetude by Lord Mackay in *Brown* v. *Magistrates of Edinburgh* 1931 S.L.T. 456.[397] Some had been repealed in part by the Statute Law Revision Act of 1906 and most of the remainder were also expressly repealed by the Statute Law Revision (Scotland) Acts 1964. But the operations of the Acts had been very erratic long before 1931. Hume for example notes that only one prosecution for profaning the Sabbath had occurred during the eighteenth century, and there the prosecution abandoned the case.[398] In the nineteenth century, despite the great argument and dispute over such matters as Sunday trains (1843–5) and the Sunday opening of Edinburgh Botanic Gardens in 1863 to say nothing of the more general arguments over Sunday, in the cases of *Bute* v. *More* (1870) 9 M. 186 and *Nicol* v. *M'Neil* (1877) 14 R. (J.) 47, it was decided that the authorities seeking to enforce the Sunday Acts had failed properly to bring the prosecutions. The attempted summary procedure was inappropriate, but one cannot imagine the more serious procedure on indictment being used in such a connection.

Of the fourteen Acts there now remains only parts of three: the Sunday Act 1579, prohibiting markets or fairs on Sunday; the Sunday Trading Act 1661 to the same effect; and those parts of the Confession in the Confession of Faith Ratification Act 1690 which relate to the keeping of Sunday. In addition to these substantive provisions, the Justices of the Peace Act 1661 includes the enforcement of the Sabbath Acts as part of the responsibilities of the Justices. It is doubtful, however, whether these remnants are of any legal importance, as following *Bute* and *Nicol* there is no enforcement machinery for them. Indeed Gordon's *Criminal Law* (1967, 1978) does not deal with sabbath breaking at all.

It is fair to say, however, that many of the areas formerly dealt with as sabbath profanation have been taken up and dealt with in their own right as matters deserving of regulation apart from their religious connotation. Fishing, labouring and other forms of work, gaming and drinking are all now pretty comprehensively regulated for reasons other than their impact on Sunday. In addition there remain a variety of contexts within which Sunday is important in legal processes, but these are largely technical and add nothing to the general picture.

The other area of control in relation to Sunday is achieved through the planning and licensing activities of local authorities, and local byelaws. Although such licensing and other legal controls are open to the criticism that they permit a lack of uniformity in the application of the law general, they have the inestimable advantage of allowing local rules to govern local matters in accordance with local views and attitudes. In the matter of Sunday this seems eminently sensible as even within the small territorial area of Scotland there are wide variations in community expectations.[399]

The future of Sunday as a special day, protected for religious reasons, is uncertain. There are few protections at present, and such as exist seem slender. Sunday is rather in law being assimilated to the general holiday, a weekly day of rest without reference to its religious origin. In marked contrast to last century, there is not the keen interest and controversy surrounding the matter, and even the churches themselves are muted on the matter. Certainly they have indicated that Sunday should be something special for the Christian, but they are unwilling to argue for a legal backing for their minority interest, and indeed are divided as to the meaning of 'special' for their own members.[400]

On the other hand it does seem that the seven day week corresponds to something innate in man, for its prevalence is not otherwise explicable.[401] It is convenient therefore that if there is to be a day of rest, which is socially desirable apart from any religious element, that the bulk of the population should have a common day. In *McGowan* v. *State of Maryland* (1961) 366 U.S. 420, 6 L. Ed. 2d 393, there was an attempt to have the Maryland Sunday Closing Laws declared unconstitutional as being contrary to the First Amendment to the U.S. Constitution. Chief Justice Warren said:

'Moreover it is common knowledge that the first day of the week has come to have special significance as a rest day in this country. People of all religions and of no religion regard Sunday as a time for family activity, for visiting friends and relatives, for late-sleeping, for passive and active entertainments, for dining out and the like . . . Sunday is a day apart from all others. The cause is irrelevant; the fact exists. It would seem unrealistic for enforcement purposes, and perhaps detrimental to the general welfare to require a State to choose a common day-of-rest other than that which most persons would select of their own accord.'[402]

Although the Chief Justice was speaking within another jurisdiction, and with a different constitutional structure, the fundamental point seems applicable to Scotland too. Sunday is now the general day of rest, whether for religious reasons or not, though its origin is clearly religious. In this area it would be best were the law to lag behind and be formed by public opinion and attitudes—not the strident views of either wing of opinion, (or of incomers impatient with a culture they do not share), either arguing for tightening or relaxing the law—but in conformity with established patterns of behaviour.

One final point : it may be argued that Scotland is trailing far behind England in this matter.[403] That is not the case. The problem which England has is that the laws on Sunday, like the rest of English law, do not fall into desuetude. This peculiar short-sighted arrogance of the English Parliament has been carried over into the activities of the Union Parliament, and the result has been that there are a number of English laws on Sunday which have to be dealt with for there to be change south of the Border. But there are few post-Union Acts which relate to Scotland, and those that exist are directed to specialised interests. The Scottish Acts on the other hand bow to public opinion, as do the bye-laws and licensing activities of local authorities, laying open the possibility of gradual change as the law alters to reflect the expectations of the citizens.

10. *Religious Discrimination*

Article V of the U.N. Draft Convention on the Elimination of All Forms of Religious Intolerance 1967 (U.N. Doc. E/4387 (1967)) insists on the right of the individual to enjoy and to exercise political, civic, economic, social and cultural rights without discrimination on the grounds of religion or belief. Article 14 of the European Convention on Human Rights[404] similarly binds the States party to that convention to secure to persons within their several jurisdictions, the rights set out in that convention, without discrimination based upon religion. Nonetheless, while as a general principle the Law of Scotland conforms to these statements, there are areas within which the law discriminates, and permits discrimination on the basis of religion.

The most obvious example of such discrimination is the requirement that the Sovereign shall be Protestant,[405] but other examples exist. While only recently was the bar on a Roman Catholic becoming Lord Chancellor lifted, and most other disabilities have been removed from Roman Catholics,[406] an adherent of that denomination would not be acceptable as Lord High Commissioner to the General Assembly of the Church of Scotland.[407] There is no requirement however, that the Commissioner be himself a member of the Auld Kirk. A further example of discrimination is the disqualification of ministers of the Church of Scotland, clergy of the Church of England, and Roman Catholic priests from sitting in the House of Commons, although ministers of other denominations are not so disqualified.[408] Again there are some discriminations operative within education—for example the requirement of approval of staff in denominational schools by the appropriate church in terms of s.21(2) of the Education (Scotland) Act 1962.

These are examples of precise discrimination, which may or may not be justified, but the question which must now arise is whether a general anti-religious discrimination statute should be introduced. We have the Race Relations Act 1976 (which usefully develops its predecessors of 1965 and 1968), prohibiting discrimination based on colour, race, nationality or ethnic or national origin in many areas of life. We have also the Sex Discrimination Act of 1975, and Commissions to oversee the operation of both statutes. Would these not be useful models for a religious discrimination law? Arguments analogous to those for the existing statutes can be constructed, and proponents can also point to anti-discrimination legislation in Northern Ireland.

However, my own feeling is that it would be very difficult to operate such a law, its application being to such a potentially contentious area. What is religion, or religious belief? At present there is insufficient evidence that a general problem exists. Until there is such evidence, the law should not be brought in. It would be the wrong instrument for the present state of the problem. We have some laws protective of religious belief,[409] and that is all that is necessary. The introduction of anti-discrimination legislation, which *ex natura* is an active, social engineering tool, would aggravate a problem which seems quiescent and perhaps moribund.

Finally let me try to draw the disparate elements of the foregoing topics together. They were arranged so as first to deal with subjects where there was a large element of institutional regulation, and then to move through to matters more affecting individual behaviour. In the order also there may be detected a departure from a common theological belief and an increase in the importance of individual conscience together with a greater concentration upon the activities of the individual. It is this aspect which explains why the treatment of Sunday Observance appears late. While that topic was once considered to be of general institutional importance it is now one of individual conscience. It is a classic example of how the main emphasis of a law can shift from the compelling of behaviour to making room and opportunity for the individual to behave as his conscience dictates or indicates.

Of course the whole law and history of Church and State is in a sense a matter of conscience, and could have been tackled expressly from that viewpoint. But Law is by its nature concerned with overt acts rather than beliefs, and prefers to deal with general propositions rather than to construct a whole mass of special instances which amount to a negation of law. It is therefore reluctant to make conscience an avowed basis either of rules, or of exemption from the normal operation of rules. There are times when that reluctance has to be overcome, but so far as possible such exceptions are well-defined and clearly limited in their compass. Some of the instances have been dealt with above, and there are other special rules such as those allowing Sikhs not to wear motor-cycle helmets, the special rules for the Kosher or Moslem slaughtering of animals, and the provision for Christian Science Nursing Homes.[410] On the other hand, where the exceptions can not be so clearly prescribed it appears that, no matter how clearly desirable, the application of a conscience provision can be difficult in individual cases. The history of conscientious objection to military service,[411] and to membership of a trade union[412] illustrate that difficulty. Putting this another way, the law is uncomfortable when it is required to take account of the requirements of conscience where those requirements can not be generalised, readily and precisely formulated, or clearly proved to apply in given instances. If one scrutinises the law, it appears that in many areas of behaviour, of which Sunday Observance is but one, private judgement is now permitted to an extent that did not formerly obtain. It is therefore all the more important that that private judgement should be made on the basis of an informed conscience.

It follows that the rôle of religion, and of religious institutions, is as important as it has ever been. Law is a neutral force, which can be used to compel behaviour, but that behaviour may not be good if it lacks the moral element of choice. Nowadays the law permits a greater variety of behaviour than it did previously but while that freedom is to be welcomed it must also be protected against those who would diminish it for the 'good' of the individual as they perceive it, whether their perceptions be based on a religious or atheistic theory of society. This is not to say that where morality can exist, the law should not enter. Other factors, such as the stability of society and the protection of the weak, require that law should exist in order to bring about behaviour which ideally would result from moral conviction alone, and to provide the detail of moral generalities. But these are secondary justifications. Unless the ethos of the community, the common belief as to what is right, underpins the dictates of the law, the law will degenerate into oppression. Obedience to law really ought to be almost accidental, and for society to be healthy people must do things because they think they are right rather than because of a fear of punishment. Where this is the case it is possible for there to be much legal freedom, and yet for common practice to approach uniformity in its morality. This can occur where religious institutions are functioning truly according to their commissions, thereby providing the basis on which the private judgement of individuals on matters of behaviour is arrived at by an informed conscience. In short, the churches and other religious groupings could maintain the ethos of our community paradoxically by withdrawing from their interference in legal and political matters, and concentrating upon the task they tell us they were set in the first place.[413]

CHAPTER VIII
Conclusion

Several considerations require that the conclusion of any work on the law relating to Church and State be tentative. Firstly it is of the nature of the subject that this should be so, for religion relates to the inward workings of heart and conscience: law is concerned with external activity. Secondly, the law in this area is partly formulated and modified by the prevailing political theory of the time. Sometimes the law is adapted to accord with a theory, and sometimes the theory is produced to justify the law, or desired changes. In Church and State in Scotland there is much truth in the observation of Charles McIlwain that:

'Political doctrines have usually been put forward not in their own interest, but to bolster up some cause'.[414]

The earlier chapters show that in the course of the years many formulae have been put forward with the aim of securing desired ends rather than on the grounds of their compelling logic.

A third reason for uncertainty in framing a conclusion is that the attitudes of any writer must affect his reading of the history, present facts and likely developments. Although a degree of detachment is possible and desirable, complete detachment in this area of law itself imports a bias. Fourthly, regard must be had to theological uncertainties, to the probable institutional development of the churches, and to the changing attitudes to religion found within society. These elements must affect this chapter, but in a sense the reader may make his own adjustments for them, according to his own opinions.

The last factor of uncertainty can not be adjusted for. We are living in and facing a 'post christian' age, an unprecedented circumstance. Society is not pagan. It has been influenced and to a degree formed by christian attitudes and beliefs and has passed on. Our legal history provides no parallels or analogues for the problems of Church and State in these conditions. In the past changes have occurred between varieties of religious faith. That is not the present pattern. There is great diversity among prevalent faiths, and in 'Christianity'. There is an even greater amount of acknowledged agnosticism. Prognostication is therefore difficult.

General

It seems inevitable that there will be further change in the Law of Scotland on Church and State. The decline of institutional Christianity, the polarisation of divergences within the denominations, the spread of the smaller and more cohesive churches, and the trend towards individualism and 'liberty' in civil life, in short the emergence of the so called 'secular society', will make that change and development necessary. Such development will affect the different

6

strands of the law in different ways. I have made some particular comments earlier; others would be appropriate in a more polemical work. Here only some general points can be made.

At a time when obedience to law is being discussed, and the nature of associations and societies within society is being reconsidered Scottish Church history may illustrate principles in action. For example the rise of modern trade unionism and the debate about its powers and immunities have strong echoes of the Disruption.

A cardinal difficulty facing government in its relations with a church or denomination is deciding the nature of the entity which it confronts. Only within the last seventy years has it come to be fully accepted in law that associations within society may have a life of their own, and be capable of growth, development, change and decline. It is only within relatively recent legal theory that there has been room for the concept of a self-generating and self-sustaining association which the law does not create but must recognise and come to terms with. The positions of the Disruption decisions were the exaggerated results of the application of a monolithic theory of sovereignty. Men analysed the facts of these disputes in accordance with an explanation of law and society which attractively explained a simple theoretical model, but that model was not a sufficiently accurate representation of life. The analysis based on sovereignty did not adequately take into consideration either the part played by allegiance to religious ideas and principles in men's minds, or people's willingness to disobey or escape from unwelcome law. Such questions go beyond religion today—one remembers the struggle about trade union registration and the Industrial Relations Act 1971—but they also affect the future of the churches.

The Church of Scotland

The Church of Scotland could present special problems, one of which is its statutory 'establishment'. The fading of the authority and position of the Church of Scotland in the life of Scotland, coupled with my own unhappiness about monolithic theory, explain why the preceding pages have not sought to define the 'establishment' of the Church of Scotland, or to deduce any special rules, concession or principles of law from the position of the Church as laid down in statute. Such definition or deduction can be perilous. To read into our law as Professor Hood Phillips did, the proposition that 'if the Church is established by statute, its rule-making authority must be a delegated power'[415] is to move from theory to practice in a way which could distort the developing reality. While there is much to be said for using the existing law to restrain undue dilution of the Church's principles, I would be loathe to assert the supremacy of law in a way which might lead either to the Church's subjection once more to the State, or to the final ossification of the life which remains in the present structure. The constitutional position of the Church of Scotland can be analysed as has been done to a degree in these pages,[416] but we must be careful to preserve in our formulations the freedom which has been achieved to date. To talk of 'establishment' is to use a term which in other jurisdictions has connotations which we would not welcome. The most that is useful is expressed in the Report of the Group on Church, Community and State, Appendix One to the Report on *Anglican–Presbyterian Conversations*, 1966:

> 'The fundamental essence of 'establishment' consists simply in the recognition by the State of some particular religious body as the 'State Church', that is, as the body to which the State looks to act for it in matters of religion, and which it expects to consecrate great moments of national life by liturgical or official ministrations.'[417]

'Establishment' should mean no more. But even the existing 'establishment' may need review.

As has been seen, the end result of the Disruption was a revision of the relations of Church and State, and a concession of freedom to the Church of Scotland. That freedom has also been adopted into the constitutions of most of the principal non-established denominations. But one may now ask whether the present law may not go too far.

If the possible doubts about the constitutionality of the 1921 Church of Scotland Act, or those about the alteration of the status of the Westminster Confession are discounted, then it may be accepted that the relationship of the Church of Scotland with the State is satisfactory from the Church's point of view. The Church has a greater degree of freedom in matters of internal self-government and in terms of constitutional flexibility than it has ever had in its previous history.

But while this freedom and independence from State control is to be welcomed, there are dangers that problems will develop which the State may have to deal with and settle. The Church is a society capable of development and modification—formulating, re-formulating and discarding doctrinal expressions. I would not deny that the Church must be free in this way. But present freedom may be either too unchecked or abused. One may question whether the Church of Scotland preserves its identity with that Church with which the State dealt in earlier years, if there is great divergence (as opposed to development) from earlier doctrinal positions.

The problem of settling what matters fall within the substance of the Faith shows some of this difficulty. It is to be regretted that there is an unwillingness on the part of the Church clearly to state the exact boundaries of doctrinal freedom. Having regard to the trend of opinion within the Church, and in modern theology, one may question whether the Church is not in danger of becoming doctrinally amorphous, despite the affirmations of the First of the Articles Declaratory of the Constitution of the Church of Scotland in Matters Spiritual.[418] The position will shortly be reached, if we are not yet there, in which the wide divergences of doctrine amongst ministers and office-bearers will raise the question whether the Church of Scotland has any title to its asserted position as National Church. Doctrinal homogeneity is essential for the Church. A claim to be 'national' merely based upon numerical membership is not adequately grounded. It may therefore be asked whether the present special position of the Church of Scotland ought to be continued. This problem will be accentuated if, as is possible, there is a disruption of the Church of Scotland over the question of the status of the Westminster Confession. Alternatively this problem may emerge in the future as the strains caused by the increasing degree of centralisation, supervision and bureaucratisation act on an institutional structure in which the basic beliefs of congregations and members are not adequately shared.

A significant secession would cast grave doubt on the propriety of continuing the present constitutional arrangements. A secession would doubtless cause a further chapter of legal difficulties, justice requiring Commissions to divide property and funds between the parties. Alternatively perhaps the whole Church of Scotland should be dissolved in anticipation so that its present constituent elements might re-group in more coherent but smaller denominations.

A further disruption of the Church, or any accentuation of its present indeterminacy of doctrine therefore raises the whole question of the National Church, and would require a revision of the statutory basis of the Church's present position. In view of the different claims of denominations, and of the spread of different religions it might be that the solution found would be an abandonment of the concept of the National Church. This would be regrettable. It would, however, be the logical outcome of present trends.

The Non-Established Churches

The relationship between the non-established churches and the State is not satisfactory. In the first place there is no machinery for determining what constitutes a church, a congregation or a denomination. As observed by Sir John Foster,[419] there are tax advantages in being classified as a church, or a body for religious purposes, but the basis of classification is not clear. In the area of marriage uncertainty exists as to the position of some 'churches' and their ceremonies. Even if a denomination is accepted as being a society, the limits of its 'jurisdiction' over its members, and the extent of any right of recourse to the civil courts available to them have not been settled. In the propagation of beliefs peculiar to any given body, problems can arise in the areas of education and broadcasting. All these difficulties exist without taking under consideration the more arcane 'religions': the divisions of 'Christianity' themselves have not been fully or properly dealt with by the law.

Secondly, the law regarding the religious association and its property is somewhat out of step with the freedom of thought of much modern theology. The 'original principles' test remains basic to this branch of the law. This means that there is a presumption against a church being an organism formulating and developing doctrine. This would seem unimportant as the

CONCLUSION   151

affirmation of truth is the function of a church, but modern fashions require as part of this process of development that propositions formerly presented as truth be discarded as timebounded, unbelievable, or otherwise incongruous with enlightened modern thought. It is possible to avoid the difficulties of the 'original principles' test by Declaratory Act, or by provision for development in the titles to property, but this can be awkward. New churches and denominations, which normally come into being to stand against the errors, heresies and infidelities of existing denominations, wish to affirm truths, not to grant themselves flexibility; and if a body wishes to bind itself restrictively, that 'is the first privilege of such a body'.[420]

It is difficult to see, however, how the law might be improved upon. The whole concept of the Law of Trusts and Succession, which is the area of law most concerned with the realm of religious property, is directed towards the performance of the wishes of the person constituting the trust. It would be unjust to make it easier for pressure groups within a denomination to change the basic tenets of the denomination and remove property which was originally devoted to other ends, even if they attain a numerical majority.[421] I am tempted to suggest that if these 'reformers' have the courage of their convictions they will not hesitate to establish themselves as a new denomination, finding their own property without seeking as it were to 'take over' (not to say misappropriate) the assets of another denomination.

Other Problems

Within those areas of general law in which there is a religious element more uncertainty exists. The former position in which a single view of Christianity dominated has now long been departed from and in any event that dominance was never absolute. Whether it is proper to seek to maintain any specifically Christian legislation in a situation in which most of the population has little or no interest in Christianity—bar some magical rite of baptism and the social function of wedding and funeral—is unclear. Certainly one cannot lay down legal propositions which will hold good for all time, but some comments may be made.

First, some legal provisions of hallowed lineage are coming under scrutiny, and it has been suggested that in some the justification for the retaining of ancient provisions is less compelling than it was. Should Prince Charles have the option of marrying a Catholic, without legal penalty? Should there be a legal impediment to his conversion from Protestantism to that church? These are matters which are bound up with history, and, to an extent, with the different relationship between the sovereign and the established Church in South Britain. But it may be observed that, within the Scottish context, there seems to be no logical reason for the continuation of the religious provisions of the Act of Settlement. The obligations of the Crown to the Church of Scotland could be discharged by a person of either 'faith' or of none, and, in that respect, were there any cogent fears, an arrangement could be made for their discharge through some other agency, as has recently been provided for if the office of Lord Chancellor is held by a Roman Catholic.[422] Of course there would be all sorts of other civil and political results of such a development. For example, it would be inappropriate for ministers of the Church of Scotland to be appointed as Chaplains to the King or Queen, which would probably distress some. Such a development would surely offend a section of the Protestant community, not to put too fine a point on the matter. I would indeed hope that such a development does not become necessary, but the fact is that the 'Catholic bar' does offend citizens of the Roman Catholic persuasion, and their voice is getting stronger as that of Protestantism diminishes in authority.

Second, it may surprise some that I have made so little reference to international standards established by treaties and other international agreements which, they would argue, are now formative of legal principle. Such international agreement may be held to be evidence of the minimum standards which a humanitarian legal system ought to adopt, without referring such matters back (or through) to a religious base. However, so to argue is to ignore history, and the extreme slowness with which change occurs in the bases which ground a nation's expectation as to the content of its Law. It is neat, orderly, and quite out of touch with reality. I did endeavour to make such reference to appropriate international agreements in my doctoral thesis,[423] but found that in the main these agreements do not contribute to the Law in Scotland, and their prescriptions are mostly met. Indeed, *per contra*, one might rather argue that religion is a very contentious area, and international agreements are adopted only where existing practices and laws make the agreement redundant. Where there may be problems, the agreement is shelved. Thus it is noteworthy that the draft International Covenant on the Elimination of All Forms of Religious Intolerance (E/4387, (1967)) is the only major human rights convention which has failed to be adopted, even in the weakened and attenuated forms of the United Nations covenants. Recent history indicates why this is so.

But what if there should be a demand that the tide of secularism be rolled back by the use of the instrument of Law? Should the Law not lead, either in revival or in reform?

It would be unwise to seek to stem the decline of institutional Christianity, however it has been known in this country, by the re-imposition of legal control in the areas of inter-action discussed in the preceding pages. A country which is predominantly of a single religious faith will naturally reflect the tenets of that faith within its legislation. A people of indeterminate religious belief will not possess that willingness to obey legislation which reflects a single religious viewpoint which is needed for the satisfactory operation of the legal system. The present trend in this country is towards diversity of religion and an emphasis upon the liberty of the individual, which leads me to suppose that the doctrines of 'individual freedom' will lead to a lessening of the rôle played by religion either in forming or in undergirding legislation. In a sense this is to be

CONCLUSION

153

welcomed, for one reading of the history of the Disruption period shows the difficulties which can be brought into being by the imposition of particular religious ideas contrary to the wishes of a large section of the population. I would hope that a similar mistake by imposing either religious or atheistic based law, will not be made in the future. On the other hand it must be recognised that there are limits to freedom and that a degree of discipline is necessary if society is to continue in its present form. In that our society was formed on a basis of principles taught in the Christian religion it is likely that for a considerable period to come the basic assumptions and the major religious background of this country will remain 'Christian'. A failure on the part of the legislature to recognise this will be productive of dissatisfaction and conflict.

Running through all this there is also the question of conscience, some aspects of which have been noted at the end of chapter VII. The circumstances under which individuals can and should be exempted from the ordinary prescriptions of the law on grounds of conscience will continue to require consideration. Further study and case law is needed here, but it does seem that such exemption cannot be large scale and must be granted on objective grounds established before some sort of tribunal, and not on a subjective assessment by the individual, and his assertions. It does seem axiomatic that in such circumstances sticking to one's convictions is bound to act to one's detriment—that is the crux of conscience. Yet the law should seek not to occasion such instances needlessly, and, where possible, should provide relief through an objective and impartial inquiry.[424]

The attaining of a working balance between liberty and discipline, reflecting the changing views of religion and religious beliefs and lack of beliefs, will therefore be difficult. Our history seems to indicate that it will be a slow process in which different aspects of the problem will be dealt with in a pragmatic rather than a logical sequence.

APPENDIX I

A General Note on the Constitution of the Church of Scotland

[Note—for detail see Cox, and Church Legislation]

The Constitution of the Church of Scotland is composed of Church legislation and custom, civil statute and case law of both jurisdictions. As such it itself is an interesting study for the constitutional lawyer. Here it is intended merely to give an outline of the Church's constitution in order to help readers acquainted with a different system. *Mutatis mutandis* this outline generally applies to all the presbyterian churches mentioned in the text.

Like all Presbyterian churches, the Church of Scotland is conciliar in its form of government. This means that the government of the Church is exercised through a hierarchy of courts. The members of the courts of the church are all elders, certain of them being set apart by the Church as ministers. In government there is equality of rank among ministers and elders, though for obvious reasons in practice a differentiation is made between the two. Ministers and elders also rank equally *inter se*. The minister of a congregation is its teaching elder, and he is assisted in the pastoral and disciplinary oversight of the congregation by elders who are elected by the congregation and are ordained for life.

Depending on the origin of the congregation the temporal affairs of the congregation are administered by the Kirk Session (early churches) or by a Deacons' Court (former Free and United Free Churches). Most congregations have, however, adopted the Model Constitution of 1965, under which temporal affairs are dealt with by an elected Congregational Board one half of whose members are Elders. Where temporal affairs are dealt with by a body other than the Kirk Session, this body is not a Court of the Church.

The elders form the Kirk Session (the lowest Court of the Church) and it is responsible for the spiritual oversight and discipline of the congregation. The minister is Moderator (chairman) of this Court.

Each congregation is represented in the local Presbytery by its Minister and an elected elder. Retired ministers, theological professors and certain ministers in secular employment may sit in the Presbytery of their residence, and elders are elected by the Presbytery to balance these numbers. (Presbyteries were re-organised in the light of the local government boundary changes which took effect in 1975 under the Local Government (Scotland) Act 1973). The Presbytery supervises the congregations within its bounds, acts as an appellate body from their courts, and deals with such matters as are sent down to it by General Assembly.

Synods are formed of the membership of at least three Presbyteries (with the exception of the Presbyteries of Orkney, Shetland and England) plus a minister and an elder appointed by the adjacent Synods. The Synod, which meets twice a year, supervises its Presbyteries, and is the final appellate body in all cases other than matters of doctrine, worship, censure, licensing and union and readjustment of parishes and congregations. Such cases go to the General Assembly. [Note: the abolition of Synods, proposed by the 1978 Assembly, failed to be approved by the requisite majority of Presbyteries, (G.A. Reps. 1979, p. 13, Report of General Administration Committee)].

The General Assembly of the Church is the supreme Court of the Church and meets annually in May. It is composed of Commissioners appointed by each Presbytery. In practice every congregation sends its minister and nominates an elder every three or four years. The Commissioners also attend the Commission of Assembly in November and February, which deals with such business arising between Assemblies as the previous Assembly has devolved on it. The Assembly is the judicial and legislative body of the Church. It disposes of appeals from the lower councils, deals with petitions, receives Reports from the Assembly Committees and debates matters of interest. Legislatively the Assembly may enact laws for the good of the Church. Any matter which will affect the constitution of the Church in regard to doctrine, worship, government or discipline must receive the approval of a majority of Presbyteries under the Barrier Act 1697, (Cox, p. 385. Curiously the Barrier Act is not itself an unalterable constitutional document, Cox pp. 15–16). In matters of urgency the Assembly may pass an Interim Act, effective for one year, during which the Barrier Act procedure is gone through.

The Moderator (chairman) of the Presbytery, Synod and General Assembly is now by tradition a minister, elected by the court concerned. He holds office for one year only, and is without function other than as such a chairman, and as the representative of the court at official occasions. Such provision distinguishes our mode of government from episcopacy. The conciliar structure of government distinguishes it from congregationalism.

[In 1978 there were 987,196 enrolled members of the Church of Scotland. The total population of Scotland was 5,179,400 (3,552,283 adults) making the Church by far the largest denomination. (Source: Comparative Statistics, Report by General Administration Committee, G.A. Reps. 1979, p. 24)].

APPENDIX II

The Church of Scotland Act, 1921 (11 & 12 Geo. 5, c.29)

An Act to declare the lawfulness of certain Articles declaratory of the Constitution of the Church of Scotland in matters spiritual prepared with the authority of the General Assembly of the Church. —[28 July 1921.]

Whereas certain articles declaratory of the constitution of the Church of Scotland in matters spiritual have been prepared with the authority of the General Assembly of the Church, with a view to facilitate the union of other Churches with the Church of Scotland, which articles are set out in the Schedule to this Act, and together with any modifications of the said articles or additions thereto made in accordance therewith are hereinafter in this Act referred to as "the Declaratory Articles":

And whereas it is expedient that any doubts as to the lawfulness of the Declaratory Articles should be removed:

Be it therefore enacted by the King's most Excellent Majesty, by and with the advice and consent of the Lords Spiritual and Temporal, and Commons, in this present Parliament assembled, and by the authority of the same, as follows:—

Effect of Declaratory Articles

1. The Declaratory Articles are lawful articles, and the constitution of the Church of Scotland in matters spiritual is as therein set forth, and no limitation of the liberty, rights and powers in matters spiritual therein set forth shall be derived from any statute or law affecting the Church of Scotland in matters spiritual at present in force, it being hereby declared that in all questions of construction the Declaratory Articles shall prevail, and that all such statutes and laws shall be construed in conformity therewith and in subordination thereto, and all such statutes and laws in so far as they are inconsistent with the Declaratory Articles are hereby repealed and declared to be of no effect.

Other Churches not to be prejudiced

2. Nothing contained in this Act or in any other Act affecting the Church of Scotland shall prejudice the recognition of any other Church in Scotland as a Christian Church protected by law in the exercise of its spiritual functions.

Jurisdiction of civil courts

3. Subject to the recognition of the matters dealt with in the Declaratory Articles as matters spiritual, nothing in this Act contained shall affect or prejudice the jurisdiction of the civil courts in relation to any matter of a civil nature.

Citations and commencement

4. This Act may be cited as the Church of Scotland Act, 1921, and shall come into operation on such date as His Majesty may fix by Order of Council after the Declaratory Articles shall have been adopted by an Act of the General Assembly of the Church of Scotland with the consent of a majority of the Presbyteries of the Church.

SCHEDULE

Articles Declaratory of the Constitution of the Church of Scotland in Matters Spiritual

I. The Church of Scotland is part of the Holy Catholic or Universal Church; worshipping one God, Almighty, all-wise, and all-loving, in the Trinity of the Father, the Son, and the Holy Ghost, the same in substance, equal in power and glory; adoring the Father, infinite in Majesty, of whom are all things; confessing our Lord Jesus Christ, the Eternal Son, made very man for our salvation; glorying in His Cross and Resurrection, and owning obedience to Him as the Head over all things to His Church; trusting in the promised renewal and guidance of the Holy Spirit; proclaiming the forgiveness of sins and acceptance with God through faith in Christ, and the gift of Eternal life; and labouring for the advancement of the Kingdom of God throughout the world. The Church of Scotland adheres to the Scottish Reformation; receives the Word of God which is contained in the Scriptures of the Old and New Testaments as its supreme rule of faith and life; and avows the fundamental doctrines of the Catholic faith founded thereupon.

II. The principal subordinate standard of the Church of Scotland is the Westminster Confession of Faith approved by the General Assembly of 1647, containing the sum and substance of the Faith of the Reformed Church. Its government is Presbyterian, and is exercised through Kirk-sessions, Presbyteries, Provincial Synods, and General Assemblies. Its system and principles of worship, orders and discipline are in accordance with "The Directory for the Public Worship of God," "The Form of Presbyterial Church Government," and "The Form of Process," as these have been or may hereafter be interpreted or modified by Acts of the General Assembly or by consuetude.

III. This Church is in historical continuity with the Church of Scotland which was reformed in 1560, whose liberties were ratified in 1592, and for whose security provision was made in the Treaty of Union of 1707. The continuity and identity of the Church of Scotland are not prejudiced by the adoption of these Articles. As a national Church representative of the Christian Faith of the Scottish people it acknowledges its distinctive call and duty to bring the ordinances of religion to the people in every parish of Scotland through a territorial ministry.

IV. This Church, as part of the Universal Church wherein the Lord Jesus Christ has appointed a government in the hands of Church office-bearers, receives from Him, its Divine King and Head, and from Him alone, the right and power subject to no civil authority to legislate, and to adjudicate finally, in all matters of doctrine, worship, government, and discipline in the Church, including the right to determine all questions concerning membership and office in the Church, the constitution and membership of its Courts, and the mode of election of its office-bearers, and to define the boundaries of the spheres of labour of its ministers and other office-bearers. Recognition by civil authority of the separate and independent government and jurisdiction of this Church in matters spiritual, in whatever manner such recognition be expressed, does not in any way affect the character of this government and jurisdiction as derived from the Divine Head of the Church alone, or give to the civil authority any right of interference with the proceedings or judgments of the Church within the sphere of its spiritual government and jurisdiction.

V. This Church has the inherent right, free from interference by civil authority, but under the safeguards for deliberate action and legislation provided by the Church itself to frame or adopt its subordinate standards, to declare the sense in which it understands its Confession of Faith, to modify the forms of expression therein, or to formulate other doctrinal statements, and to define the relation thereto of its office-bearers and members, but always in agreement with the Word of God and the fundamental doctrines of the Christian Faith contained in the said Confession, of which agreement the Church shall be sole judge, and with due regard to liberty of opinion in points which do not enter into the substance of the Faith.

VI. This Church acknowledges the divine appointment and authority of the civil magistrate within his own sphere, and maintains its historic testimony to the duty of the nation acting in its corporate capacity to render homage to God, to acknowledge the Lord Jesus Christ to be King over the nations, to obey His laws, to reverence His ordinances, to honour His Church, and to promote in all appropriate ways the Kingdom of God. The Church and the State owe mutual duties to each other, and acting within their respective spheres may signally promote each other's welfare. The Church and the State have the right to determine each for itself all questions concerning the extent and the continuance of their mutual relations in the discharge of these duties and the obligations arising therefrom.

VII. The Church of Scotland, believing it to be the will of Christ that His disciples should be all one in the Father and in Him, that the world may believe that the Father has sent Him, recognises the obligation to seek and promote union with other Churches in which it finds the Word to be purely preached, the sacraments administered according to Christ's ordinance, and discipline rightly exercised; and it has the right to unite with any such Church without loss of its identity on terms which this Church finds to be consistent with these Articles.

VIII. The Church has the right to interpret these Articles, and, subject to the safeguards for deliberate action and legislation provided by the Church itself, to modify or add to them; but always consistently with the provisions of the first Article hereof, adherence to which, as interpreted by the Church, is essential to its continuity and corporate life. Any proposal for a modification of or addition to these Articles which may be approved of by the General Assembly shall, before it can be enacted by the Assembly, be transmitted by way of overture to Presbyteries in at least two immediately successive years. If the overture shall receive the approval, with or without suggested amendment, of two-thirds of the whole of the Presbyteries of the Church, the Assembly may revise the overture in the light of any suggestions by Presbyteries, and may transmit the overture when so revised to Presbyteries for their consent. If the overture as transmitted in its final form shall receive the consent of not less than two-thirds of the whole of the Presbyteries of the Church, the General Assembly may, if it deems it expedient, modify or add to these Articles in terms of the said overture. But if the overture as transmitted in its final form shall not receive the requisite consent, the same or a similar proposal shall not be again transmitted for the consent of Presbyteries until an interval of five years after the failure to obtain the requisite consent has been reported to the General Assembly.

IX. Subject to the provisions of the foregoing Articles and the powers of amendment therein contained, the Constitution of the Church of Scotland in matters spiritual is hereby anew ratified and confirmed by the Church.

[Note: the Act was brought into force on 28 June 1926 by The Church of Scotland Order in Council, 1926 (S.R. & O. 1926, No. 841).]

APPENDIX III

The Procurator's Opinion on Questions anent the Westminster Confession of Faith

At the meeting of the Sub-Committee of the Panel on Doctrine on Wednesday, 22nd October 1969, I was asked to consider the following three questions:—

Is it within the power of the General Assembly of the Church of Scotland:—

(1) to delete reference to the Westminster Confession of Faith as the principal subordinate standard of the Church of Scotland in Article II, and substitute therefor the third paragraph of the suggested new Preamble for use at Ordination and Induction which is set out on page 210 of the 1969 volume of the Reports to the General Assembly?

(2) to delete reference to "subordinate standards" in Article V?

(3) to approve of a new Preamble as set out on the said page of the Reports referred to in (1) *supra*?

All three questions in my opinion are concerned with matters spiritual and accordingly the proper approach is to consider whether, on a proper construction of the Articles Declaratory, the Church has power to do what is proposed. I say this in light of the terms of Section I of the Church of Scotland Act 1921 which declares that the said Declaratory Articles are lawful and that the matters set forth in them are matters spiritual. It goes on to declare that all statutes and laws affecting the Church of Scotland in matters spiritual, in so far as they are inconsistent with the Declaratory Articles, are repealed and are of no effect. It follows in my view, that it is idle to consider, for instance, the status accorded to the Westminster Confession of Faith in, for example, the Act of Union, if on a proper construction of the said Articles, the Church of Scotland is empowered to declare what that status is in relation to its belief. "Section I is a clear and unambiguous affirmation of the supremacy of the Articles in every conflict with existing laws or statutes touching the matters with which they deal." (*Ballantyne* v. *Presbytery of Wigtown*, 1936 SC 625 per Lord Justice Clerk Aitchison at page 654.)

(1) By Article IV the Church is given "power . . . to legislate and to adjudicate finally in all matters of doctrine . . ." In my opinion this article gives the Church a general power to declare the status to be accorded to the Westminster Confession of Faith as an expression of the doctrine to which it adheres.

The ambit of this general power is set out in Article V with particular relation to certain matters which include the subordinate standards of the Church. The said article empowers the Church, *inter alia*, "to declare the sense in which it understands its Confession of Faith . . . always in agreement with the Word of God and the fundamental doctrines of the Christian Faith contained in the said Confession, of which agreement the Church shall be the sole judge. . . ." The Confession of Faith referred to can only be the Westminster Confession of Faith because that is the only confession of faith referred to in the preceding articles.

The proposed alteration to Article II is to the effect that the Church acknowledges the Westminster Confession of Faith as a historic statement of its (the Church's) abiding faith. In so far as it only seeks to do that it is clearly doing something it is specifically empowered to do by Article V, namely to declare the sense in which it understands that confession. The matter however does not end there because the proposal entails the equation of the Westminster Confession with the Apostles' Creed, the Nicene Creed and the Scots Confession, and the consequent demotion of the Westminster Confession from its position as the principal subordinate standard of the Church of Scotland. Furthermore no specific reference is made in the Articles to the Apostles' Creed, the Nicene Creed or the Scots Confession. However, in addition to the power referred to in the preceding paragraph of this opinion Article V also empowers the Church ". . . to adopt its subordinate standards. . . ." The only "subordinate standard" specifically referred to is the Westminster Confession, referred to as the "principal" subordinate standard. In my opinion the use of the word "principal" in Article II read with the phrase "subordinate standards" (plural) in Article V is indicative of the recognition of the existence of one or more subsidiary subordinate standards in the expression of the doctrinal beliefs of the Church of Scotland, albeit these standards are not specified in the Articles Declaratory. It is now proposed to specify them, and by so doing as I see it to adopt them as subordinate standards at the same time maintaining the Westminster Confession as a Confession of Faith.

Provided that, in the judgment of the Church, the Apostles' Creed, the Nicene Creed, and the Scots Confession are not in disagreement with the Word of God, and the fundamental doctrines of the Christian Faith contained in the Westminster Confession, nor inconsistent with the first of the Articles Declaratory, I am of opinion that the Church of Scotland has power to alter the first sentence of Article II in the way proposed. This of course would involve a modification of the Articles, and therefore, as provided by Article VIII, Presbytery consent would have to be sought and received by means of the procedure set out in Article VIII before an Act of Assembly could be passed giving effect to the proposal.

(2) The deletion of the words "subordinate standards" in Article V would entail other alterations in that Article and no proposals for such alterations is before me. As I understand it however, the question on which my advice is really sought is whether some reference to subordinate standards as such has to be maintained in the Articles. The inherent powers claimed in the Articles and recognised by Act of Parliament are very wide indeed, and appear to have been

designed to give the Church not only wide powers with regard to matters spiritual but considerable room for manoeuvre in the exercise of these powers. This is exemplified particularly by the terms of Article V and the phrase in it "of which agreement the Church shall be sole judge." In my opinion there is nothing in the Articles which enjoins the Church for all time to subscribe to and recognise, subordinate standards as such, and therefore nothing sacrosanct about the use of the phrase "subordinate standards." The Word of God as it is contained in the Scriptures is the supreme rule of Faith and life. Any doctrinal statement made or recognised by the Church must be subordinate to that supreme rule no matter what that doctrinal statement may be called.

In the sense set out above I answer this question in the affirmative subject, of course to compliance with the provisions of Article VIII. That is the view I have reached on the question put and without specification of the modification proposed.

(3) Article IV gives the Church power . . . "to adjudicate finally" in matters which include "the right to determine all questions concerning membership and office in the Church . . . and the mode of election of its office-bearers." Article V gives it power to define the relationship of its office-bearers to the sense in which it understands its confession of faith and doctrinal statements which it has formulated subject to the provisos at the end of the Article to which I referred in the last paragraph of the answer to question (1). The powers sought do not appear to conflict with the provisos (in any event that is really a matter for the Church to decide), and I am of opinion that the said Articles empower the Church to introduce the proposed new Preamble.

Strictly speaking this of itself would not involve a modification of, or an addition to, the Articles and therefore the procedure enjoined by Article VIII would not require to be carried out. The association between the alterations to the articles and the new Preamble is so close however that I am of opinion that the same procedure should be followed with regard to both.

The opinion of,

W. R. GRIEVE

EDINBURGH,
12th November 1969.

[Note: the above Opinion was given as noted on proposals of the Panel on Doctrine as they stood in 1969. Subsequently the proposed alterations to the Preamble for Ordination and to the Declaratory Articles were somewhat modified, but not sufficiently to make the Opinion irrelevant].

Source: *Reports to the General Assembly of the Church of Scotland,* 1970, Report of the Panel on Doctrine, p. 171 at 180–2.

APPENDIX IV

Opinion secured by the National Church Association

The Westminster Confession of Faith Today

The Legal Position

The Church of Scotland is a confessional, as distinct from a credal, Church, and the proposal of the Panel on Doctrine, to replace the Westminster Confession by the Creeds, is contrary to law, for the following reasons—

(1) The proposal is contrary to the express enactments of the Parliaments of Scotland and the United Kingdom, which recognise and establish the Westminster Confession as the Confession of the Church of Scotland, these enactments being as follows—

(a) The Confession of Faith Ratification Act, 1690;
(b) The Protestant Religion and Presbyterian Church Act, 1706;
(c) The Union with England Act, 1707; and
(d) The Church of Scotland Act, 1921, and Declaratory Articles scheduled thereto.

(2) The Panel's proposal contravenes also the contractual Basis of Union on which the then Church of Scotland and the United Free Church united in 1929, and which expressly recognises the Westminster Confession, and does not refer to any Creed.

(3) The Panel's statement as to the place of Scripture contravenes Declaratory Article I, which provides that the Church of Scotland received the Word of God which is contained in the Scriptures of the Old and New Testaments as this supreme rule of faith and life.

(4) The Panel's proposed demotion of the Westminster Confession from being the principal subordinate standard of the Church is contrary to Article II.

(5) The Panel's proposals concerning the Scriptures and the Confession, and their introduction of the Creeds, involve a fundamental change in the identity of the Church, expressly preserved by Articles III, VII and VIII.

Incidentally, this question of the legality of altering the Confessional Church to a Credal Church has not been put to the Procurator, whose opinion, sent down to Presbyteries and Sessions with the Panel's 1970 proposals was given, not on these proposals, but on the more limited proposals of 1969.

(6) The Preamble, Questions and Formula, "though adding nothing to the material of the Church's constitution, are of the highest importance with reference thereto, because in a measure they summarise the main elements of that constitution (Cox edn. 5 p. 5). It follows therefore, that they must fall within the terms of the Articles and Confession. The Panel's proposed Preamble, Questions and Formula do not do so, and are accordingly incompetent.

(7) The Articles cannot be modified or added to by any redrafting of Preamble, Questions and Formula, but only by the procedure laid down in Article VIII, i.e. on approval by Presbyteries on a reference under the Barrier Act on three distinct occasions.

[Note: Subsequent to this Opinion the proposed alterations to the Preamble for Ordination and to the Declaratory Articles were somewhat modified, but not sufficiently to make the Opinion irrelevant.]

Notes on Text

1 G. Marshall, *Constitutional Theory*, 1971, pp. 13-34.

2 J. Highet, *The Churches in Scotland Today*, 1950, and *The Scottish Churches*, 1960, are general reviews of the recent scene. See also App. I.

3 Written between AD 412 and 426. On the sources of its concepts see E. Gilson's Introduction to the Fathers of the Church, Inc. translation of 1950; L. S. Mazzolani, *The Idea of the City in Roman Thought*, trans. S. O'Donnell 1962, pp. 242-79; and, J. N. Figgis, *The Political Aspects of St. Augustine's City of God*, 1921.

4 Ehler p. 11; *Enchiridion Symbolorum* 374 (reference is to paragraph).

5 Ehler, p. 12

6 Cf. his letter to the Bishop of Metz, 15th March 1081: Ehler pp. 30-9, Bettenson, pp. 104-10.

7 In his letter, *Sicut universitatis conditor*, 3rd November 1198: Ehler, p. 73; Bettenson, p. 112; Migne, *Patrologica Latina*, ccxiv, 377; *Enchiridion Symbolorum* 767.

8 Ehler pp. 90-2; Bettenson, pp. 115-16; *Enchiridion Symbolorum* 870-975.

9 J. Calvin, *Institutes of the Christian Religion*, ed. J. T. McNeill, trans. F. L. Battles, 1960, Book IV, Ch. XX. The Catholic attitude in these matters is summarised in J. Lecler, *The Two Sovereignties*, 1952. Cf. the statements in the *Syllabus of Errors* issued by Pius IX in 1864: Ehler, pp. 282-5; Bettenson, pp. 272-3; *Enchiridion Symbolorum* 2901-80.

10 Lecler, op. cit., is a useful short introduction.

11 J. N. Figgis, 'Erastus and Erastianism' in *The Divine Right of Kings*, 2nd ed. 1914 rep. 1965, p. 293.

12 Selden, Table Talk, Op. III 2067, quoted by Figgis, ibid. p. 291.

13 See C. Cross, *The Royal Supremacy in the Elizabethan Church*, 1969.

14 J. N. Figgis, *The Divine Right of Kings*, 1914 rep. 1965, p. 293. Cf. Figgis 'The Great Leviathan' in *Churches in the Modern State*, 1913, pp. 54-98.

15 Only in this century has the Church of England made proper progress to independence, with the notable hiccup of Parliament's rejection of a revised Prayer Book in 1927 and 1928 although it had been approved by a large majority in the National Assembly and in both Convocations. The existence of the National Assembly as a legislative body dated only from 1919, and the Church of England Assembly (Powers) Act. Recent development has been swift. The Synodical Government Measure 1969 (1969 No. 2) revised the Church's legislative machinery, and the Church of England (Worship and Doctrine) Measure 1974 (1974 No. 3, in force 1 September 1975) gave powers at last over doctrine. (See debates (1974-5) 354 H. L. Deb. 867-945; 901 H. C. Deb. 1567-1698). A new court system created by the Ecclesiastical Jurisdiction Measure 1963 (1963 No. 1) has also been working independent of the state. These measures are to be welcomed, in general. Constitutionally properly, but nevertheless regrettably, the appointment of bishops remains a matter for the Crown acting on the advice of the Prime Minister. The proposals of the Archbishops' Commission on *Church and State*, 1970 were not accepted, although a new procedure for advising the Prime Minister has been established to allow the will of the Church fuller expression (see (1975-6) 912 H. C. Deb., W. A. cols 612-4).

On doctrine see the Gorham judgements, (1849) 2 Rob. Ecc. 2, 163 E.R. 1221, I Cripps Church and Clergy Cases 233; (1850) 19 Q.B. 279; 19 C.P. 200; 19 Exch. 367. Cf. *Bishop* v. *Stone* (1808) 1 Hag. Con. 424, where a clergyman was sentenced to deprivation from office after criminal trial under The Ordination of Ministers Act 1571: *Banister* v. *Thompson* [1908] P. 362, *The King* v. *Dibdin* [1910] P. 57 and *Thompson* v. *Dibdin* [1912] A.C. 533. Cf. L. T. Dibdin, *Establishment in England*, 1918; C. Garbett, *Church and State in England*, 1950; *Church and State: The Report of the Archbishops' Commission*, 1970.

16 F. Wendel, *Calvin*, trans. P. Mairet 1963.

17 Civil effects were given to church decrees by such Acts as 1572 c. 14 (Excommunication) and 1593 c. 7 (Church tax), both repealed by s. 12 of the Scottish Episcopalians Act 1711.

18 8 *Works* 113.

19 See *McCollum* v. *Board of Education* (1948) 333 U.S. 203; *Zorach* v. *Clauson* (1952) 343 U.S. 306; *Engele* v. *Vitale* (1962) 370 U.S. 421; *Abington School District* v. *Schempp* (1963) 374 U.S. 203; *Lemon* v. *Kurtzman* (1971) 403 U.S. 602; *Tilton* v. *Richardson* (1971) 403 U.S. 672; *Levitt* v. *Committee for Public Education*, (1973) 413 U.S. 472; *Committee for Public Education* v. *Nyquist*, (1973) 413 U.S. 756.

20 See P. G. Kauper, 'The Constitutionality of Tax Exemptions for Religious Activities' in *The Wall between Church and State*, D. H. Oaks ed. 1963, pp. 95-116.

21 J. Locke, *Two Treatises of Government*, 1690; R. Williams, *The Bloudy Tenent, of Persecution for cause of Conscience*, 1644. On these and other writers see A. P. Stokes, *Church and State in the United States*, 1950, Vol. I, ch. III, pp. 65-257.

22 Art. VI of the Articles Declaratory of the Constitution of the Church of Scotland in Matters Spiritual, scheduled to the Church of Scotland Act 1921. See App. II.

23 Discussion of these lies outside the scope of the present enquiry. For them see Sir J. Connell, *The Law of Scotland regarding Tithes and the Stipends of Parochial Clergy*, 1815, 1830; W. Buchanan, *Treatise on the Law of Scotland on the subject of Teinds or Tithes*, 1862; J. M. Duncan, *The Parochial Ecclesiastical Law of Scotland*, ed. C. N. Johnston 1903; W. G. Black, *Parochial Ecclesiastical Law*, 4th ed. 1928 for post-1925 law; A. J. H. Gibson, *Stipend in the Church of Scotland*, 1960. Cf. nn. 90 and 207.

24 H. Geffken, *Church and State*, trans. F. Taylor 1877, is an early general survey; cf. A. R. Vidler, *The Church in an Age of Revolution*, 1961 rev. 1971.

25 See Vidler, pp. 11-21, 68-78, 146-56, 179-89; J. N. Figgis, 'Ultramontanism' in *Churches in the Modern State*, 1913, pp. 135-74; Lord Acton, 'Ultramontanism' in *Essays on Church and State*, ed. D. Woodruff 1952, pp. 37-85; H. J. Laski 'De Maistre and Bismark' in *Studies in the Problem of Sovereignty*, 1917 rep. 1968, pp. 211-66.

26 Cf. S. T. Coleridge, *On the Constitution of the Church and State*, 1st ed. 1830, and W. E. Gladstone, *The State in its Relations with the Church*, 1st ed. 1838. (Both books went through later editions, but were contributions first to the discussion in the pre-Disruption period). See also O. Chadwick, *The Victorian Church*, 2 vols. 1966 and 1970, and Vidler, op. cit.

27 Cf. J. Austin, *The Province of Jurisprudence Determined*, 1832 and E. Rubin, 'John Austin's Political Pamphlets 1824-1859' in *Perspectives in Jurisprudence*, E. Attwooll, ed., 1977; cf. also, J. Bentham, *Of Laws in General*, (H. L. A. Hart, ed. 1970). See also n. 67.

28 J. N. Figgis, *Churches in the Modern State*, 1913; H. J. Laski, *Studies in the Problem of Sovereignty*, 1917 rep. 1968.

29 G. Donaldson, *The Scottish Reformation*, 1960, p. 74 makes the point that the Scottish Reformation was essentially moderate and gradual.

Donaldson's book, W. C. Dickinson, *Scotland: From the Earliest Times to 1603*, 2nd ed. 1965, and G. S. Pryde, *Scotland: From 1603 to the Present Day*, 1962 (vols. I and II of *A New History of Scotland*), and P. Hume Brown, *History of Scotland*, are the principal general sources for this chapter.

30 Sir David Lindsay's *Ane Satyre of the Thrie Estaits* is the example most commonly referred to. W. C. Dickinson's Introduction to his edition of Knox's *History* reviews much of the material.

See also documents collected in Kidd, esp. nos. 334 and 341, as well as the S.S.C. and S.B.S.H. II pp. 98-116.

31 Thus Hamilton's Catechism of 1552, Kidd, no. 342. Cf. Statutes of the Provincial Council,

1549, S.S.C. pp. 84-134; of the General Provincial Council 1551, pp. 135-48, and of the General Provincial Council 1558-9, particularly pp. 163-90.

32 On 17th July 1525 the Scots Parliament prohibited the import of Lutheran books: Act 1525 c. 4, Kidd no. 335. In 1528 Patrick Hamilton was burned at St. Andrews.

33 Knox, *History* I pp. 60-97, (Book I).

34 Kidd, no. 344.

35 Ibid. no. 347. II S.B.S.H. pp. 180-4 includes the 'Concessions to the Scots' attached to the Treaty.

36 These points, together with Mary's failure to assent to the Acts led to the ratifying legislation of 1567.

37 See Knox, *History*, I, pp. 337-9 (Book II). *The Scots Confession* 1560, G. D. Henderson ed., and J. Bulloch, trans., 1960; App. VI to Dickinson's ed. of Knox's *History* (printed in the original *in gremio* of Book III).

38 Innes I pp. 12-17, II pp. 10-15.

39 Scots Confession arts. XVI and XVIII.

40 Ibid., art. XXIV.

41 Commonly called 'First' to distinguish it from Melville's *Book* of 1578. *The First Book of Discipline* is printed as App. VIII to Dickinson's ed. of Knox's *History*, (in the original it is placed at the end of Book III). J. K. Cameron, *The First Book of Discipline*, 1972 is an excellent modern edition and commentary based on the available texts. Cameron, pp. 3-14, reviews what is known of the drafting and revision of the *Book*.

42 See Ch. VII, 'Education', pp. 115-23.

43 Poor relief was later entrusted to the Church's administration. See Dunlop's *Parochial Law* or W. G. Black *Parochial Law other than Ecclesiastical*, 1893.

44 See *The First Book of Discipline*, introduction to the Fifth Head, and the Sixth Head 'Of the Rents and Patrimony of the Kirk'.

45 In 1561 the Privy Council passed an Act under which ministers were to receive thirds of the benefices (a tax originally payable to the Crown) for their support as a temporary measure: Donaldson op. cit. pp. 69-71; Knox *History*, app. IX; II S.B.S.H. pp. 192-3. This Act had to be reinforced in 1566, (II S.B.S.H. p. 197) and was replaced by the Act 1567 c. 7 *infra*.

46 George Buchanan's *De Iure Regni apud Scotos*, (Eng. trans. D.H. McNeil, 1963) was written partially to justify Mary's forced abdication, although the work was not published until 1579. The Abdication document is printed II S.B.S.H. pp. 200-3.

47 III S.B.S.H. p. 12; B.U.K. I, p. 220.

48 B.U.K. II, pp. 488 ff; III S.B.S.H. pp. 22-31.

49 See G. D. Henderson, *Presbyterianism*, 1954, and J. Kennedy, *Presbyterian Authority and Discipline*, 1960.

50 See the First Chapter of the *Book* on the Two Kingdoms.

51 III S.B.S.H. pp. 32-5; App. I to J. D. Douglas, *Light in the North*, 1964. This Confession was the basis of the National Covenant, 1638, and the Solemn League and Covenant, 1644.

52 III S.B.S.H. pp. 54-61.

53 For the whole of this period see J. D. Douglas, *Light in the North*, 1964.

54 J. N. Figgis, *The Divine Right of Kings*, 2nd ed. 1914, rep. 1965.

55 Act of Assembly 1647, August 27. Sess. 23. S.S.F.C.S pp. xxvii-xxviii. Important modifications relate to the claim of the Crown to call Assemblies of the Church stressing the right of the Kirk itself to meet irrespective of the will of the Civil Magistrate, and other points relating to their relations.

56 Lord Stair, one of the institutional writers in Scots Law, was active in the debates on the

Test Act, and secured that the standard of Protestantism in the Act was Scots Confession. This made the Test rather self-contradictory as the Scots Confession placed the Church in an independent position while the Test asserted Royal Supremacy. See A. J. G. Mackay, *Memoir of Sir James Dalrymple, First Viscount Stair*, 1873, pp.144-7.

57 See Innes I, p. 68, II, p. 39, noting that the Scots Confession's introduction into the Test Act was made easy because it had fallen into such oblivion after the introduction of the Westminster Confession.

58 Technically this is an Act of a Convention of Estates rather than a Parliament cf. the Acts of 1560.

59 A reference to the Coronation Oath Act 1567 c. 8.

60 Innes I, pp. 71-2, II, pp. 42-3 notes that the adoption of the Confession differs from that of the Protestant religion. The Scots Confession was ratified in 1560 as the Confession of the members of Parliament. The 1690 Act ratifies the Reformed faith, and binds the State to maintain the Confession. A distinction is present between the State and its members, and the Church and its members. This could be argued to be the beginning of modern concepts of Church and State in our legal system.

61 S. Mechie *The Office of Lord High Commissioner*, 1957, pp. 51-2.

62 See n. 172.

63 For this reason Acts 1700 c. 2, and 1702 c. 3 are Acts of Security for the Church.

64 Cf. The Maintenance of the Church of England Act 1706.

65 One effect of this language would seem to be that the provisions of the Ministers Act 1693 c. 38, allowing for the development of worship, (p. 20), vanished. The worship of the Church is made unalterable.

66 A. V. Dicey and R. S. Rait, *Thoughts on Union between England and Scotland*, 1920, pp. 282-3, cite also the Yule Vacance Act 1711 repealing the Act 1690 c. 23 which forbad the Scottish courts to abstain from sitting on Christmas day and some other English holidays, as also being seen as an attack on Presbyterianism.

67 J. Austin, *The Province of Jurisprudence Determined*, 1832. His *Lectures in Jurisprudence* were published posthumously by his wife along with a second edition of the *Province* in 1862. The best edition of the *Lectures* is by R. Campbell, 1885. Cf. also J. Bentham, *The Limits of Jurisprudence Defined*, ed. C. W. Everett, 1945. See also n. 27.

68 This is reflected in the titles of the two principal authorities on the period. Robert Buchanan, *The Ten Years' Conflict; being the History of the Disruption of the Church of Scotland*, new ed. 1856, 2 Vols., gives an account from the viewpoint of the Evangelical party. James Bryce, *Ten Years of the Church of Scotland from 1833 to 1843 with a Historical Retrospect from 1560*, 1850, 2 vols. gives the Moderate viewpoint. Both accounts must be treated with some caution, being partisan. G.I.T. Machin "The Disruption and British Politics" (1972) 51 Scot. Hist. Rev. 20, and his *Politics and the Churches in Great Britain*, 1977, pp. 112-47, places the affair in its political context; cf. Bulloch I.

69 I. D. L. Clark, 'From Protest to Reaction: The Moderate Regime in the Church of Scotland, 1752-1805', in N. T. Phillipson and R. Mitchison eds., *Scotland in the Age of Improvement*, 1970, pp. 200-24; Buchanan I, pp. 144-51; Cockburn II, pp. 289-91; Bulloch I, s.v. Moderates, but esp. pp. 45-81.

70 Dunlop, pp. 174-308; Erskine I. 5. 10-20; Stair II. 8. 27-35; More's Notes cxlii. Patronage was a matter of civil law and therefore amenable to the jurisdiction of the civil courts—see cases cited in above references, and below n. 96.

71 Buchanan I, pp. 151-61. Sir George MacKenzie, *Observations on the Acts of Parliament made by James I—Charles II*, 1686, Observation on Act 1592 c. 121 (c. 13 Record). Cf John Galt, *The Annals of the Parish*, 1st ed. 1821.

72 Erskine I. 5. 16.

73 Erskine I. 5. 13; Stair II. 8. 35; Dunlop p. 180.

74 *First Book of Discipline* 4. 1. 2; *Second Book of Discipline* c. 3. 4. The 1649 act is quoted Buchanan I, p. 103, and *Kinnoull* v. *Presbytery of Auchterarder* (the First Auchterarder case) (1838) 16 S. 661 at 674.

75 Only a few patronages had been bought out by the time the Act was repealed in 1711; First Auchterarder case (1838) 16 S. 661 at 680-1.

76 Act of Assembly 1715, IX. Buchanan I, 127-31; Innes I, p. 119.

77 Buchanan I, pp. 151 7; Burleigh, pp. 280-5. See also narration in the First Auchterarder case, (1838) 16 S. 661 at 682-6.

78 Macaulay, *Speeches*, 1866, II, p. 301, (as to the date of the Act see the note to Table of Statutes). Innes I, p. 120; II, p. 60. Cf. Bulloch I, pp. 259-60.

79 Bryce, *Hist. Ret.*, pp. 221-56; Buchanan I, pp. 173-89; Burleigh, pp. 309-33; Bulloch, I, pp. 180-219.

80 Chalmers *Lectures on the Establishment and Extension of National Churches*, delivered in London April 25th—May 12th 1838, Glasgow 1838. W. Hanna, *Memoirs of Thos. Chalmers*, 1852, vol. IV, p. 45; Bryce I, p. 12; Buchanan I, pp. 314-18.

81 Buchanan I, pp. 198-210. The operation of the Call at this time is explained in (1838) 16 S. 685-6.

82 Acts of Assembly 1833, pp. 45-6. Cockburn *Journals*, I, pp. 44-5, notes that the minority contained a majority of ministers. He suggests that had this motion been successful it would have deprived the anti-patronage movement of much of its strength. The defeat of the motion was therefore rather a defeat of the Moderates. Buchanan I, pp. 210-38.

83 Acts of Assembly 1833, p. 46. Bryce I, p. 15.

84 Cockburn, *Journals* II, p. 73 gives examples of the sort of objections offered under the Scotch Benefices Act 1843, which may reflect the objections under the 1833 Declaratory Act. These included bodily infirmity, weakness, stuttering, lameness, disagreeableness of manner, occasional exuberance of animal spirits, musical illiteracy and tone deafness. Cf. objections to the ordination of 'Jupiter' Carlyle in 1748, quoted by I. D. L. Clark, (n. 69 above) at p. 201 (n.3).

85 Act XII 1834, Overtures and Interim Act on Calls, and Regulations; Acts of Assembly 1834 pp. 31-36; Act IX, 1835. Bryce I, p. 21; Buchanan I, p. 255, note; Robertson *Auchterarder* I, app. 1; the First Aucherarder Case (1838) 16 S. 661 at 686; The *Free Church Case* [1904] C. 514 at 529.

86 Buchanan I, p. 258. This view of 'qualification' was roundly dismissed by Lord Brougham in the House of Lords in the First Auchterarder Case, (1839) McL. & Rob. 220 at 267-77, esp. pp. 272-3, *infra* at p. 32.

87 Bryce I, p. 25; Buchanan I, p. 246-68; Cockburn, *Journals* I, p. 160.

88 Buchanan I, pp. 268-9. His father, Charles Hope, the Lord President, was the first to express the restriction of the powers of the Church by reason of its establishing statutes in an Assembly debate in 1826 (Buchanan I, pp. 182-3).

89 Bryce I, pp. 18-20; Buchanan I, pp. 269-96.

90 Buchanan I, 229; N. Elliot *Teinds or Tithes and Procedure in the Court of Teinds in Scotland*, 1893, and *The Erection of Parishes Quoad Sacra*, 1876. Jurisdiction in the matter was given to the Court of Session by the Act 1706 c. 10, later modified by the Act 48 Geo. 3 c. 151, and by the Judicature Act 1825. Heritors were property owners of a certain value in the parish and were legally liable for the construction and maintenance of the parish and church buildings irrespective of their own beliefs.

91 Cf. W. Kennedy, *Annals of Aberdeen*, 1818, I, p. 387, on the origin of Gilcomston Chapel of Ease.

92 Buchanan I, pp. 230-1—a rather scathing attack, and p. 233. Chalmers was a major force in the established church response, and very active in the period 1834-40.

93 Ibid., p. 282-3.

94 After the Disruption Cockburn wrote (*Journals* II, pp. 40-1): 'On looking back at the whole matter, what I am chiefly sorry for is the Court of Session. The mere purity of the Judges it would be ludicrous to doubt. They all delivered what each, after due inquiry, honestly believed to be the law; but passion sometimes invades the Bench; and when it does it obstructs the discovery of truth as effectually as partiality can. The majority of the court may have been right at first, and to a certain extent; but they soon got rabid, inso much that there seemed to be no feeling except that winging Wild-churchmen. The apology was that they were provoked by their law being defied; but a Court has no right to be provoked.'
Cf. *Journals* II, p. 56, where in another connection Cocky refers to 'these inexorable revolutionists—the steady Tories, who will change nothing voluntarily, and thus compel everything to change itself forcibly.'

95 Acts of Assembly 1835 pp. 68-9. Buchanan I, pp. 348-9; First Auchterarder Case (1838) 16 S. 661 at 695; Robertson *Auchterarder* I, App. p. 31-2, where the minutes of Assembly are narrated in the minutes of the Auchterarder Presbytery, and ibid. I, p. 11 (Mr. Whigham's speech).

96 E.g. *Dunse* (1749) Mor. 9911: *Culross* (1751) Mor. 9951: *Dick* (1752) Mor. 9954: *Unst* (1795) Bell's Cases 169: *Moncriffe* (1735) Mor. 9909: *Strathbogie* v. *Forbes* (1776) Mor. App. Patronage 3: Cf. other cases sub nom. Patronage in Morison's Dictionary; (1838) 16 S. 714 note; Stair II. 8. 27-35; Dunlop, pp. 299-308.

97 Buchanan I, p. 353. (1838) 16 S. 661 at 696-7; Robertson, *Auchterarder* I app. II, p. 6 at p. 11.

98 Lord President Hope, Lord Justice-Clerk Boyle, Lords Gillies, Meadowbank, Mackenzie, Medwyn, Cuninghame and Corehouse formed the majority; Lords Fullerton, Moncreiff, Jeffrey, Cockburn and Glenlee the minority.

99 Robertson, *Auchterarder* II, p. 20. Buchanan I, p. 400 is a little inaccurate in the propositions stated.

100 Buchanan I, pp. 442-59.

101 Acts of Assembly 1839, p. 39. Buchanan I, pp. 451-2, 466.

102 The facts of the case are recited in the cited Reports, in Bryce I, pp. 73-80, and Buchanan II, pp. 1-17. It appears from the Claim of Right 1843, that there were four Lethendy cases, but only the given case is reported. The other cases were the interdicts against Assembly and Presbytery proceedings. The 1 D. report is abbreviated; Robertson's is full (the Lethendy Report).

103 Buchanan II, p. 8.

104 Ibid. II, p. 15. (1839) 1 D. 955 at 1020-3.

105 Ibid. II, p. 16.

106 Buchanan II, pp. 17-52, 125-207, 245-85, 298-306, 345-56. Bryce I, pp. 101-58, 195-216; II, pp. 53-80, 92-107, 120-70, 181-2, 203-4.
The cases listed 1-3 form the First Strathbogie case, No. 4 is the Second Strathbogie case and no. 6 the Third Strathbogie case, corresponding with usual treatment. The cases are known in the literature as either 'Marnoch' (the name of the parish) or 'Strathbogie' (the name of the presbytery).

107 The description of Edwards in Bryce I, p. 101 and Buchanan II, p. 18, are not readily recognisable as being of the same individual.

108 Buchanan II, pp. 48-9; Bryce I, 133-5.

109 Buchanan II, pp. 172-82.

110 Buchanan II, pp. 192-206; cf. Bryce II, p. 93.
111 Buchanan II, pp. 245-81; Bryce II, pp. 120-60.
112 Buchanan II, pp. 281-5; Bulloch I, p. 238.
113 Buchanan II, pp. 346-9; Bryce II, pp. 254-60.
114 (1840) 3 D. 282: (1843) 5 D. 909. Cockburn, *Journals* II p. 29 notes that fines of £5 were imposed for this breach.
115 This case was also published separately, but the Dunlop report is full. Buchanan II, pp. 313 23; Bryce II, pp. 236-53. The facts resemble the settlement at Glass, which did not give rise to court action; Bryce II, p. 253.
116 Buchanan II, pp. 315-18.
117 Bryce II, pp. 252-3.
118 *Gordon* v. *Trustees of the Widows' Fund,* (1836) 14 S. 509; *Irving* v. *Trustees of the Widows' Fund,* (1839) 16 S. 1024; *Panmure* v. *Sharpe,* (1839) 1 D. 840; *Bell* v. *Bell,* (1841) 3 D. 204.
119 Bryce II, pp. 288-9; cf. *Smith* v. *Presbytery of Abertarff,* (1842) 4 D. 1476, where interdict was granted by a majority on grounds of urgency and without fully argued opinion, against a Presbytery whose members included the minister of a parliamentary charge.
120 *Livingstone* is quoted for its effect on the progress of the conflict. It may be noted that in later proceedings ((1846) 8 D. 898; affirmed, (1849) 6 Bell 469) the civil courts refused to reduce the sentence of deposition passed by the Church courts in Livingstone's absence, in disregard of the interdict. The argument that the proceedings were vitiated *ipso facto* by the presence of 'ministers' whose rights to sit were based on the Chapel Act, (which by then had been declared *ultra vires* in the Stewarton case) was not valid. These persons had been acting *bona fide,* and had a colourable title to act. Cf. also *Campbell* v. *Presbytery of Kintyre,* (1843) 5 D. 657, where the acts of a 'proper' presbytery were held not vitiated by association with an Assembly and Commission partially composed of ministers of *quoad sacra* charges. The Presbytery had been instructed to proceed, but not how to proceed.
121 Bryce II, pp. 286-8.
122 Buchanan II, pp. 402-12. Opinions are published only in the Stewarton Report, not in 5 D.
123 These seceders had split on the question of the legality of the Burgess Oath. The Associate Synod considered it lawful; Burleigh pp. 281-2.
124 Stewarton Report p. 53; quoted Buchanan II, p. 407.
125 In so doing I follow Innes I, p. 182; II, p. 89.
126 Stewarton Report, p. 73.
127 (1843) 1 Bell 662 at 733-4.
128 *Cruickshank* v. *Gordon,* (1843) 5 D. at 964-5.
129 *Clark* v. *Stirling,* Lethendy Report, p. 217. See n. 102.
130 *Report of the Select Committee on Church Patronage in Scotland,* 1834, H.C. 512 p. iii-iv.
131 Buchanan I, pp. 472-3. On all governmental moves see G.I.T. Machin, "The Disruption in British Politics" (1972) 51 *Scot. Hist. Rev.,* pp. 20-51.
132 'A Letter to the Lord Chancellor, on the Claims of the Church of Scotland in regard to its Jurisdiction, and, on the propose Changes in its Polity,' by John Hope. Esq., Dean of Faculty. Edinburgh and London, 1839. The 'letter' is 290 pages long, plus 11 pages of appendices. However objective one may wish to be in discussing the *lex lata* and *lex ferenda,* after reading the letter, and reviewing the other acts of John Hope, one is left with the feeling that personal elements played a part in his conduct.

172

OF PRESBYTERS AND KINGS

133 Buchanan I, p. 203. To follow all the negotiations and attempts at solutions would be to lose track of the point. They are all dealt with in Buchanan and Bryce. See next note.

134 Lord Aberdeen's Act. Discussion of the Bill is chronicled, Buchanan II, pp. 98-122, 218-23; 324-43; Bryce II, pp. 2-37, 194-218; Cf. Cockburn, *Journals* I, pp. 259-60; Bulloch I, pp. 239-40. I omit from consideration a Bill prepared by the Duke of Argyle, as it was in no way legally effective.

135 General Assembly 1842, Act XIX. Printed *inter alia* S.S.F.C.S. pp. 235-55; Buchanan II, pp. 471-85. See also the *Free Church Case* [1904] A.C. 515 at 737; Innes I, pp. 162-7; II pp. 176-83. Cf. *A Vindication of the Free Church Claim of Right*, by Sir H.W. Moncrieff, 1877.

136 Buchan, II, pp. 419-27. Hansard 3rd series, H.C. Deb. vol. 67, 354-422, 441-510. Machin, (1972) 51 *Scot. Hist. Rev.* 20 at pp. 46-50.

137 General Assembly 1843, Act I. S.S.F.C.S. pp. 257-62; Buchanan II, pp. 485-8. See also the *Free Church Case* [1904] A.C. 515 at 741; Innes I, pp. 167-71; II, pp. 183-7. The Disruption was legally completed by the Act of Separation and Deed of Demission, Act IV, registered in the Books of Council and Session 8th June 1843, (Innes I, pp. 171-172, *Free Church Case* [1904] A.C. 515 at 532 n. 1), and a Supplementary Act of Separation and Deed of Demission, Act VI, (S.S.F.C.S., pp. 263-280).

138 Buchanan II, pp. 431-49; Bryce II, pp. 357-91; Cockburn, *Journals* II, pp. 18-46; Rev. T. Brown, *Annals of the Disruption,* pp. 81-96. There is debate about exact numbers. For our purposes it suffices to note that around one third of the ministers left the established church. Bulloch I, p. 250 notes that had the voting been by Presbyteries 60 would have had a majority for remaining and 18 would have voted to secede.

139 Cf. Bulloch I, pp. 257-64.

140 Ibid., pp. 256-7.

141 See nn. 27 and 67.

142 Bulloch II and III, passim.

143 Cf. Cockburn, *Journals* II, pp. 28-32, and his report of the reaction of his friend in his *Life of Lord Jeffrey,* 1872, p. 382.

144 Buchanan II, pp. 450-62; Bryce II, pp. 375-412. The 1843 Assembly revived the Act V, 1799, barring all but duly licensed Church of Scotland ministers from taking church services. There was much bitterness even after the Free Church had problems in getting sites for its churches: see *Reports of the Select Committee on Sites for Churches (Scotland)* 1847, H.C. 247, 311 and 613; *Bain* v. *Black,* (1849) 11 D. 1286; T. Brown, *Annals of the Disruption, 1843,* 1892, pp. 246-90.

145 The third case in this sequence is *Smith* v. *Presbytery of Auchterarder,* (1849) 12 D. 296, where Mrs. Smith failed properly to allege malice in an action for damages in respect of her being mentioned in the Presbytery proceedings against Dunbar.

146 E.g. in *Sturrock* itself an action was allowed in respect of the 'official' reiteration of the sentence of the Kirk Session by the minister on the authority of the Session after the sentence had been reversed by Presbytery and Synod on appeal.

147 Cf. *Dunbar* v. *Skinner* (1849) 11 D. 945; *Edwards* v. *Begbie* (1850) 12 D. 1134; but cf. *Murray* v. *Wyllie* 1916 S.C. 356. See Ch. VI, pp. 91 ff.

148 This applies to all judicial bodies, not just church courts.

149 The preceding discussion is of the absolute privilege of a church court decision. It is clear that such absolute privilege would not apply to communications within the court, or on church business. Whether such communications were afforded qualified privilege (i.e. actionable only if malice and want of probable cause are averred and shown) depends on the nature of the occasion. See *Smith* v. *Presbytery of Auchterarder,* (1849) 12 D. 296; *Rankine* v. *Roberts* (1873) 1 R. 225; *Croucher* v. *Inglis* (1889) 16 R. 774; *Jack* v. *Fleming* (1891) 19 R. 1; *A.* v. *B., (Macleod* v. *Munro)*

(1895) 22 R. 984; *Doig* v. Thomson (1898) 15 Sh. Ct. Rep. 59; *Barclay* v. *Manuel* (1902) 10 S.L.T. 450 and *Murray* v. *Wyllie* 1916 S.C. 356.

150 (1849) 11 D. 1220 at 1242.

151 Ibid. at pp. 1231-2.

152 Ibid. at pp. 1233-4.

153 (1851) 13 D. 1296 at 1299. This case differs from the reduction in *Dunbar* v. *Stoddart* (1849) 11 D. 587 (*supra* p. 54) being a matter of discipline and not statutory duty.

154 Id.

155 Ibid. at 1301.

156 Ibid at 1302.

157 (1861) 23 D. 720 at 723.

158 Cf. the dicta of Lord Medwyn in *Sturrock* noted *supra* n. 152. One might compare this with the rule of exhaustion of local remedies in International Law.

158a Wight, minister of Auchtergaven, being charged by Presbytery with fornication, indecent and scandalous familiarity with a female parishioner, pleaded guilty to the least charge (scandalous familiarity) and not guilty to the others. He was suspended for 6 months. Nothing was officially done regarding the other charges, though Wight said he was told they were to be dropped. No appeal was taken by any member of Presbytery. Four months later, on the petition of 5 elders of his congregation the General Assembly ordered the remaining charges to be dealt with, due to allegations of irregularities in the Presbytery proceedings. Wight argued that he had been tried and sentenced by a judgement which had become final, that the elders had had no standing to petition thus, and that matters were closed. He asked the Court of Session, therefore, to bar further proceedings against him.

159 Quoted *infra* pp. 95-6 Cf. the argument of the Pursuer in *Edwards* v *Begbie*, (1850) 12 D. 1134, and the cases on the Church (Patronage) Scotland Act 1874, to which we are coming.

160 See N. Elliot, *The Erection of Parishes Quoad Sacra, and Feuing of Glebes*, 1879. Further developments and modifications, not of immense importance for our purposes, were contained in the United Parishes (Scotland) Acts of 1868 and 1876. The 1844 Act did not put an end to all the difficulties and hostility of the older churches, cf. *Hutton* v. *Harper* (1876) 3 R. (H.L.) 9.

161 Statutory intervention was also needed for the reconstruction of certain parishes, e.g. Annuity Tax Acts 1860 and 1870.

162 Fleming I, p. 125. In order to get the bill through a clause giving powers of compelling witnesses in ecclesiastical cases was dropped, but on that point see *Presbytery of Lews* v. *Fraser*, (1874) 1 R. 888, where the Court of Session held that the civil authorities could compel witnesses to attend Church courts and give evidence.

163 See *Paterson* v. *Paterson*, (1888) 15 R. 1060; *Earl of Strathmore* v. *Heritors of Rescobie*, (1888) 15 R. 364.

164 Innes II, p. 115. The Assembly Committee on Patronage published in 1870 its examination of the topic, and this report served as the basis on which the Bill was drawn.

165 (1878) 6 R. 221 at 237.

166 Per Lord Ormidale, ibid. at 238.

167 See Note by Lord Kyllachy in *Craig* v. *Anderson*, (1893) 20 R. 941 at 944.

168 G.A. 1711, Act X. See the *Free Church Case*, [1904] A.C. 515 at 536n.

169 Innes II, pp. 136-7.

170 The Opinion is printed in the Proceedings of Assembly 1900, Innes II, p. 138-9, and as an appendix to Sheriff R. Vary Campbell's article 'Spiritual Independence Constitutionally Considered' (1900) 12 J.R. 194, which reviews the whole question, as does Innes loc. cit. See also C. N. Johnston, 'Doctrinal Subscription in the Church of Scotland', (1905) 17 J.R. 201.

171 Innes II, pp. 187-202, prints the minute of the debate.

172 See C. N. Johnston, op. cit. The 1905 Act s.6 and sch.2 repealed two important provisions: 1. that part of the 1693 Act requiring that a minister had to subscribe the Confession declaring 'the same to be the Confession of his faith, and that he owns the doctrine therein contained to be the true Doctrine, which he will constantly adhere to', and 2, that part of the Protestant Religion and Presbyterian Church Act 1706 c.6 requiring ministers to acknowledge and profess the Confession as the confession of their faith.

173 See Sjölinder, pp. 84-92; Fleming II, pp. 26-34; Burleigh, pp. 335-6, 364-6, 398-9; Bulloch III, pp. 79-125; and next note. Disestablishment Bills were introduced annually from 1883 but did not progress.

174 P. M. H. Bell, *Disestablishment in Ireland and Wales*, 1969. The Churches were disestablished by the Irish Church Act 1869, and the Welsh Church Act 1914.

175 On moves towards Union in this period see Sjölinder, pp. 58-104; Fleming II, pp. 35-55, 81-94, 103-25; Bulloch III, pp. 298-322.

176 See App. II.

177 The Act came into force on 28 June 1926 (S.R. and O. 1926, No. 841), following the General Assembly's approval of the Declaratory Articles under Barrier Act procedure.

178 Sjölinder is the best available account. A biography of a leading figure in the Union is: Augustus Muir, *John White*, 1958.

179 See also Ch. VI 'The Church outside Establishment' p. 101 ff, for greater detail.

180 Fleming I, pp. 72-6, 123-39, 174-90; II, pp. 35-56, 81-94, 103-25; Bulloch II, pp. 298-341, III, pp. 298-322.

181 *General Assembly of the Free Church of Scotland* v. *Lord Overtoun (Bannatyne* v. *Overtoun)* : *MacAlister* v. *Young* (1904) 7 F.(H.L.)1; [1904] A.C. 515. (The 'Free Church case'.) See p. 105 ff.

182 See Appendix to the Basis and Plan of Union, 1929, Cox, pp. 392-3.

183 See pp. 105-6.

184 The Memorandum is printed as an Appendix to the Report of the Committee of the Church in Conference with the Representatives of the United Free Church of Scotland, 1912 *Reports to the General Assembly of the Church of Scotland,* 1205 at 1216. See Sjölinder, pp. 214-33.

185 Sjölinder, pp. 252-308.

186 Sjölinder, pp. 309-58. Second Reading, Commons, 1921 H.C. Deb. vol. 143, cols. 1397-1469: Lords, 1921 H.L. Deb. vol. 45, cols. 1339-64. C. N. Johnston, (1920) 233 Quart. Rev. 205.

187 The Memorial and Opinion of Counsel are printed as an Appendix, pp. 13-31, to the Report of the Committee for Conference with the Church of Scotland on Union, *United Free Church Reports,* no. XXVII, 1928. See also Sjölinder pp. 365-6.

188 Article VIII. On the arguments and debate as to the relations of Article I and Article VIII, see Sjölinder, pp. 252-308; Cox, p. 14.

189 Standardisation resulted in a loss to the Church of around one-sixth of its income from these sources. Sections 2, 4 and 5 of the Land Tenure Reform (Scotland) Act 1974, prohibit the creation of new teinds and similar feudal burdens, and provide machinery for their redemption at the option of the person liable, or on the first transfer for value of the burdened land.

190 The responsibility of the heritors is phased out under procedures laid down in ss. 26-33, thus ending a system of support for the church which had given rise to many court cases. An important case in the politics of the matters, which does not appear in the court reports, was that of Shettleston church, Glasgow, where John White secured a court order for the building of a new

church largely at heritors' expense, they having refused an offer to permit them to contribute only one third, and denying liability. Many strands were drawn into the general argument, including disestablishment, but the law was simple. See A. Muir, *John White*, 1958, pp. 19-37.

191 *Church of Scotland General Trustees, Petitioners*, 1931, S.C. 704; 1931 S.L.T. 526. The General Trustees are constituted presently under the Church of Scotland (General Trustees) Order Confirmation Act 1921 c.cxxv, as amended, the Church of Scotland Trust Order Confirmation Act 1932 c.xxi, as amended, and other Acts relating to particular Trust funds.

192 1936 S.C. 625 at 678.

193 Ibid. at 679. Lord Mackay's opinion in the *Church of Scotland General Trustees Petitioners*, 1931 S.C. 704 at 711 12 makes the same point about repeal, though there he comes to a different conclusion on the facts of the case.

194 1936 S.C. 625 at 642.

195 See Opinion of Lord President Inglis in *Hastie* v. *McMurtrie* (1889) 17 R. 715 at 730-2: Lord Mackay in *Ballantyne* v. *Presbytery of Wigtown* 1936 S.C. 625 at 686-7. But cf. the Opinion of Lord President Clyde in *Church of Scotland General Trustees* v. *Inland Revenue* 1932 S.C. 97 at 101.

196 See the Preamble, Questions and Formula to be used for Admission to Office in the Church, Cox, pp. 568-75, and Art. V, *ad fin.*, Declaratory Articles 1921.

197 The Opinion of the Procurator is printed in an Appendix to the Report of the Panel on doctrine, G. A. Reps. 1970, p. 171 at 180-2. See App. III. *Barker* v. *O'Gorman* [1971] Ch. 215 for observations on the English Methodist position. The Methodist Church Act 1976, c. xxx solves many problems both in England and for the projected union of the Scottish Methodists and the Church of Scotland.

198 Cf. Opinion of Counsel obtained by the National Church Association, dated October 3, 1971. See App. IV.

199 Sjölinder, pp. 351 and 356.

200 1921 H. C. Deb. vol. 143 col. 1461. Cf. Westminster Confession, ch. xxiii, 3, as to the powers of the civil magistrate in such a case.

201 1921 H. L. Deb. vol. 45 col. 1161.

202 Ibid. col. 1164.

203 Ibid. cols. 1151-2.

204 *Nairn* v. *University of St. Andrews*, 1909 S.C. (H.L.) 10 : *Viscountess Rhondda's Claim* [1922] 2 A.C. 339. Clearly the abolition of synods, recommended by the Assembly in 1978, is a different matter, being one merely of internal organisation. Sufficient Presbyteries did not support the recommendation (G.A. Reps. 1979 p. 13).

205 Questions might also arise as to the Baird Trust, constituted by Deed of Trust, dated 24 July 1873, and registered in the Books of Council and Session, which refers to the Westminster Confession and conservative principles as being those 'sound religious principles', on which purposes and institutions to be supported are to be judged. This is repeated in the Baird Trust Order Confirmation Act 1939, c.cv.

206 T. B. Smith, *The United Kingdom : Scotland*, 1955, pp. 641-50; 'Two Scots Cases' [1953] 69 L.Q.R. 512; 'The Union of 1707 as Fundamental Law' [1957] 2 P.L. 99: K. W. B. Middleton, 'Sovereignty in Theory and Practice,' (1952) 64 J.R. 135; 'New Thoughts on the Union between England and Scotland,' (1954) 66 J.R. 37: G. Marshall, 'Parliamentary Supremacy and the Language of Constitutional Limitation,' (1955) 67 J.R. 62 (Cf. 'What is Parliament? The Changing Concept of Parliamentary Sovereignty,' (1954) 2 Pol. Stud. 193): D. N. MacCormick, Review of S. A. De Smith, *Constitutional Law*, [1972] P.L. 174-9; 'Does the United Kingdom have a Constitution? Reflections on MacCormick v Lord Advocate', (1978) 29 Northern Ireland Law Quart. 1-20.

207 (1808) Mor. App. 'Stipend' No. 6. The Opinions are reprinted in full from Session Papers in J. Connell, *The Law of Scotland regarding Tithes and the Stipends of Parochial Clergy*, 1815, vol. III p. 310 ff. (There is also a 2 vol. ed. 1830, which I have not seen.) The quotation from Lord Justice-Clerk Hope appears at p. 320.

208 Connell, Vol. III, 376.

209 J. D. B. Mitchell, *Constitutional Law*, 2nd ed. 1968, pp. 71-2, n. 34, notes several cases from the Disruption. See also T. B. Smith, [1957] 2 P.L. 99 p. 115.

210 Thus MacCormick, [1972] P.L. 174 at 177 quotes 1872 H.L. Deb. vol. 210 col. 1990; 1873 H.L. Deb. vol. 214 col. 1738.

211 1953 S.C. 396 at 409 (Argument of Respondent), L. P. Cooper at 411-2.

212 R. F. V. Heuston, 'Sovereignty' in *Oxford Essays in Jurisprudence*, 1961, A. G. Guest ed. at p. 198. I see no reason why Scotland should not adopt a position 'completely contrary to the whole tenor of English authorities on the point' (ibid. p. 206). The doctrine is merely a theoretical extrapolation designed to justify and dignify the exigencies of government. It would be proper to decide this matter on utility and justice, not doctrinal theory.

213 T. B. Smith, [1957] 2 P.L. 99 at 114.

214 1952 S.C. 396 at 412-3. Cf. Mitchell pp. 82-91.

215 *Ex parte Canon Selwyn*, (1872) 36 J.P. 54. P. M. H. Bell, *Disestablishment in Ireland and Wales*, 1969; O. Chadwick, *The Victorian Church*, vol. I, 1966, pp. 47-60. It may be noted that the passing of the Irish Church Act 1869 and of the Roman Catholic Emancipation Act 1829 show clearly that the Sovereign's Oath of Accession protecting ecclesiastical interests is without any legal importance (cf. Chadwick, pp. 14-15.).

216 *Bergman* v. *Minister of Finance* (1969) 23 P.D. 693 (I), known to me only through M. B. Nimmer, 'The Uses of Judicial Review in Israel's Quest for a Constitution' (1970) 70 Col. L.R. 1217.

217 Cf. Lord Russell in *MacCormick* 1953 S.C. 396 at 417.

218 E.g. by the 1711 Patronage Act, and the abolition of University Tests by the Universities (Scotland) Act 1853. T. B. Smith, [1957] 2 P.L. 99 at 112, goes rather far in suggesting that patronage was not covered by the Union agreements. It may be noted that by the time of the Universities (Scotland) Act 1889 the Church seems not to have pressed the question of University Tests, and in its evidence to the Committee on University Tests in Scotland, 1892, C.6970, acquiesced in their removal.

219 A. V. Dicey and R. S. Rait, *Thoughts on the Scottish Union*, 1920, pp. 252-4. (This seems to modify Dicey's previous statements in his *Introduction to the Study of the Law of Constitution*, 10th ed. by E. C. S. Wade 1959, pp. 64-70, cf. ibid., pp. lxiv-lxvi.)

220 Innes I, p. 126; II, p. 66.

221 C. N. Johnston, *A Handbook of Scottish Church Defence*, p. 203, 1892, (quoted by T. Johnston during the Second Reading of the Church of Scotland (Property and Endowments) Bill 1925, 1924-25 H.C. Deb. vol. 180, col. 58).

222 Quoted *supra* p. 77.

223 Gen. Ass. Sess. 3, 23 May 1974, Report of the Committee of Forty, proposed new section 3, and relative minute (1974 Gen. Ass. Minutes, 693-9, 703-5, 713-5).

224 Church of England (Worship and Doctrine) Measure, No. 3 of 1974; cf. also the Methodist Church Act, 1976 c.xxx.

225 *Ballantyne* v. *Presbytery of Wigtown* 1936 S.C. 625 at 657-8.

226 See p. 111.

227 Fleming II, p. 121, See p. 111.

228 But see n. 215.

229 In England the Moderator takes precedence after Bishops of the Church of England but before Barons; Cox, p. 777. The Coronation is really an Anglican ceremonial (some would say arrogantly so). See C. Garbett, *Church and State in England*, 1950; T. Beeson, *The Church of England in Crisis*, 1973. I intend to discuss this point in another work on the Church of Scotland itself.

230 The Lord High Commissioner may not be a Roman Catholic; Roman Catholic Emancipation Act 1829 s. 12. His allowance is regulated under the Lord High Commissioner (Church of Scotland) Act 1974.

231 See S. Mechie, *The Office of Lord High Commissioner*, 1957, pp. 51-2.

232 An allied curiosity is that responsibility for the Crown Copyright in the Authorised Version in Scotland is vested in the Bible Board, regulated by Royal Warrant of 1839. The members of the Board are the Moderator of the General Assembly of the Church of Scotland, the Lord Advocate and the Solicitor General *ex officio*. Messrs. Bell and Scott, Bruce and Kerr, W.S., 16 Hill Street, Edinburgh are the Clerks to the Board, and I am grateful to W. M. Kerr, Esq., for information. The permission of the Board is necessary for the printing of new editions of the Authorised Version in Scotland.

233 Innes I, p. 242; II, p. 209.

234 The Confession of Faith Ratification Act 1560 c. 1.

235 The Papal Jurisdiction Act 1560 c. 2, confirmed Act 1567 c. 3.

236 Act 1560 c. 3.

237 Act 1560 c. 4, confirmed Act 1567 c. 5.

238 Confirmed Act 1579 c. 7.

239 Naturally this period was extremely important in general history, but has left little legal trace, apart from the more severe establishment of Presbyterianism at its end, and a certain amount of legislation on such topics as clandestine marriages, on which see ch. VII, p. 130 ff.

240 14 March 1689, Act 1689 c. 28.

241 The history of the Cameronians is reviewed by Lord President Inglis in *Wallace* v. *The Ferguson Bequest Fund* (1879) 6 R. 486 at 501, and more extensively in the Note of Lord Curriehill, the Lord Ordinary at p. 495 ff.

242 Innes II, p. 288. Contrast the Ecclesiastical Titles Act 1851, repealed by the Ecclesiastical Titles Act 1871.

On the restoration, see D. McRoberts 'The Restoration of the Scottish Catholic Hierarchy in 1878', (1978) 29 Innes Rev. 1-29; Cf. Peter F. Anson, *Underground Catholicism in Scotland*, 1970. The bull is printed as App. 1 to the *Acta et Decreta Concilii Scotiae Plenarii Primi Post Redintegratum Hierarchiam*, 1888. A major extract is translated as App. XIX of A. Bellesheim, *History of the Catholic Church of Scotland*, 4 vols. 1887-90, trans. D. O. Hunter Blair, vol. IV pp. 414-21.

243 Adam Gib's case, Elchies' *Decisions*, voce Title to Sue, p. 487, 30 June 1752; see D. M. Forrester, 'Adam Gib, the Anti-Burgher' (1941) VII R.S.C.H.S. pp. 141-69. *Pollock* v. *Maitland*, ibid., p. 488, 8 July 1752 is to like effect.

244 Now s.26 of the Tithes to Land Consolidation (Scotland) Act 1868.

245 It may be more difficult to sue the U.P. church for debt, *Aitken* v. *Harper*, (1865) 4 M. 36. Individuals may find themselves liable on promissory notes signed on behalf of congregations, although the congregation itself is not: *McMeekin* v. *Easton*, (1889) 16 R. 365, a Reformed Presbyterian church case.

246 G.A. Reps. 1912, pp. 1216-21, para. 11.

247 Hume, *Decisions*, 595 at 596 also notes the case of *Brownlee and Scott* v. *Kirk-session of Carluke*, to the same effect. Cf. *Grieve* v. *Smith*, Hume, p. 637.

248 See the note of *Auchinloss* in *Dunn* v. *Brunton*, (1801) Mor. App. Soc. 10 at 16.

249 Unreported. See the note to the argument of the defenders in *McMillan* v. *Free Church of Scotland*, (First Cardross case) (1859) 22 D. 290 at 310-11, also noted Innes I p. 263 note. (Innes II, 217 n. 3 refers to a later page, but there is no later reference.)

250 Per Lord Fullerton, (1849) 11 D. 945 at 961; cf. Lord President Boyle, ibid. at 958, quoted *supra* p. 87.

251 (1849) 11 D. 945 at 962.

252 A harbinger of the decision is to be found in *Mathers* v. *Laurie* (1849) 12 D. 433, where it was held that an extract of a Free Church Kirk Session minute was not evidence, that Kirk Session not being a court recognised by law. Eventually the point had to be proved by parole evidence; the clerk not having been present at the meeting, the minute book itself was not evidence either. Cf. *Dunbar* v. *Skinner* (1849) 11 D. 945 discussed above.

253 *The General Assembly of Baptist Churches* v. *Taylor* (1841) 3 D. 1030, and similar cases may be distinguished as not raising questions of damages.

254 *MacMillan* v. *The Free Church of Scotland* (1864) 2 M. 1444, (the Fourth Cardross Case). On the whole saga see Fleming, I pp. 127-30; N. L. Walker, *Chapters from the History of the Free Church of Scotland*, pp. 212-25; A. M. Hunter 'The Cardross Case' (1941) VII R.S.C.H.S. pp. 247-258.

255 *Supra* at p. 92.

256 1940 S.C. 376 at 382.

257 Ibid. at 383.

258 Ibid. at 383-4. Cf. *Bell* v. *The Trustees*, 1975 S.L.T. (Sh. Ct.) 60.

259 *Supra* at p. 90.

260 See the Cardross cases generally; *Gall* v. *Loyal Glenbogie Lodge of the Oddfellows Friendly Society* (1900) 2 F. 1187; *Skerret* v. *Oliver* (1896) 23 R. 468 *infra*.

261 Cf. *McGonagle* v. *Glasgow Unitarian Church* 1955 S.L.T. (Sh.Ct.) 25; *Mackintosh* v. *The Trustees of the Scottish Episcopal Fund* (1801) (unreported: noted A. McWhirter, 'Lesser known Church Law Cases' (1955) 11 R.S.C.H.S. 149-59, at 149); *Aitken* v. *Associated Carpenters and Joiners of Scotland* (1885) 12 R. 1206. Following the property cases discussed *infra*, it would have been better for Forbes to have claimed the property of the Scottish Episcopal Church, on the basis that the new canons meant Eden etc. had forfeited their rights to property having departed from the original principles of the Church. Cf. n. 258.

262 *Skerret* v. *Oliver* (1896) 23 R. 468, opinion of Lord Kincairney at 481-2; *Mulcahy* v. *Herbert* (1898) 25 R. 1136; *Brook* v. *Kelly* (1893) 20 R. 470, 20 R. (H.L.) 104; *MacMillan* v. *General Assembly of the Free Church*, (1859) 22 D. 290, (1861) 23 D. 1314.

263 1940 S.C. 376 at 387. Analogously, it was held in *Gibb* v. *Stanners*, 1975 S.L.T. (Notes) 30, that a trustee of a meeting hall should be given notice of a move to remove him from office.

264 *Supra* p. 32. (First Auchterarder Case appeal, (1839) McL. & Rob. 220 at 314-5.).

265 Inferences from the opinions of Lord Kincairney in *Skerret* v. *Oliver*, (1896) 23 R. 468 at 474, and from Lord Salvesen in *Bridge* v. *South Portland Street Synagogue*, 1907 S.C. 1351, (both *supra* p. 89), would indicate this solution. Lord Kincairney, at 475, indicated that it may be necessary to call all the individuals in a damages action. Cf. *Bannatyne* v. *Overtoun* (1902) 4 F. 1083, (1904) 7 F. (H.L.) 1, [1904] A.C. 515, where the Third Defenders included the individual members of the 1900 U.F. Assembly.

266 Cf. the argument to this effect of the Free Church in the Cardross cases.

267 (1849) 11 D. 945 at 962, quoted *supra* at p. 92.

268 1940 S.C. 376 at 384 (*supra* p. 96).

269 Cf. his observations in *MacMillan* v. *The General Assembly of the Free Church of*

Scotland (1895) 22 D. 290 at 323, quoted *supra* p. 93. Lord Ardmillan is generally broader. In *Presbytery of Lews* v. *Fraser* (1874) 1 R. 888 at 894, he would have the civil courts compel witnesses for non-established as well as established Church courts.

270 1940 S.C. 376 at 383-4 (*supra* pp. 94-6).

271 *Supra* pp. 87-8. *Bryson* v. *Wilson* (1752) Elchies Dec. p. 487; *Pollock* v. *Maitland*, ibid. p. 488; *Wilson* v. *Jobson* (1771) Mor. 14555; *Allan* v. *Macrae* (1791) Mor. 1583.

272 Mor. App. Soc. 10 at 17.

273 Per Lord Justice-Clerk Hope in *Craigie* v. *Marshall*, (1850) 12 D. 523 at 536.

274 Ibid.

275 Also known as *Davidson* v. *Aikman*; (1805) Mor. 14584; (1813) 1 Dow 1, 5 Paton 719 (1820) 2 Bligh 529, 6 Paton 618.

276 Per Lord Meadowbank in the Campbeltown case, *Galbraith* v. *Smith*, (1837) 15 S. 808 at 827.

277 These are reviewed Innes I, p. 327-43; II, p. 222-31, and in Lord Meadowbank's opinion just cited.

278 This is the basis of each of his Lordship's opinions in the case. Cf. Eldon's opinion in the English case, *Att. Gen* v. *Pearson* (1817) 3 Mer. 353, 36 English Reports 135.

The great difficulty of the application of the original principle test is exemplified by the Craigdallie case itself, where the interlocutors of the Court of Session and of the House of Lords, 2 Bligh 537, reflect the perplexity of the Court. Their Lordships find 'as far as they are capable of understanding the subject', that the pursuers had failed to condescend on facts establishing deviation from original principles, and that they 'have failed in rendering intelligible to the Court, on what ground it is that they aver, that there does at this moment exist any *real* difference between their principles and those of the defenders'. But, of course, the title or Trust Deed may provide for the case of deviation, union or schism—*Kennedy* v. *Morrison and Lee*, (1879) 6 R. 879; *Lyon's Trustees* v. *Aitken*, (1904) 6 F. 608; *Craig* v. *Mackersy*, (1823) 2 S. 198.

279 (1837) 15 S. 808 at 820.

280 Lord Meadowbank in effect stated that one must assume that the governing body of a church will continue to adhere to the principles of the sect, and hence adherence to it, and therefore the will of the majority in Presbyterian systems, involves adherence to the original principles. (It may be noted that at the end of his opinion, p. 831, he confesses that he had only opened the record in the case on the previous day.)

281 (1850) 12 D. 523 at 524.

282 Per Lord Justice-Clerk Hope, ibid. at 539-43.

283 Ibid. at 547-48.

284 Ibid. at 558-61, 567.

285 The Carnoustie case, *Cairncross* v. *Lorimer*, or *Cairncross* v. *Meek* (1858) 20 D. 995; aff'd (1860) 22 D. (H.L.) 15, 3 McQ. 827.

286 The Appeal Cases report is more satisfactory than that of Session Cases as it prints and indexes all the documentary material in the case. The case is also printed, with full argument of counsel in *The Free Church of Scotland Appeals, 1903-4*, R.L. Orr ed, 1905. This report is not so easy to use as it prints material *in gremio* of the speeches.

287 Diagrams of the principal schisms and union in Scotland are printed: Burleigh, insert; Sjölinder, p. 379; and Innes I, p. 418.

288 A lesser union with the Reformed Presbyterian Church in 1876 gave rise to the Ferguson Bequest case of 1879, *Wallace* v. *The Ferguson Bequest Fund*, (1879) 6 R. 486, (*supra* p. 104), and also *Kennedy* v. *Morrison and Lee* (1879) 6 R. 879 on church titles: cf. *Lyon's Trs.* v. *Aitken* (1904) 6 F. 608; *Craig* v. *Mackersy* (1823) 2 S. 198; and *Presbytery of Edinburgh* v. *De La Condamine*

7

(1868) 7 M. 213. The 1876 Uniting Act is Free Church 1876, Act III, printed Cox p. 415. On progress to union see Fleming I, pp. 72-6, 174-90; II, pp. 35-56, 81-94, 103-25; Bulloch II, pp. 298-311; III, pp. 298-322.

289 Young was selected from four cases raised as test cases by the United Free Church. One of these is reported; *The United Free Church of Scotland* v. *McIver* (Aultbea), (1902) 4 F. 1117, which was simply decided in accordance with *Bannatyne*. The Free Church Model Trust Deed is discussed Innes II, pp. 249-53.

290 United Presbyterian Church Basis of Union, [1904] A.C. 515 at 752, App. J.; and more fully: United Free Church 1900, Act I; Cox, pp. 437-8.

291 U.P. Church Declaratory Act 1879; [1904] A.C. 539; Cox pp. 435-6.

292 Orr's Report pp. 254-55, speech of Mr. Johnston.

293 [1904] A.C. 543. This Act was modified in 1894, [1904] A.C. 544. Cox pp. 436-7.

294 (1902) 4 F. 1083.

295 Ibid. at 1110.

296 Ibid. at 1114.

297 T. M. Taylor, 'Church and State in Scotland' 1957 J.R. 121 at 131. Fleming, II, ch. V, esp. pp. 64-5. Lord Robertson's comment appears (1904) 7 F. (H.L.) 1 at 53; [1904] A.C. 515 at 686.

298 I have not sought to refer to particular parts of these judgements as they require to be read as units.

299 J. Ferguson, 'The Scottish Church Case' (1904) 16 J.R. 347; cf. A. T. Innes, 'Church Law and Trust Law' (1904) 16 J.R. 314; F. C. Lowell, (1906) 6 Col. L.R. 137 for a U.S. view.

300 *Kennedy* v. *Morrison and Lee* (1879) 6 R. 879, which also illustrates the point that even where a Model Trust Deed is not adhered to by a congregation title, that title may nonetheless separately provide for the case of union or schism. A deed of trust may similarly provide—*Bannerman* v. *Bannerman's Trustee* (1896) 23 R. 959. Where the constitution is a private Act of Parliament, or in other cases as a final resort, a Private Act of Parliament may be required. Thus the difficulties exposed for the Methodist Church in *Barker* v. *O'Gorman* [1971] Ch. 215, and in discussion about union with the Church of Scotland, have been met by the Methodist Church Act, 1976 c. xxx.

301 See Appendix to the Basis and Plan of Union, 1929; Cox, pp. 392-3.

302 *Ness* v. *Miller*, (1912) 2 S.L.T. 263.

303 *General Assembly of the Free Church* v. *Lord Overtoun* (1904) 7 F. 202. Overtoun asked for delay as there were moves to overrule the decision by parliamentary action, which eventually produced the 1905 Churches (Scotland) Act as described below.

304 *General Assembly of the Free Church* v. *Johnston*, (1904) 7 F. 517; *General Assembly of the Free Church* v. *Rainy*, (1904) 12 S.L.T. 387. A list of the actions was compiled for the House of Commons, *United Free Church and the Free Church of Scotland (Litigation)* 1905 H.C. 148, for the use of Sir John Cheyne's Commission to settle interim possession of the properties at issue pending final determination; see the *Interim Report of the Departmental Commission on the Free and United Churches*, 1905 Cd. 2510.

305 *Report of the Royal Commission on Churches (Scotland)* 1905, Cd. 2494, (Evidence printed Cd. 2495).

306 *Report of the Royal Commission appointed under the Churches (Scotland) Act 1905*, 1910 Cd. 5060, (Proceedings printed Cd. 5061).

307 Fleming, II p. 121.

308 *Burgess' Trustees* v. *Crawford*, 1912 S.C. 387. *Forrest* v. *Forrest*, 1960 S.L.T. 88, gives procedure.

309 *Connell* v. *Ferguson*, (1857) 19 D. 482, a multiple-poinding, where there were claims to the whole fund, or return of a part. But cf. *Bain* v. *Black* (1849) 11 D. 1286, where the established Church was held entitled to a fund which had been collected to build a church, although one basis of the collection was the intention to erect a church under the Chapel Act, subsequently held void by the Stewarton case. This decision caused much ill-feeling as the Free Church adherents claiming the property felt, with some reason, that they had been harshly treated. Cf. also *Peake* v. *The Association of English Episcopalians in Scotland* (1884) 22 S.L.R. 3, where a minority was held entitled to interdict against dissolution of the Association on the grounds that its purposes had not failed. *Obiter* Lord McLaren suggested at p. 5 that surplus revenue might be redistributed to contributing congregations without recourse to the civil courts. Cf. *Edinburgh Young Women's Christian Institute* (1893) 20 R. 894.

310 See *dicta* of Lord Cullen, the Lord Ordinary, in *Anderson's Trustees* v. *Scott*, 1914 S.C. 942, Lord Dunedin in *The Incorporation of Maltmen of Stirling*, 1912 S.C. 887 at 891, and Lord Sands in *The Caledonian Employees' Benevolent Society*, 1928 S.C. 633 at 637. There are no reported cases in which such trust property has actually fallen to the Crown. See A. R. G. McMillan, *The Law of Bona Vacantia in Scotland*, 1936, pp. 35-38.

311 *Anderson's Trustees* v. *Scott*, 1914 S.C. 942.

312 Cf. the successive Reports of the Committee of Forty, Gen. Ass. Rpts., 1973 pp. 625-35; 1974 pp. 519-31; 1975 pp. 509-56; 1976 pp. 479-504; 1977 pp. 473-503; 1978 pp. 489-516.

313 The most recent general account is J. Scotland, *The History of Scottish Education*, 2 vols. 1969, (cited hereafter as Scotland I and II).

314 See ch. II, p. 14 and n. 41.

315 Scotland I, pp. 1-21, 71-87, 209-27. Cf. J. Grant, *History of the Burgh Schools in Scotland*, 1876. Private Schools were also active : Scotland I, pp. 90-113, 261-301. The Reports of the Argyll Commission (*infra* n. 319) also give much data.

316 T. Brown, *Annals of the Disruption, 1843*, 1892, pp. 309-26; N. L. Walker, *Chapters from the History of the Free Church of Scotland*, 1895, pp. 113-30; D. J. Withrington, 'The Free Church Educational Scheme, 1843-50', (1966) XV R.S.C.H.S. 103-16. Other special societies such as the Gaelic Schools Society and the Scottish Society for the Propagation of Christian Knowledge were also important.

317 Judgement was acquiesced in, and the case appears only at (1861) 23 D. 287 at 299, as a reference in the Note of the Lord Ordinary in the *Elgin Academy* case to which we are just coming.

318 (1861) 23 D. 287 at 288.

319 Reports of the Education Commission (Scotland), Chairman, The Duke of Argyll. First Report : Evidence, 1865, 3483 and 3858; Second Report : Elementary Schools, 1867, 3845, with Reports of Assistant Commissioners, 3845—I to IV; Third Report : Burgh and Middle Class Schools, 1867-8, 4011.

320 H. Craik, *The State in its Relation to Education*, 1896, pp. 154-60, compares the two Acts, as does Scotland I p. 366. On the formation of the Scottish Act, see: J. D. Myers, 'Scottish Nationalism and the Antecedents of the 1872 Education Act', (1972) 4 Scot. Educ. Stud. 73-92; B. Lenman and J. Stocks, 'The Beginning of State Education in Scotland' (1972) 4 Scot. Educ. Stud. 93-106; D. J. Withrington, 'Towards a National System, 1867-1872: The Last Years in the Struggle for a Scottish Education Act', (1972) 4 Scot. Educ. Stud. 107-24; D. J. Withrington, 'The Making of the 1872 Act'. Times Educ. Supp., Scot., 18 Aug. 1972.

321 The custom is noted in the Second Report of the Argyll Commission at xxx. It is interesting to find that the 1872 conscience provision was introduced only in the later stages of the Bill, and carried by the votes of English Members.

322 Brother Kenneth, 'The Education (Scotland) Act, 1918, in the Making', (1968) 19 Innes Rev. 91-128.

323 *Moral and Religious Education in Scottish Schools.* The Report of a Committee appointed by the Secretary of State for Scotland, 1972. (The Millar Report).

324 Millar Report, p. 121 : Problems in Future Developments, para. 13.

325 Cf. Head V (5) of the *First Book of Discipline (ad. med.)* '. . . this must be carefully provided, that no father, of whatever estate and condition that he ever be, use his children at his own fantasy, especially in their youth-head; but all must be compelled to bring up their children in learning and virtue.' P. Fraser, *The Law of Scotland applicable to Personal and Domestic Relations,* 1st ed. 1846, vol. 2 (Parent and Child) pp. 30-1; and *Parent and Child,* 3rd ed. by S. Clark, 1906, pp. 89-91, cites instances of such 'compelling'.

326 The Millar Report 1.4 indicates that the Scottish solution has led to a decline in religious education in the state school system.

327 Apart from material already cited, see also: J. Murphy, *Church, State and Schools in Britain, 1800-1971,* 1972; J. J. Robertson, 'The Scottish Solution', Yearbook of Education, 1951, 329-48; and the Durham Report, *The Fourth R,* 1970, the Report of the Commission on Religious Education in Schools, appointed by the Church of England, 1967. At the time of writing (1979) there is a move to consider the introduction of examinations in religious education through a committee under L. B. Young, set up with the approval of the Secretary of State for Scotland.

328 Innes I, pp. 122-3 and 158-61, the latter being a note on the whole matter of Professor Blackie, including data on the otherwise unreported case. Bulloch II, pp. 300-1; Bryce II, pp. 172-3.

329 *Presbytery of Edinburgh v. Magistrates of Edinburgh and Macdouall* (1847) 10 D. 247; *Tullis v. Macdouall* (1847) 10 D. 261; Cockburn, *Journals* II, pp. 49-53.

330 Report of the Committee on University Tests in Scotland, 1892, C.6970; cf. A. T. Innes, 'University Tests in Scotland' (1892) 4 J. R. 301.

331 The Agreement between the Courts of the Scottish Universities which have divinity Faculties, and the Church of Scotland, is registered in the Books of Council and Session, 28th March 1951. I have used the Ordinance of the University Courts available to me as Ordinance No. 284 (General No. 10), in the Acts and Ordinances affecting the University of Aberdeen, 1858-1965. The 'General No. 10' reference is to the series of Ordinances affecting all Scottish universities, and both reference systems have ceased current use following the Universities (Scotland) Act 1966.

332 Cf. M. Dinwiddie, *Religion by Radio,* 1968, and R. Falconer, *The Kilt beneath my Sporran,* 1978. The major work on U.K. Broadcasting is Asa Briggs, *The History of Broadcasting in the United Kingdom,* 1. *The Birth of Broadcasting,* 1961, 2. *The Golden Age of Wireless,* 1965, 3. *The War of Words,* 1970, 4. *Sound and Vision,* 1979, (cited as Briggs I, II, III and IV).

333 Independent Television began under the Television Act 1954.

334 I.B.A. Annual Report and Accounts, 1975-76, pp. 125-9, (App. X); also published separately by the Authority.

335 Advertising was not accepted for the New English Bible (1960), *The Bible Today* (a weekly instalment publication of the Bible, 1969) or J. Allegro *The Sacred Mushroom and The Cross* (1969). However, *Man, Myth and Magic* was considered to be factual and objective, and so advertising that work was permissible: see on these the *Report of the Independent Television Authority, 1969-70* (1970-1 H.C. 177), pp. 46-7. (cf. also n. 358, below).

336 *Report of the Broadcasting Committee, 1935,* 1936, Cmd. 5091, para. 100.

337 Briggs III, pp. 622-3.

338 *Report of the Broadcasting Committee, 1949,* 1951, Cmd. 8116, rec. 60, but cf. para. 252.

339 *Report of the Committee on Broadcasting, 1960. Appendix E: Memoranda submitted to the Committee*, 2 vols. 1962, Cmnd. 1819 and 1819-I, vol. 1, memo. no. 53.

340 *Report of the Committee on Broadcasting, 1960*, 1962 Cmnd. 1753, para. 288.

341 *Report of the Committee on the Future of Broadcasting*, 1977 Cmnd. 6753, para. 20.11, (hereafter cited as 'Annan').

342 Ibid., para. 20.12.

343 Ibid., para. 20.13.

344 1954-5 H.L. Deb. vol. 192, cols. 3-4.

345 1971-2 H.C. Deb. vol. 829, col. 478.

346 B.D.C. Annual Report, 1975-76, in *B.B.C. Handbook 1977*, pp. 34-5; *I.B.A. Annual Report 1975-76*, p. 26; Annan para. 20.4.

347 Supra n. 343.

348 Annan, para. 20.24. The C.R.A.C. is appointed by the Authorities in consultation with major churches. This has been criticised, but it is difficult to see how better things could be arranged. The Committee is representative, not a conglomerate of delegates. (Cf. Annan, para. 20.23).

349 Annan, para. 20.22; governmental response in *Broadcasting*, 1978, Cmnd. 7294.

350 Cf. Pilkington Committee (*supra* n. 340), para. 289; evidence submitted to that Committee (*supra* n 339), vol. 2, Paper no. 154; and evidence of W. Brown, Chairman of Scottish Television Ltd., *Independent Broadcasting Authority, Second Report from the Select Committee on Nationalised Industries*, 1972, 1971-72 H.C. 465, qus. 664-71.

351 Annan, para. 20.18.

352 Cf. Church Rates Acts 1833 and 1874.

353 *Belhaven-Westbourne Church* v. *Glasgow Corporation*, 1965 S.C. (H.L.) 1, (house of church officer); *Worldwide Evangelisation Crusade* v. *Glasgow Corporation*, 1965 S.L.T. 339, (college and offices of missionary organisation); *Scottish Burial Reform and Cremation Society Ltd.* v. *Glasgow Corporation*, 1967 S.C. (H.L.) 116, (cremation society offices).

354 The first permanent Income Tax Act, that of 1842, made provision for the exemption of charities—e.g. ss.88 and 105.

355 *Pemsel* itself marked a change in Scots Law, for it overset *Baird's Trustee* v. *Lord Advocate* (1888) 15 R. 682, which had held that religious purposes were not charitable under the then taxation legislation.

356 Cf. *Registration of Charities in Scotland*, the Report of a Working Party of the Scottish Council of Social Service, Chairman, Prof. A. W. Bradley, 1972; *Charity Law and the Voluntary Organisations*, the Report of an Independent Committee of Inquiry set up by the National Council of Social Service, Chairman, Lord Goodman, 1976; *Charity Commissioners and their Accountability*, the Tenth Report from the H.C. Expenditure Committee, 1974-5 H.C. 495-1, with evidence (H.C. 495-11), and comment by A. H. Sherr, (1976) 39 Modern Law Rev. 77-84; and material cited *infra* n. 360. Cf. also H. Picarda, *The Law and Practice relating to Charities*, 1977; M. Chesterman, *Charities, Trusts and Social Welfare*, 1979.

357 *Enquiry into the Practice and Effects of Scientology*, Report by Sir J. G. Foster, Q.C., M.P., 1971-2 H.C. 52, para. 263; cf. paras, 4 and 263-7.

358 Buckley, L. J. [1970] 2 Q.B. 697 at 709:

'Worship I take to be something which must have some at least of the following characteristics: submission to the object worshipped, veneration of that object, praise, thanksgiving, prayer or intercession. . . . [Acts] which [contain] none of these elements cannot in my judgement, answer to the description of an act of worship.'

Lord Denning, M.R. ibid. at 707:

'Religious worship means reverence or veneration of God or of a Supreme Being. '. . . In Scientology . . . '[t]here may be belief in a spirit of man, but there is no belief in a spirit of God.'

Winn, L. J. ibid. at 709:

'. . . they do not humble themselves in reverence or recognition of the dominant power and control of any entity or being outside their own body and life.'

Cf. F. H. A. Micklewright, 'Place of Worship' (1971) 115 Sol. J. 197. Note, the I.B.A. considers that Scientology advertising on television is banned under para. 8 of Sch. 2 of the 1973 Independent Broadcasting Act, (letter from I.B.A. Advertising Control, dated 22nd February 1974). Cf. as to 'Place of Worship' under English Rating Law, *Henning* v. *Church of Jesus Christ of Latter-Day Saints,* [1962] 1 W.L.R. 1091; aff'd. [1964] A.C. 420.

359 Foster Report, (*supra* n. 357), paras. 258-61.

360 Today there is much concern about a whole variety of movements, e.g.: Scientology—see the Foster Report (*supra* n. 357); *The Report of the Board of Inquiry into Scientology,* (the Anderson Report), 1965, Government Printing Office, Victoria, Australia; *Hubbard Scientology Organisation in New Zealand,* 1969, Government Printing Office, Wellington N.Z.; and the report of an Ontario Committee referred to in paras. 28-30 of the Foster Report. The Children of God have also caused concern (e.g. Oral Answers, 9 Dec. 1974, 883 H.C. Deb. cols. 23-4; cf. *Final Report on the Activities of the Children of God,* submitted by the Charity Frauds Bureau to Hon. L. F. Lefkowitz, Attorney General of the State of New York, to whom I am grateful for the sight of a copy.)

It should be said that the Foster Report, paras. 210-4, recommended that the ban on alien scientologists entering the country to study scientology, should be lifted. This has not yet been done. The ban on entry is the only thing the State can do in such a case, where other laws are not infringed. It seems odd to refuse entry to those who wish to study something which it is not unlawful for nationals to study.

There is also the problem of the U.K. obligation under arts. 9 and 14 the European Convention on Human Rights, 1950, Cmd. 8969, though see *Church of X against the United Kingdom* (1969) 12 Y.B. Eur. Conv. H.R. 306, and cf. *Van Duyn* v. *Home Office* [1974] 1 C.M.L.R. 1 and 347. Such international obligations could affect this area but would require extensive discussion if not just noted in this way.

361 Cf. C. S. Lewis, *Screwtape proposes a Toast,* 1965; and 'The Humanitarian Theory of Punishment' in his *Undeceptions* 1971, pp. 238-49.

362 Cf. C. S. Lewis, *The Abolition of Man,* 1947, 1978.

363 P. Fraser, *Husband and Wife according to the Law of Scotland,* 2nd ed. 1876; F. P. Walton, *The Law of Husband and Wife in Scotland,* 3rd ed. 1951; E. M. Clive and J. G. Wilson, *The Law of Husband and Wife in Scotland,* 1974. For the development of the Law of Incest see *infra* n. 382.

364 Fraser, op. cit., vol. I, pp. 391-414; Walton op. cit. pp. 34-7; Stair I. 4.6 and IV. 45.19 (thirdly); Erskine, I. 6.6; D.I.C. Ashton Cross 'Cohabitation with habit and repute' 1961 J.R. 21-31; *Leslie* v. *Leslie* (1859) 22 D. 993, *Nicol* v. *Bell* 1954 S.L.T. 314. The parties have to be free to marry, *Low* v. *Gorman* 1970 S.L.T. 356, though continued cohabitation after the parties become free to marry will suffice, even though the cohabitation commenced earlier, *Campbell* v. *Campbell* (1866) 4 M. 867, (1867) 5 M. (H.L.) 115.

365 per Lord Deas, *Leslie* v. *Leslie* (1859) 22 D. 993 at 1011. Cf. Matt. 19:4-6; Erskine, *Inst.* I. 6.2. Stair, *Inst.* I. 4.5.—'consensus, non coitus, facit matrimonium'—using an old maxim of

Canon Law (cf. C.I.C. 1015). Cf. also D. M. Walker, *Principles of Scottish Private Law*, 2nd ed. 1975, I, p. 252.

366 Cf. 1, the definition of 'family' in the Family Allowances Act 1965, s.3, the National Insurance Act 1965, s.114 (2)(c), and s.86 (2)(c) of the National Insurance (Industrial Injuries) Act 1965; 2. the concept of 'household' and related arrangements under s.5 and Sch.2, and ss. 22-4 of the Ministry of Social Security Act 1966, and in para. 3 of the Sch. I to the Supplementary Benefits Act 1976; 3. the notion of cohabitation *inter alia* in ss.19 (2), 20 (3) and 21 (3) of the Social Security Act 1973. Cf. also the definitions in the various statutory instruments which regulate social security benefits, and the decisions of the Commissioner under the various Acts.

See also H. Calvert, *Social Security Law*, 2nd ed. 1978; A. I. Ogus and E. M. Barendt, *The Law of Social Security*, 1978; M. A. Glendon, *State, Law and Family* . *Family Law in Transition in the United States and Western Europe*, 1977.

367 E.g. *H.M.A.* v. *Dickson*, (1844) 2 Broun 278; the Appendix to vol. 3 of Irvine's Justiciary Reports; and *H.M.A.* v. *Ballantyne* (1859) 3 Irv. 352.

368 The Marriage (Prescription of Religious Bodies) (Scotland) Regulations 1977, S.I. 1977, No. 1670.

369 Cf. *R.* v. *Registrar General ex parte Segerdal*, [1970] 1 Q.B. 430; [1970] 2 Q.B. 697.

370 See the Supplication to the Queen's Majesty by the General Assembly, 29th June 1562, text printed Knox *History* pp. 47-51, at 51.

371 *First Book of Discipline*, (*supra* ch. II p. 14 and n. 41), Head IX (3).

372 D. B. Smith, 'A Note on Divorce for Desertion' (1939) 51 J.R. 254-9.

373 The Church of Scotland permits re-marriage under rules contained in the Act 26, 1959. Full inquiry into each case by the minister is required, and the minister need not act against his conscience (see Cox pp. 63-4). The provision for re-marriage after divorce is not limited to the Confessional grounds of divorce. Cf. the Report of the Special Committee on the Re-marriage of Divorced Persons, 1957 Gen. Ass. Rpts. pp. 825-73.

374 *Supra* n. 366.

375 Scottish Law Commission, memorandum no. 41, Family Law: Occupancy Rights in the Matrimonial Home and Domestic Violence, vol. 2, Part 8. The proposal for comment on protection devices is at 8.13, while the arguments against property consequences normally being imposed in cohabitation is at 8.5 and 8.6. Cf. the English Law Commission's *Family Law* (third report) Law Comm. no. 86, 1977-8 H.C. 450.

376 *Report of the Committee on the Working of the Abortion Act* (the Lane Committee) 1974, Cmnd. 5579, 5579 I-II; and Reports and minutes of evidence to the House of Commons Select Committee on Abortion, 1974-5 H.C. 253 i-xiv, 496, 552 and 692 I-II; 1975-6 H.C. 250 i-ix, 573 I-II, 737.

377 *Finlayson* v. *H.M. Advocate* 1978 S.L.T. (Notes) 60. Cf. surrounding facts of *Atkins* v. *London Weekend T.V.* 1978 S.L.T. 76.

378 Cf. *On Dying Well*, (Anglican) Church Information Office, 1975; and the Incurable Patients Bill (1975-6 H.L. no. 21) introduced by Baroness Wooton, 1976. *On Dying Well*, ch. 2, outlines the discussion of earlier bills of 1936 and 1969.

379 Cf. J. G. Gardiner, 'The Influence of the Law of Moses', in *The Sources and Literature of Scots Law*, 1936, (Stair Soc. vol. no. 1) pp. 235-40. Apart from such statutes as noted below, it was also possible to ground a criminal charge on the Bible alone: e.g. *Argyll Justiciary Records*, *1705-1742*, 1969 (Stair Soc. vol. no. 25), pp. 220 (adultery) and 224 (bestiality); J. M'Laurin, *Decisions in Remarkable Cases before the High Court of Justiciary, 1670-1773*, 1774, p. 18 (incest).

380 Erskine I. 1.45; *Brown* v. *Magistrates of Edinburgh* 1931 S.L.T. 456.

381 Noted Erskine's *Institute*, 2nd ed. 1785, IV. 4.52, note.

382 The Marriage Enabling Act 1960 consolidated earlier extensions of the law by the Deceased Wife's Sister Act 1907, the Deceased Brother's Widow Act 1921 and the Marriage (Prohibited Degrees of Relationship) Act 1931. See now the Marriage (Scotland) Act 1977 s.2 and Sch. I. Cf. J. Gibson, *The Marriage Affinity Question*, 1854; Lord Salvesen 'The Law of Incest in Scotland' (1941) 53 J.R. 112, 262; D. Sellar 'Forbidden Degrees of Matrimony' 1977 S.L.T. (News) pp. 1-4.

383 Hume, *Commentaries on the Law of Scotland respecting Crimes*, 1797, vol. I, pp. 318-9.

384 Ibid. pp. 560-2; Arnot, *Criminal Trials*, 1785, pp. 322-7, could only find three prosecutions. Apart from Aitkenhead, one person was fined and one was outlawed. Cf. R. Chambers, *Domestic Annals of Scotland*, 1859, II, pp. 160-6, and Bulloch I, pp. 13-15.

385 J. H. A. MacDonald, *The Criminal Law of Scotland*, 5th ed. by J. Walker, 1948, p. 153.

386 *Thomas Paterson* (1843) 1 Broun 629; *Henry Robinson* (1843) 1 Broun 643. Note: non-Christian and anti-Christian trust purposes are valid; *General Assembly of Baptist Churches* v. *Taylor* (1841) 3 D. 1030; *Bowman* v. *Secular Society* [1917] A.C. 406.

387 For trial see *The Times* 5-12 July 1977: appeal to Court of Appeal, Criminal Division, unsuccessful, *R.* v. *Lemon: R.* v. *Gay News* [1978] 3 All E.R. 175; further appeal to House of Lords also unsuccessful, [1979] 1 All E.R. 898 (H.L.). Cf. G. Maher, 'Blasphemy in Scots Law', 1977 S.L.T. (News) 257-60.

388 Kramer and Sprenger wrote the *Malleus Maleficarum*, 1487 (trans. M. Summers, 1928, 1971), the authoritative text of the time on witchfinding.

389 Arnot (*supra* n. 384), pp. 347-70; Sir G. Mackenzie, *Criminal Law*, 1699, tit. X; G. F. Black, *A Calender of Scottish Witchcraft Cases, 1510-1727*, 1938; M. Summers, *A Geography of Witchcraft*, 1927, 1978, pp. 201-53.

390 E.g. the Sovereign's Oath under The Protestant Religion and Presbyterian Church Act 1706 c.6, in respect of the Church of Scotland; the Coronation Oath Act 1567 c.8 (English Act, 1688); The Regency Oath, scheduled to the Regency Act 1937; the Oath of Allegiance taken by a naturalised person under ss. 6 and 10 and sch. I of the British Nationality Act 1948. In the past oaths were also used as shibboleths to bar certain persons from public life—notably under the Test Acts, 1681 c.6, and 1685 c.13 (repealed by the Acts 1690 cc.9 and 58), and were used in covenanting times to detect covenanters. The Statutory Declarations Act 1835 reduced the occasions on which oaths had to be taken in official business.

391 See Lord Moncrieffe in *Pattinson* v. *Robertson* (1846) 9 D. 226 at 229; *Longworth* v. *Yelverton* (1865) 3 M. 645, aff'd (1867) 5 M. (H.L.) 144; *Perdikou* v. *Pattison*. 1958 S.L.T. 153. See also ch. 14 of Research Paper on the Law of Evidence of Scotland, by Sheriff I. D. MacPhail, Scottish Law Commission, April 1979. Sheriff MacPhail recommends the abolition of the Oath on Reference at para. 14.01.

392 3rd ed. para. 1432 (*s. v. Witness*) Cf. W. G. Dickson, *The Law of Evidence in Scotland*, 2nd ed. 1864, s. 1968 (vol. 2, p. 959).

393 A. Alison, *Practice of the Criminal Law in Scotland*. 1833, p. 437.

394 *Clarke* v. *Bradlaugh* (1881) 7 Q.B.D. 38; *Bradlaugh* v. *Clarke* (1883) 8 App. Cas. 354; *Bradlaugh* v. *Gossett* (1884) 12 Q.B.D. 271.

395 G. Gordon, *Criminal Law*, 1978, pp. 1063-80 treats of perjury. Cf. *False Witness*, 1973, a Report by a Committee of Justice, Chairman, R. Muir Hunter, Q.C., pp. 21-7. Many declarations, e.g. income tax returns, contain such warning. Cf. MacPhail, *supra* n. 391, at para. 8.05-8.

396 R. Cox, *Literature on the Sabbath Question*, 2 vols. 1865; Bulloch II, pp. 21-5, 306-13; Fleming I, 212-20.

397 As narrated by Lord Mackay the Acts were: 1503 c.83 (c.28); 1579 c.70 (c.8); 1592 c.124 (c.17); 1593 c.163 (c.6); 1594 c.201 (c.8); 1661 c.18 (c.281); 1661 c.38 (c.338); 1663 c.19 (c.43); 1672 c.22 (c.58); 1690 c.5 (c.7); 1693 c.40 (c.64); 1696 c.31 (c.31); 1701 c.11 (1700 c.12)—the

citation in brackets being to the Record edition of the Scottish Acts. See also analysis of the principal Acts in the Report from a Committee of the Gen. Ass., on the Sabbath Observance (Scotland) Bill, 1834: 1834 H.C. 405.

398 Hume, op. cit. *supra* n. 383, vol. 1 p. 563.

399 Cf. the *Report of the Departmental Committee on Scottish Licensing Laws*, (the Clayson Committee), 1973 Cmnd. 5354, and s.53 and Sch.4 of the Licensing (Scotland) Act 1976.

400 See Gen. Ass. Rpts. 1946, 1947, 1962, culminating in 1964 p. 359.

401 W. Rordorf, *Sunday* (trans. A. A. K. Graham, 1968) pp. 9-38, quotes or refers to most of the basic material.

402 361 U.S. 420 at 451-2; 6 L. Ed 2d 393 at 414.

403 Cf. *Report of the Departmental Committee on the Law on Sunday Observance*, Chairman, Lord Crathorne, 1964 Cmnd. 2528.

404 European Convention on Human Rights, 1950, 213 U.N.T.S. 221; (1953) G.B.T.S. No. 71, Cmd. 8969.

405 Ss. 1 and 2, Act of Settlement 1700. Similarly a Roman Catholic may not act as Regent, s.3(2), Regency Act 1937.

406 The Lord Chancellor (Tenure of Office and Discharge of Ecclesiastical Functions) Act 1974; Roman Catholic Emancipation Act 1829; Roman Catholic Relief Act 1926. See also ch. VI, p. 87 and n. 242.

407 Roman Catholic Emancipation Act 1829, s.12.

408 The House of Commons Disqualification Act 1975, s.10(3), preserves these disqualifications which were first imposed under the House of Commons (Clergy Disqualification) Act 1801, and s.9 of the Roman Catholic Emancipation Act 1829. Ministers are not disqualified from election to local government bodies; or to the European Assembly: European Assembly Elections Act 1978 c.10, s.3 and Sch.I, para 5 (3)(*b*). One consequence of the establishment of the Church of England in England is the presence of twenty-six bishops in the House of Lords. Their impact on the House is out of all proportion to their numbers: see, G. Drewry and J. Brock, 'Prelates in Parliament', (1971) 14 Parl. Affairs 222. Reduction of their number has been proposed (*Reform of the House of Lords*, 1968, Cmnd. 3799), and accepted (*Church and State*, 1970. Report of the Archbishop's Commission, pp. 45-7).

409 For examples, see nn. 410-12 *infra*.

410 On Sikh's turbans see: Motor-cycle Crash-helmets (Religious Exemption) Act 1976; on slaughter see: Slaughter of Animals (Scotland) Act 1928 s.2(6) and s.8, and the Slaughter of Animals (Prevention of Cruelty) (Scotland) Regulations 1955 (S.I. 1955 No. 1993) reg. 13 (cf. for England, the Slaughterhouses Act 1974 s.36(3) and sch.1, and the Prevention of Cruelty (Slaughter of Animals) Regulations 1958 (S.I. 1958 No. 2166) regs 17 and 19); on Christian Science Nursing Homes see: the Public Health Act 1936 s.193, and the Nursing Homes Registration (Scotland) Act 1938 ss.6 and 7, as amended, (cf. for England, s.18 of the Nursing Homes Act 1975).

411 On conscientious objection to military service see: for 1914-18, J. W. Graham, *Conscription and Conscience*, 1922, D. Boulton, *Objection Overruled*, 1967; J. Rae, *Conscience and Politics*, 1970. For 1939-45 see, D. Hayes, *Challenge of Conscience*, 1949. A comparative survey is P. Schaffer and D. Weissbrodt, 'Conscientious Objection to Military Service as a Human Right', (1972) The Review (Int. Commission of Jurists) 33-47.

The latest U.K. law is contained in s.1(1) and s.17 of the National Service Act 1948, which repeat earlier provisions. Cases reported include *Guy* v. *Mackenna* 1917 J.C. 59, *Saltmarsh* v. *Adair*, 1942 J.C. 58 and *Walsh* v. *Lord Advocate*, 1956 S.C. (H.L.) 126, (all three being on the position of Jehovah's Witnesses elders), *Montgomerie* v. *Mackenna*, 1918 J.C. 55 (Plymouth Brethern) and *Marshall* v. *Haig*, 1918 J.C. 47 (divinity student acting as locum minister). There are no relevant reported cases on lay persons, but see the books cited above, and cf. *Newell* v. *Gillingham Corporation*, [1941] 1 All E.R. 552, and *Downsborough* v. *Huddersfield Industrial Society Ltd.* [1941] 3 All E.R. 434.

On the position now under the European Convention on Human Rights (1953, Cmd. 8969) see *Grandrath* v. *Germany*, (1965) 8 Y.B. Eur. Conv. H. Rts. 324, (1967) 10 Y.B. Eur. Conv. H. Rts. 626.

412 *Report of the Royal Commission on Trade Unions and Employers Associations, 1965-68,* Chairman Lord Donovan, 1968 Cmnd. 3623, paras. 563-4 and 614. See now s.58(3) of the Employment Protection (Consolidation) Act 1978, formerly para 6(5) of Sch. 1 to the Trade Union and Labour Relations Act 1974 (amended from the provision in ss.6, 9 and 10 of the 1971 Industrial Relations Act), *Saggers* v. *British Railways Board* [1977] I.R.L.R. 266, [1978] I.R.L.R. 435; *Hynds* v. *Spillers-French Baking Ltd.* [1974] I.R.L.R. 281.

413 Cf. E. Norman, *Christianity and the World Order,* Oxford U.P. 1979, (the Reith Lectures, 1978). Ch.xxxi, 5 of the Westminster Confession of Faith reads:

> 'Synods and councils are to handle or conclude nothing but that which is ecclesiastical: and are not to intermeddle with civil affairs which concern the commonwealth, unless by way of humble petition in cases extraordinary; or by way of advice for satisfaction of conscience, if they be thereunto required by the civil magistrate.'

414 *The Political Works of James I*, ed. by C. H. McIlwain, 1918, xxix, quoted by D. Shaw, *The General Assemblies of the Church of Scotland 1560-1600 : Their Origins and Development,* 1964, p. 21.

415 O. Hood Phillips, *Constitutional and Administrative Law,* 5th ed. 1973 p. 571 n. 11.

416 Also R. King Murray, 'The Constitutional Position of the Church of Scotland', [1958] P.L. 155 (cf. Hood Phillips loc. cit.)

417 *The Anglican Presbyterian Conversations*, St. Andrew Press and S.P.C.K., 1966, at p. 42; also printed as an Appendix to the Supplementary Report of the Special Committee on Anglican-Presbyterian Relations, G.A. Reps. 1966, pp. 618-662, the quotation appearing at p. 649. The definition is there quoted from Prof. N. P. Williams. On the whole business of these conversations, see I. Henderson, *Power without Glory. A Study in Ecumenical Politics,* Hutchinson, 1967.

418 *The Report of the Multi-lateral Conversations*, G.A. Reps. 1972, and the plans for Union with the Methodist Church in Scotland 1977, do not reassure in this respect. The 1976 Assembly's decision and debate on the question of 'second baptism' may have opened an alternative way of defining the substance of the Faith. A series of cases could be brought to appeal on questions of doctrine, with the effect of building definitions by case law. This would, however, be a divisive and regrettable way of proceeding. (See the Appeal: Presbytery of Hamilton against the decision of the Synod of Clydesdale, 25 May 1976: G.A. 1976, sess. 7 and relative minute).

419 *Supra* p. 128 and n. 357.

420 Per L. J. C. Hope, *Craigie* v. *Marshall* (1850) 12 D. 523 at 547-8.

421 Incorporation does not remove these problems. On the U.S. experience see Paul G. Kauper and S. C. Ellis 'Religious Corporations and the Law' (1973) 71 Mich. L.R. 1500-74.

422 The Lord Chancellor (Tenure of Office and Discharge of Ecclesiastical Functions) Act 1974.

423 *Church and State in Scotland*, thesis presented in candidature for the degree of Doctor of Philosophy, University of Aberdeen, October 1972, on file at the University Library.

424 Pp. 145-6, nn. 410-12.

Table of Cases

Italic number after n refers to Notes on the Text.

Viscountess Rhondda's Claim, [1922] 2 A.C. 339   n. *204*.

Wallace *v.* The Ferguson Bequest Fund, (1879) 6 R. 486   104, n. *241, 288*.

Walsh *v.* Lord Advocate, 1956 S.C. (H.L.) 126; S.L.T. 283; [1956] 3 All E.R. 129   n. *411*.

Wight *v.* Presbytery of Dunkeld, (1870) 8 M. 921   58, 59, n. *158a*.

Wilson *v.* Jobson, (1771) Mor. 14555   86-7, n. *271*.

Wilson *v.* Presbytery of Stranraer, (1842) 4 D. 1294   43, 47.

Worldwide Evangelisation Crusade *v.* Glasgow Corporation, 1965 S.L.T. 339   n. *353*.

Young *v.* MacAlister—see Bannatyne *v.* Lord Overtoun.

Zorach *v.* Clauson, (1952) 343 U.S. 306; 96 L Ed 954   n. *19*.

Table of Statutes
Acts of the Parliament of Scotland

In the text and in this index I have used the short titles of Acts where these have been given. In other cases I have listed the title or subject matter as noted in the Table of the Acts of the Scottish Parliaments in the Second Revised Edition of *The Acts of the Parliaments of Scotland, 1424–1707*, H.M.S.O. 1966. In the text, unless quoting, I have used the Record Edition chapter numbers, and have given the duodecimo citation in brackets in this index where it differs. Most older works cite to the duodecimo edition, but the Record is becoming standard.

Note: Italic number after n. refers to Notes on Text.

Acts of the Parliament of England

1571 The Ordination of Ministers Act, 13 Eliz. I c. 12   n. *15.*

1688 Coronation Oath Act, 1 Will & Mary c. 6   n. *390.*

1695 Quakers Oaths Act, 7 & 8 Will. 3 c. 2   140.

1700 Act of Settlement, 12 & 13 Will. 3 c. 2   151, n. *405.*

1706 The Maintenance of the Church of England Act, 6 Anne c. 8   n. *64.*
      Union with Scotland Act, 6 Anne c. 11   21, 78.

Statutes of the Parliament of Great Britain

In dating Acts I have used the correct legal date, which in places means that an Act cited in older or non-legal works is differently cited here. For example, the Church Patronage (Scotland) Act, 10 Anne c. 21, is cited as 1711, whereas many other works cite it as 1712. The discrepancy occurs because, until the passing of the Acts of Parliament (Commencement) Act 1793, 33 Geo. 3 c. 13, Acts legally came into force from the beginning of the term of Parliament in which they were enacted. The Patronage Act was actually passed in 1712, and therefore became effective then in practice. Technically it became effective from 1711.

   Citation by regnal years ceased from, and including, 1963.
   Church of England Measures are included in this Table.

1711 Scottish Episcopalians Act, 10 Anne c. 10 (c. 7 in some eds.)   22, 25, 87, 91, n. *17.*
      Yule Vacance Act, 9 Anne c. 13   n. *66.*
      Church Patronage (Scotland) Act, 10 Anne c. 21   22, 25, 31, n. *218.*

1735 Witchcraft Act, 9 Geo. 2. c. 5   139.

1790 Scottish Episcopalians Relief Act, 32 Geo. 3 c. 63   87.

1793 Acts of Parliament (Commencement) Act, 33 Geo. 3 c. 13   *supra.*

1801 House of Commons (Clergy Disqualification) Act, 41 Geo. 3 c. 63   n. *408.*

1803 Parochial Schools (Scotland) Act, 43 Geo. III c. 54   116.

1808 Administration of Justice (Scotland) Act, 48 Geo. III c. 151   n. *90.*

1812 Doctrine of the Trinity Act, 53 Geo. 3 c. 160   139.

1819 Criminal Libel Act, 60 Geo. 3 & 1 Geo. 4. c. 8   139.

1825 Leasing Making (Scotland) Act, 6 Geo. 4 c. 47   139.
      Judicature Act, 6 Geo. 4 c. 120   n. *90.*

1828 Justiciary Courts Act, 9 Geo. 4 c. 29   140.

1829 Roman Catholic Emancipation Act, 10 Geo. 4 c. 7   n. *215, 230, 406, 407, 408.*

1830 Court of Session Act, 11 Geo. 4 & 1 Will. 4 c. 69   133.

1832 Representation of the People (Reform) Act, 2 & 3 Will. 4 c. 45   23, 52.
      Representation of the People (Scotland) Act, 2 & 3 Will. 4, c. 65   23, 52.

Index of People

Note: The name of parties to court cases (see Table of Cases, p. 189), of judges, and of legislators have been omitted from this index, unless otherwise of note. Italic number after n. refers to Notes on Text.

Aberdeen, Lord   n. *134.*
Argyle, Duke of   n. *134.*
Argyll, Duke of   n. *319.*
Augustine, St.   3.
Austin, John   10, 22, 52, n. *27, 67.*

Beaton, David, Cardinal   12.
Begg, Dr James   66, 106.
Beza, Theodore   4.
Bismarck, Otto von   10.
Blackie, Professor J. S.   121.
Boniface VIII, Pope   3.
Bradlaugh, Charles   141.
Brougham, Henry, Lord   32, 34, 50, 98, n. *86.*
Buchanan, George   n. *46.*
Bullinger, Heinrich   4.

Calvin, John   1, 3, 4, 7, 134.
Carstares, William, Principal   25.
Chalmers, Thomas   23, 26, 32, 33, 39, 40, 43, n. *92.*
Charlemagne   3.
Charles I   7, 18.
Charles II   19.
Cockburn, Henry, Lord   27, 56, n. *82, 84, 94.*
Constantine   5.
Cook, Dr George   29.
Cunningham, John, Principal   40.

Dunlop, Alexander M.   40.
Dupanloup, Felix A. B.   10.

Elizabeth I   9, 13.
Erastus, Thomas   4-5, 6.
Erskine, Ebenezer   43.

Farel, Guillaume   7.
Figgis, John N.   4, 6.
Finlay, R. B. (Viscount)   68, 77.

Gelasius I, Pope   3.
Gregory VII, Pope   3.

Haldane, James A and Robert   26.
Haldane, Richard B. D., Viscount   77, 82.
Halsbury, Hardinge S. B., Earl   109.
Hamilton, John, Archbishop   n. *31.*
Hamilton, Patrick   n. *32.*
Hobbes, Thomas   6, 22.
Hooker, Richard   2, 5-6.

Index of Subjects

Note: Roman numerals alone are a general reference to a chapter. Italic number after n. refers to Notes on Text.

£1.50